RIGHTS AND RESPONSIBILITIES OF DOCTORS

RIGHTS AND RESPONSIBILITIES OF DOCTORS

From the **BMA Professional Division**

Project director	Dr FLEUR FISHER
Project editor	Dr NATALIE–JANE MACDONALD
Consultants	BOB GANN JANE FERGUSON
Editorial secretariat	ANN SOMMERVILLE HENRIETTA WALLACE JOANNA THOMPSON

Published by the BMJ Publishing Group
Tavistock Square, London WC1H 9JR

ERRATUM TO SECTION 5.2 ON
SURROGACY, PAGES 66 AND 67.

LAST SENTENCE SHOULD READ...

The court may make an order for a child to be treated in
law as the child of a married couple where the gametes of
the husband or the wife are used and another woman
carries the child through pregnancy, provided that the
couple:

First printed 1988
Second impression 1990
Second edition 1992

British Library Cataloguing in Publication Data
Rights and Responsibilities of Doctors

ISBN 0–7279–0753–0

Printed by Latimer Trend & Company Ltd, Plymouth
Typeset by Apek Typesetters, Nailsea, Bristol

Contents

Table of cases

Table of circulars and notices

Table of statutes

Table of statutory instruments (SI)

Introduction to the second edition

The rights and responsibilities of doctors have developed in parallel with their ability to intervene, to identify, and cure or alleviate disease. For example, scientific advances in the understanding of infectious organisms were accompanied by a series of Public Health Acts during the nineteenth and twentieth centuries. Many of the powers and duties laid down in the Acts are beyond the scope of the individual—for instance, supervision of housing, control of sewage, drainage and water supplies, inspection of foodstuffs—but others impose specific obligations on doctors. Thus several diseases must, by law, be notified to the appropriate officer of the local authority by the doctor in charge of the case.

More recently, the trend in legislation has been to increase the rights of the patient. This is exemplified in the step-by-step legislation surrounding access to medical records—from the Data Protection Act 1984 and related provisions of the mid-1980s, to the Access to Health Records Act of the early 1990s.

The doctor's relationship with his patient is very special, but the two sides of the relationship are not always equally balanced. In the same way as the lawyer knows more about law than his client, the doctor knows more about medicine than the patient. Rapid developments in medicine have been accompanied by a tendency in patients to ask for greater involvement and control over what happens to them. This is reflected in the gradual evolution of legal controls of medical practice.

Doctors practising today must therefore be aware of their rights and responsibilities, and the duties and powers which require them to do, or not to do certain things in certain circumstances.

The British Medical Association (BMA) is a voluntary association which was set up in 1832 "To promote the medical and allied sciences, and to maintain the honour and interests of the medical profession." The BMA is the professional association of doctors in the United Kingdom and advises doctors every day, both collectively and individually, on the professional and ethical aspects of their work and actions in relation to their patients, their colleagues, and society as a whole. It receives a constant stream of enquiries about all non-clinical aspects of medical practice. Many are dealt with on the spot but some require painstaking research and consultation with lawyers or other specialists.

The first edition of this book was published in 1988 and has proved a remarkably successful and useful resource not just for doctors but for many others whose work involves medical practice and the law to some extent. These include medical students, health service administrators, lawyers and local authority officers. The introduction to that edition recognised its somewhat limited scope and called for suggestions for entries to be included in later editions. This second edition reflects many of these suggestions as well as the extensive amount of new medical law which has emerged over the past four years. Major alterations in this edition include a reorganisation of most of the existing chapters and new chapters on children, fertility and birth, and death. There are extensive additions relating to consent, confidentiality and young people, medical research, the law and those with learning disabilities and European Community legislation.

How to use this book

This book intends to provide a practical and concise guide to certain aspects of the law as it affects doctors. It is not, of course, possible to deal with everything. Even with the extensive revision and additions for this second edition, there are still areas where more could be said. Indeed, many areas of medical practice remain unregulated by the law. It is hoped, though, that the book will cover the main areas that most doctors need to know about. As the BMA receives numerous queries about legal matters some idea can be gleaned of the questions most often asked. (Readers are encouraged to write to the Association with suggestions for inclusions or deletions for future editions.)

As noted above, the law is continually evolving and any doctor with a specific problem should check that no amendment has occurred following the publication of this edition.

Every person has a duty to behave lawfully and the sanctions for not doing so can be considerable. If a criminal offence has been committed the offender can be prosecuted in the criminal courts where a penalty such as a fine or, in serious cases, a prison sentence could be imposed. Other breaches of the law could result in a civil law suit and an award of damages against the wrongdoer.

Doctors have additional codes of conduct to observe. The General Medical Council (GMC) is the governing body of the medical profession and has a statutory power to suspend or erase the registration of any registered medical practitioner who is found "to have been convicted in the British Islands of a criminal offence," or who is judged "to have been guilty of serious professional misconduct." Doctors working in the National Health Service (NHS) can be referred to the GMC as a result of investigation by a service committee of allegations of breaches of terms and conditions of service. This book is not intended to be a comprehensive guide to the sorts of misconduct which could lead to disciplinary proceedings and readers should refer to the current GMC advice in *Professional Conduct and Discipline: Fitness to Practise*, referred to as the "blue book."

Doctors also have the issue of medical ethics to consider. What the law expects of doctors may mirror closely what codes of medical ethics expect but sometimes the law may conflict with what doctors sees as their ethical duty. This book is not intended to be a guide to medical ethics and readers should refer to published BMA ethical guidance for further help.

The book has 13 chapters each containing a number of related subtopics. The issue of confidentiality, for instance, is first discussed in general and then considered particularly in relation to—for example, the difficulties doctors may face when confronted with a patient who they suspect has committed a serious crime, or who has a disease which must by law be notified to an outside authority.

The topics and subtopics covered are listed in the contents pages, but if the subject you wish to know about does not seem to be there then turn to the index, which we have tried to make as comprehensive as possible: The topic that you are interested in is probably referred to in one of the chapters. In fact, some topics, crop up in several different chapters, and wherever possible cross-references are made to other entries.

Finally, although, only the masculine gender is used throughout this book, it should be read as referring to both sexes, and no sexism is implied.

A brief guide to United Kingdom and European Community law

Some people who use this book will have extensive knowledge of the law but others will not and it is for the benefit of the latter that the following paragraphs are included.

United Kingdom law

The sources of law in England and Wales are, firstly, legislation and, secondly, decided court cases. Sometimes a situation crops up which is not covered by any existing statute nor by any decided court case. The reader will find several instances of such legal vacuums while consulting this book. When this occurs all a lawyer can do is to look at the other authorities which are not law but which may well influence a judge's decision. Examples of such are the opinions of academic lawyers as expressed in recognised law text books, decisions made in law courts in other countries, and, of particular relevance in the field of medical law, circulars emanating from official bodies such as the Department of Health. To assist those readers who know very little about our legal system, further explanation is given below about the process of legislation and the role of decided court cases.

At various times throughout this book we shall be referring to acts or statutes (both words mean the same thing). Acts of Parliament are primary legislation and become law after they have been passed by both Houses of Parliament and have received Royal Assent. An Act may come into force immediately or at a later date, or it may be introduced in stages. This can make life very difficult for the writers of guides to the law. They may know that there is a new statute waiting in the wings to be brought into operation whereas at the time of writing the old law still applies. When we have set out the law as it will be in the future rather than as it is at present we have, of course, made that clear, and readers who are members should refer to the BMA for guidance as to the current state of the law.

We shall also be referring the reader to numerous Statutory Instruments (SI). These are usually known as regulations or orders and are sometimes called "delegated legislation" because when an Act has been passed by parliament to deal with a particular situation, parliament can, at the same time and in the body of the Act, delegate to the Secretary of State the right to draw up regulations to deal with details or future situations which it is not possible or appropriate to include in the main Act. The Statutory Instruments Act 1946 provides for various procedures by which a statutory instrument can come into force and become law. There is not space here to explain fully these procedures which are complicated. Briefly the statutory instrument must either:

1 Be laid before parliament before it comes into operation (which means parliament must legislate to revoke it), or

2 Be laid before parliament with forty days' time limit being given within which objections can be made, or

3 Be laid before parliament in draft and approved by resolution.

Regulations have the force of law but they can only be drawn up if there is an Act of Parliament already in existence from which the right to make the particular regulation derives.

Decisions made in the English courts are an important source of law. Blackstone defined the common law as "the ancient unwritten law of this kingdom". Common law is the law of the land embodied in judicial decisions as opposed to statutory law or law enacted by parliament. Court decisions may be the only authority concerning a particular issue or they may be the authority which decides how a particular piece of legislation is to be interpreted, as it is not possible to legislate for every situation that might occur. Legislation can be passed to change the rule of law in a decided court case and to that extent court cases are subordinate to the rule of Parliament. Courts must follow decisions made by courts superior in the hierarchy. To avoid a complete stalemate, however, the House of Lords can in certain circumstances decide not to follow a decision that it made previously.

Scotland: The law in Scotland differs fundamentally from that in England and Wales. Different statutes apply, and the system of courts and legal officers is different—for example, in Scotland there are procurators fiscal, *some* of whose powers and duties are similar to those of English coroners. A volume of this size, cannot describe all the relevant differences between Scottish and English law, but some representative examples are mentioned. Thus this book should be used only for general guidance in Scotland; people requiring definitive information are strongly advised to consult a Scottish lawyer or the Scottish Office of the BMA.

Northern Ireland: Similarly, the law in Northern Ireland frequently differs from that in England and Wales. Many statutes do not have force in Northern Ireland and where similar legislation exists—for example, that governing mental health—the provisions may be different. Where possible, reference is made in the text to differences in law in Northern Ireland, but as with Scotland the book can only be relied on as a superficial guide and recourse to the Northern Ireland office of the BMA for members or Northern Irish lawyers, is recommended for detailed advice.

European Community law

The entry into the European Economic Community (EEC) in 1972 has necessitated changes in United Kingdom law to effect harmonisation between its member states. The founding EEC treaties were reinforced by the Single European Act in 1987, and the evolution of the Community continues.

Five permanent institutions have been set up to apply the treaties establishing the Community, and to work out and implement common policies.

The **European Commission** is the "executive" body of the Community. It proposes and carries out policies and is responsible for monitoring the implementation of Community legislation by member states. It can take governments or firms to the European Court of Justice for breaches of law. It has a central and very powerful role.

There are 17 commissioners, each with responsibility for a particular area of policy. They are obliged to act independently of their own national governments. The Commission itself is divided into 23 directorates-general (DG), which administer general policy areas. There is *no* directorate-general for health – health care *systems* do not fall within the remit of the Community – but a number of directorates-general produce policy which has a potential impact on the health care sector. The following directorates general produce policy which has some impact on medicine and health:

DG III   Internal market and industrial affairs. (Directorate D is responsible for free movement and the mutual recognition of diplomas, including the "doctors' directives".)

DG V   Employment, industrial relations and social affairs. (The Europe Against Cancer programme is run by this DG.)

DG XI   Environment, consumer protection and nuclear safety.

DG XII   Science, research and development. (This includes medical research.)

DG XII   Telecommunication, information industries and innovation. (This DG is responsible for Advanced Informatics in Medicine, a major research programme.)

The **European Parliament** does not have the legislative powers of a national government, but its opinion must be sought on nearly all proposals. It is a powerful consultative body, which has already increased its powers and seems set to do so further. It is also responsible for approving the budget of the European Commission and has the right to make alterations to certain aspects of the budget. Its members are elected by citizens of member states for five year terms; they sit in political party groups, rather than in national delegations. The allocation of its 518 seats is as follows:

France, Germany, Italy, United Kingdom (81); Denmark (16); Spain (60);

Ireland (15); the Netherlands (25); Luxemburg (6); Belgium, Greece, and Portugal (24).

The **Council of Ministers** is the Community's principal decision making body and most powerful institution. Each national government has a seat on it, and for the subject under discussion each national government is represented by the government minister responsible for this area. Legislation is proposed and drafted by the Commission and voted on by the Council. In practice, unanimity tends to be the rule but decisions can be taken by a qualified majority. For this the votes of members are weighted according to population: France, Germany, Italy and the United Kingdom have ten votes each; Spain eight votes; Belgium, Greece, the Netherlands and Portugal five each; Denmark and Ireland three each, and Luxembourg two. Out of the 76 votes 54 are required for a majority. Presidency of the Council is held by each member state in turn for six month periods. Its meetings are prepared by COREPER, the Committee of Permanent Representatives, which is composed of member states' ambassadors to the EC.

The European Council is the term given to the 12 heads of government, who hold twice yearly summit meetings.

The **Court of Justice** rules on questions of Community law and whether actions by the Commission, Council of Ministers, member governments and other bodies are compatible with the various treaties. It is based in Luxemburg. It should not be confused with the European Court of Human Rights, which is part of the Council of Europe, a body separate from the European Community. Judgements are by majority vote and are directly binding on all parties. National courts faced with a question of Community law can ask the court for a preliminary ruling. Such a request is obligatory where the national court is the final court of appeal in its particular member state.

The **Economic and Social Committee** (ECOSOC) is an advisory body, which was established by the treaties, and is consulted by the Commission and the Council. Moreover, it can elaborate opinions on its own initiative. ECOSOC was set up to involve the various categories of economic and social activity of the Common Market; its membership therefore comprises three groups – representatives of employers (group I), workers (group II), and various interest groups (group III). Members are proposed by national governments and appointed by the Council for four year terms. Members may be reappointed. ECOSOC must be consulted by the Council or the Commission where the treaties so provide and may also be consulted if the Council or Commission think it appropriate in other cases.

Legislation

Much national legislation now has its origin in Brussels. Once a text has been formally adopted, member states may face infraction procedures if they do not comply within specified time-limits. (In practice, this applies almost exclusively to directives.) The following forms of legislation may be issued:

Regulations immediately become law in member states, in the form in which they are issued.

Directives are binding on member states as far as intended results are concerned, but national authorities may decide how best to achieve these results.

Decisions are binding on all those to whom they are addressed, which may be member states or particular groups within them.

Opinions and Recommendations are not binding; they are advice to governments.

A term much used is "subsidiarity". This is a principle of de-centralisation, by which responsibility for action in particular areas is devolved from central Community institutions to national and regional authorities.

1 Consent

1.1 Consent to treatment

It is the right of an adult to decide what is done to his or her body. A mentally sound adult generally has the right to give or refuse consent to be examined or treated. And, if a doctor were to examine or treat a patient against a patient's wishes, the doctor could find himself at risk of an action for battery or negligence.

Consent need not be written. It can be implied from the circumstances: a patient opening his mouth so that the doctor can examine his sore throat, or an injured person visiting casualty with a bleeding wound implicitly agree to examination and treatment. In an American case a patient who rolled up her sleeve and held her arm out to the doctor was held to have consented to vaccination.

The *Guide to Consent for Examination or Treatment* (NHS management executive, 1990) recommends that there should be *written* consent for any procedure or treatment carrying any substantial risk or substantial side effect, including general anaesthesia, surgery, certain forms of drug treatment, such as cytotoxic drugs, and treatment involving the use of ionising radiation.

The use of a standard consent form provides evidence that the procedure has been explained and that the patient understands the nature and purpose of the proposed treatment.

Consent, even in writing, is not valid unless the patient is informed about the procedure and why it is to be performed.

There have been several court cases concerning the issue of what is sometimes called "informed consent." Patients who have sustained injury as a result of receiving medical treatment have attempted to sue a surgeon for battery or negligence on the basis that they were not given adequate information about the risks involved. The argument is that had they been fully informed they would never have agreed to have the treatment in question and the doctor is negligent in not having given sufficient information. The legal position at the moment can be summed up best as follows.

A doctor does have a duty to warn the patient of risks inherent in the procedure so that the patient can make an informed decision as to whether or not to consent. If, however, the doctor warns of all the risks which a recognised body of medical opinion considers the patient should be warned of, as opposed to every possible risk, then the patient probably will not succeed in any action for medical negligence (see chapter 2 on medical malpractice, where the case of Bolam *v* Friern Barnet hospital management committee is discussed. The principle laid down in that case has been applied to the issue of informed consent).

In the case of Sidaway *v* Bethlem Royal Hospital, the House of Lords considered the issue in detail. A patient became paralysed after surgery to her cervical vertebrae. The operation carried a small risk of damage (about 2%) to the nerve root or spinal cord. Damage to the cord would produce a far more serious result and the risk of that happening was less than 1%. The surgeon warned of the risk of damage to the nerve root but not of the risk to the spinal cord.

The operation was carried out with due care and skill but unfortunately resulted in damage to the spinal cord. The patient failed in her claim for damages. The court laid down general principles on the provision of information to patients. It confirmed that a doctor has a legal duty to warn a patient of the risks of treatment and to provide information on the alternatives and options available. It is a matter of clinical judgement. A doctor must exercise his professional skill in deciding the risks of which the patient should be warned and the degree of disclosure necessary to assist the particular patient in making a rational choice on whether to undergo treatment. Having listened to expert medical opinion, a court may conclude in certain circumstances that disclosure of a particular risk was so obviously necessary to an informed choice that no reasonably prudent doctor would fail to make it—for example, an operation carrying substantial risk of grave adverse consequences.

There may be a greater obligation to provide information if the patient questions the risks of treatment. If the patient specifically asks the doctor about the risks of a particular treatment the doctor's duty is "to answer truthfully and as fully as the questioner requires" (Sidaway case). In the case of Blyth *v* Bloomsbury Area Health Authority the patient (a nurse) had prolonged bleeding after receiving the contraceptive Depo-Provera. Despite her questions she was not told of the potential side effects. On the facts, the Court of Appeal held that the doctor had not been negligent. Even when the patient asks for information, the amount given is still a matter of clinical judgement. The doctor does not have to pass on *all* the information available in response to a general enquiry, or even a specific one, but the doctor must not lie when giving information.

In a later case (Gold *v* Haringey Health Authority) Mrs Gold brought an action for damages when she became pregnant three years after she had been sterilised. It was admitted that the operation had failed and that she had not been advised either that this might happen or that her husband, alternatively, could have had a vasectomy. Her action was successful at first instance but she lost in the Court of Appeal on the basis that there was a responsible body of opinion which did not believe women should be warned that surgery for sterilisation might fail. The outcome of the case is important because it challenges the principle of informed consent. Fortunately, the standard consent forms for sterilisation and vasectomy now warn of the possibility of failure.

1.2 Refusing treatment

A patient has the right to refuse all or part of the treatment proposed by a doctor. The patient should be given a detailed explanation of the nature of the illness and the need for the treatment proposed. The patient should also be warned of any possible consequences. Refusal on the part of the patient to be treated must then be respected. The doctor should record this decision in the patient's clinical notes, and it is sensible to have this witnessed.

1.2.1 *Jehovah's Witnesses*

If any adult refuses to consent to treatment then legally that treatment cannot be given. Even if the person is mentally confused there is still no mechanism for imposing treatment on someone who has refused consent except the limited provision of treatment for mental disorder under the Mental Health Act (see chapter 8). Jehovah's Witnesses present a special problem in that they do not permit any form of tissue transplantation, including blood transfusion.

The BMA gives guidance to doctors in the event of a Jehovah's Witness refusing to consent to a transfusion being given in cases which would normally involve this procedure. The BMA advises that if the doctor decides to continue treating the patient despite the risk arising from the refusal, then the patient should be warned of the extent of this risk. It is advisable to give such a warning in the presence of a witness. If despite the warning the patient still does not agree to recommended procedures being taken, he should be asked to sign a written acknowledgement to that effect stating that he understands the nature of the increased risks which result from such refusal.

The position regarding children of Jehovah's Witnesses is governed by common law, there being no relevant statute. The issue of children and their ability to consent to treatment on their behalf is considered in chapter 7. A minor can be made a ward of court in order for treatment to be authorised contrary to parental wishes, or a specific issue order can be obtained (Children Act 1984, 5.8(1)).

1.3 Emergency treatment: unconscious patients

A doctor should not treat a patient without the latter's consent. A patient might be brought into hospital unconscious, urgently needing treatment but in no fit state to consent to anything. In a 1989 case relating to the sterilisation of an adult with a learning disability (Re F), the House of Lords considered the question of the lawfulness of treatment given to a patient who for any reason, temporary or permanent, lacks the capacity to give consent to treatment. The court advised that treatment necessary to preserve the life, health, or well being of the patient may be given without consent in such cases. Any doctor who acted with due care and skill in such circumstances would be immune from liability in battery or negligence. In fact, not only would the doctor be immune from liability but it would be the common law duty of the doctor to give treatment to an unconscious or otherwise incapacitated patient in the doctor's care, if that treatment were in the best interests of the patient. This only applies to treatment which is carried out to save lives or to ensure improvement or prevent deterioration in physical or mental health. The doctor should not give more extensive treatment than is necessary to cope with the particular emergency. Nevertheless, a doctor should not treat a patient if it is clearly known and stated in writing that the latter would, if conscious and competent, object to the treatment—for example, if the patient had left explicit written instructions saying he did not wish to be treated if admitted to hospital, (see chapter 6.2.3 for living wills and advance directives). Other cases, such as Jehovah's Witnesses, present a difficult dilemma. The doctor should not automatically assume that a Jehovah's Witness would refuse treatment, and a court would probably support a doctor who did undertake treatment in an emergency.

In a 1988 Canadian case, however, the Ontario High Court found a doctor liable in damages for giving an unconscious patient a life-saving blood transfusion. The patient carried a card saying she was a Jehovah's Witness and the doctor saw the card before deciding to give her blood. The court held that although the doctor had acted promptly and professionally he was guilty of battery and the patient was awarded $Can 20000 for mental distress (*Medico Legal Journal* 1989; **58**: 1407-8). The decision was subsequently upheld on appeal.

In any event it would be advisable for the doctor to try to get a view from the next of kin if possible. No other person can give consent for an adult, but people close to the patient may be helpful in providing insight to the patient's opinions.

1.4 Consent to transplantation of organs and tissue

The Human Organ Transplants Act 1989 prohibits commercial dealings in human organs, reinforcing the voluntary basis of donations of organs and tissue. The Act, and regulations made under it, also place restrictions on transplants between living persons who are not genetically related. These are discussed below.

Further regulations under the Act require doctors to supply specified information about transplants to the United Kingdom Transplant Service (UKTS).

1.4.1 *Live donors*

The Human Organ Transplants Act 1989 restricts transplants between people who are not genetically related (specified in the Act as natural parents and children, brothers and sisters, nephews and nieces, aunts and uncles and cousins, all of whole or half blood). The relationship must be tested by an approved tester using tests specified in the regulations. A person is guilty of an offence if he removes from a living person an organ intended to be transplanted into another, or transplants an organ removed from a living person into another person who is not genetically related, unless the approval of the Unrelated Live Transplant Authority (ULTRA) has been obtained. In every case where the transplantation of an organ is proposed between a living donor and a recipient who are not genetically related the proposal must be referred to ULTRA. As an independent authority its function is to consider cases where no genetic relationship exists or where a claimed relationship cannot be established.

In deciding whether to approve a transplant between people who are not genetically related, ULTRA needs to be satisfied that:

(i)   no payment has been made or is proposed (although reasonable expenses are permitted);

(ii) the doctor who referred the matter to the authority has clinical responsibility for the donor;

(iii) the doctor has given the donor an explanation of the nature of the procedure, and the risks involved;

(iv) the donor understands the nature and risks of the procedure and consents to the removal of the organ;

(v)   the donor's consent was not obtained by coercion or the offer of an inducement;

(vi) the donor understands that he is entitled to withdraw consent.

Even where the donor and recipient are genetically related the doctor should still abide by these principles of full, free and informed consent.
Note: The Human Organ Transplants Act 1989 does not cover bone marrow transplantations.

1.4.2 *Dead donors*

If the transplanted organ is to be taken from a cadaver then the Human Tissue Act 1961 (not applicable in Northern Ireland where the situation is regulated by the Human Tissue Act (Northern Ireland) 1962) and the Corneal Tissue Act 1986 (not applicable in Northern Ireland) regulate the position. The sections of the Human Organ Transplant Act 1989 which prohibit commercial dealings in human organs also apply.

Express consent of donor

Section 1(1) of the Human Tissue Act 1961 states: "If any person, either in writing at any time or orally in the presence of two or more witnesses during his last illness, has expressed a request that his body or any specified part of his body be used after his death for therapeutic purposes or for the purposes of medical education or research, the person lawfully in possession of the body after his death may, unless he has reason to believe that the request was subsequently withdrawn, authorise the removal from the body of any part or, as the case may be, the specified part, for use in accordance with the request."

It should be noted that there is no specific wording that the deceased must have used, and the request can be made orally during a terminal illness if witnessed by at least two people. DHSS circular HSC(IS)156 advises that those wishing to donate their bodies should be asked to make a written statement to that effect and to carry this on their person. Would-be donors should also be encouraged to discuss their wishes with their family or anyone close to them. Donors should be advised to take their donor card with them if ever admitted to hospital and once there they should tell staff that they have made such a request. If they make one while in hospital that fact should be included in the patient's medical records. Hospitals are warned that patients should not be pressed to complete donor cards, although it is acceptable for a hospital to display posters and have kidney donor cards freely available.

Consent of relatives

The second set of circumstances in which tissue may be removed under the Human Tissue Act 1961 is specified in section 1(2). This states that the person lawfully in possession (see discussion below) of the body can authorise the removal of any part of the body for the same purposes as mentioned above if, "having made such reasonable enquiry as may be practicable, he has no reason to believe:

(a) that the deceased had expressed an objection to his body being so dealt with after his death, and had not withdrawn it; or

(b) that the surviving spouse or any surviving relative of the deceased objects to the body being so dealt with."

The Act does not state what a reasonable enquiry should consist of, but DHSS circular HSC(IS)156 gives guidance on this point: "...in most instances it will be sufficient to discuss the matter with any one relative who had been in close contact with the deceased, asking him his own views, the views of the deceased and also if he has any reason to believe that any other relative would be likely to object. In certain circumstances it might be necessary for such discussion to take place on the telephone. Potential organ donors will often have spent some hours or even days in hospital and in such cases hospitals will have sufficient opportunity to take steps to contact relatives. Where, after such reasonable enquiry as may be practicable, there is no evidence that the donor has any relatives, authority may be given under section 1(2) in the absence of any other evidence which suggests to the contrary. Where it is known that a potential donor has relatives but it has not been possible to contact any of them, a person giving authority for organ removal must be especially careful to ensure that the requirements of the Act with regard to the making of enquiries have been met. It is not enough to say in a case where organs must be removed very soon after death that no enquiry is practicable. Any objections made by patient or relatives should be noted immediately in the patient's notes. The word "relatives" is not defined in the Act, but there are some circumstances in which it ought to be interpreted in the widest sense, eg. to include those who although claiming only a distant relationship are nevertheless closely concerned with the deceased."

As long as the terms of the statute are adhered to there is no legal requirement that relatives consent in writing to tissue removal. However, DHSS circular HC(77)28 states in relation to proposed removal of tissue for transplant purposes at post mortem examinations that the Department "considers it desirable" that relatives should be invited to sign a post mortem declaration form. The form contains a consent to remove "amounts of tissue for the treatment of other patients and for medical education and research." The circular also states, however, that "it is accepted that there will be occasions when only verbal enquiry is possible."

If the deceased is known to have followed a particular religion then consultation with an appropriate religious leader might well be advisable. Some Hindus, for example, might object to the removal of an organ after death, and in Judaism, as the question of when life is extinct might not accord with that given below, the deceased person might have objected.

"Lawfully in possession"

The question of who is "lawfully in possession" and may thus give the necessary authorisation has given rise to much debate. Is it the person or authority which has control over the premises in which the person died or is it the deceased's executor or next of kin? DHSS circular HSC(IS)156 offers the following guidance:

"If a person dies in hospital, the person lawfully in possession of the body, at least until the executors or "relatives" ask for the body to be handed to them, is the Area Health Authority or the Board of Governors responsible for the hospital. In the case of a private institution or a Services hospital, the person lawfully in possession would be the managers and commanding Officer, respectively."

If a person dies elsewhere than in hospital the question of who is lawfully in possession should not normally give rise to difficulty. Thus, it may be the husband in the case of a deceased wife, the parent in the case of a deceased child, the executor, if any, or even the householder on whose premises the body lies. If a person is brought into hospital dead the Health Authority will be lawfully in possession of the body..., although in such cases the Coroner will normally be involved.

In those cases where a body is lawfully in the possession of a hospital, nursing home, or other institution the Act permits the managers to delegate the right to give authority to remove tissue under the Act to a designated person.

The person "lawfully in possession" is under no obligation to authorise tissue removal even if the deceased made it clear that this was his wish. Thus the question of who has the right to make this authorisation could be important. There could, in theory, be a dispute between the hospital and the relatives as to which of them was "lawfully in possession" for these purposes. In *Law and Medical Ethics* (third edition) by J K Mason and R A McCall Smith (London: Butterworths, 1991) the authors state: "We believe that to accede to the relatives in such circumstances would be the lesser of two evils but it is fortunate that such conflicts are very rare in practice."

If a person has reason to believe that the coroner or procurator fiscal may require an inquest, or inquiry, or a post mortem examination to be held tissue cannot be removed without their consent. There is no statutory requirement that this consent be in writing. This applies equally if tissue is removed in the circumstances set out below.

General requirements

When it comes to the removal of the organs, section 1(4) of the Human Tissue Act 1961 (as amended by the Corneal Tissue Act 1986) states: "No such removal, except of eyes, or parts of eyes shall be effected except by a registered medical practitioner who must have satisfied himself by personal examination of the body that life is extinct." Section 1(4)(A) states that eyes or parts of eyes can only be removed as above or by "a person in the employment of a health authority acting on the instructions of a registered medical practitioner who must, before giving those instructions, be satisfied that the person in question is sufficiently qualified and trained to perform the removal competently and must also either:

(i) have satisfied himself by personal examination of the body that life is extinct; or

(ii)   be satisfied that life is extinct on the basis of a statement to that effect by a registered medical practitioner who has satisfied himself by personal examination of the body that life is extinct."

An appendix to Department of Health circular HC(90)7 sets out the procedure for allocating organs removed from patients in NHS hospitals. In the first instance they should be used for transplantation into patients who are eligible for NHS treatment.

1.5 *Brain death*

There is no legal definition of death. In 1983 a revised edition of the *Code of Practice on the Removal of Cadaveric Organs for Transplantation* was drawn up by a working party on behalf of the health departments of Great Britain and Northern Ireland. This includes a section on diagnosis of death and reproduces the texts of the papers "Diagnosis of Brain Death" and "Diagnosis of Death" by the Conference of Royal Colleges and Faculties of the United Kingdom as appendices. The "Code of Practice" was commended to hospital doctors by the Chief Medical Officer in January 1980 (CMO(80)1). For a more detailed discussion of the legal issues surrounding the diagnosis of death see chapter 6.

1.6 Police and Criminal Evidence Act 1984

1.6.1 *Intimate body searches*

By virtue of the Police and Criminal Evidence Act 1984 doctors may be involved in performing intimate body searches and taking intimate body samples from persons in police custody. As this would normally constitute assault unless the person consented in the usual way, it is worth noting when such searches, etc, are, in fact, lawful.

Section 55 deals with "intimate searches" defined by section 118 as "a search which consists of physical examination of a person's body orifices." Such searches may be carried out only if a officer of the rank of superintendent or above has reasonable grounds for believing:

(a)   that an article which would cause physical injury to a detained person or others at the police station has been concealed or;

(b)   that the person concealed a Class A drug which he intends to supply to another or to export (see also Schedule to *Misuse of Drugs Act*, chapter 9)

(c)   that in either case an intimate search is the only practicable means of removing it.

9

Intimate searches may only be carried out by a registered doctor or a registered nurse (RGN) unless an officer of at least the rank of superintendent considers that this is not practicable and the search is conducted under (a) above. A search under (a) or (b) may only take place at a hospital, surgery or other medical premises. It cannot take place at a police station. Action in connection with intimate and strip searches is set out in a code of practice for the detention, treatment, and questioning of persons by police officers issued under the Act. The code of practice also deals with medical treatment of persons detained in custody.

Section 62 deals with the taking of intimate samples from persons in police detention. Under section 65 these are defined as a "sample of blood, semen or any other tissue fluid, urine, saliva or pubic hair, or a swab taken from a person's body orifice." All such samples (except for urine or saliva) must be taken by a registered doctor and either the consent of the prisoner must be obtained or the authorisation of a police officer of at least the rank of superintendent. The prisoner's consent is needed if he has attained the age of 17. If he is under 17 but has attained the age of 14, not only his consent but that of his parent or guardian is also required. If the prisoner is under 14 the parent's or guardian's consent only is required. If the consent is not forthcoming then a senior police officer may authorise the taking of the sample only if he has reasonable grounds to do so.

Any person held in police custody will have a custody record which should detail the time of arrest and any treatment, interview, telephone calls and the like which take place during the period in custody. Any authority for the taking of intimate samples or for the carrying out of an intimate search should be recorded in that custody record. The record should record which part of the person's body was searched, by whom, and details of anyone else who was present together with reasons for the search and its result.

BMA policy on the issue, agreed in 1989, states that "no medical practitioner should take part in an intimate body search of a subject without that subject's consent." Guidelines for doctors asked to perform intimate body searches are available from the BMA.

1.6.2 *Provision of medical treatment*

A police surgeon or other doctor must be called, or the prisoner taken to hospital if he

(a)   appears physically or mentally ill;

(b)   is injured;

(c)   shows no signs of awareness;

(d)   fails to respond to conversation (unless drunk);

(e)   appears to need medical treatment for other reasons (apart from minor ailments or injuries).

A detainee can also request a medical examination, in which case the police surgeon must be called as soon as practicable. Alternatively, the prisoner can be examined by a doctor of his own choice at his own expense.

1.7 *Notifiable diseases*

Statutory powers under public health legislation in respect of individuals with notifiable diseases provide for compulsory examination and compulsory removal and detention in hospital. (Notification by registered medical practitioners is referred to in the section on confidentiality in chapter 3. In England and Wales the law on this subject is presently contained in the Public Health (control of disease) Act 1984 and various regulations.

Section 35 states that if a Justice of the Peace (JP) has received a written certificate, issued by a registered medical practitioner who has been nominated by the local authority and is satisfied:

"(a)   that there is reason to believe that some person in the district

    (i)   is or has been suffering from a notifiable disease, or
    (ii)   though not suffering from such a disease, is carrying an organism that is capable of causing it, and

(b)   that in his own interest, or in the interest of his family, or in the public interest, it is expedient that he should be medically examined, and

(c)   that he is not under the treatment of a registered medical practitioner or that the registered medical practitioner who is treating him consents to the making of an order ..."

then the court may order such an examination. The Act states that the examination may include subjecting the patient to bacteriological and radiological tests and similar investigations.

Similarly, section 36 provides that compulsory medical examinations can be imposed on groups of persons if the group is believed to comprise carriers of notifiable diseases.

The JP must be satisfied:

(a)   that there is reason to believe that one of a group of persons, though not suffering from a notifiable disease, is carrying an organism that is capable of causing it, and

(b)   that in the interests of those persons or their families, or in the public interest, it is expedient that those persons should be medically examined."

Section 37 of the Act provides for the compulsory removal to hospital of those with notifiable diseases. If, on the application of a local authority, a JP thinks that a person has a notifiable disease and that proper precautions to prevent the spread of infection cannot be or are not being taken, and that the person is a serious risk of infection to others, then the JP may order the person's removal to hospital provided there is space available and the district health authority consents.

Under section 38, if a JP thinks that the patient "... would not on leaving the hospital be provided with lodging or accommodation in which proper precautions could be taken to prevent the spread of the disease by him," the JP may order further detention in hospital for as long as is necessary in his opinion. A patient thus detained would be guilty of an offence if he discharged himself.

It should be noted that sections 35, 36, 37 and 38 all provide that "if he deems it necessary" the JP may act ex parte. This means the JP may make these orders without the person affected thereby being present in court or represented.

The Act makes many other provisions in respect of notifiable disease. These include the prosecution of those who, knowing that they have a notifiable disease, act in such a way as to expose others to risk of infection (section 17). Persons with notifiable diseases can also be stopped from trading (section 19) and such persons can be forced to stop working (section 20). This would affect, for instance, those involved in food preparation. (Such people are entitled to statutory sick pay if they are eligible under the Social Security and Housing Benefits Act 1982, and also compensation according to the Public Health (Control of Disease) Act 1984.)

Public Health (Infectious Diseases) Regulations 1985 (SI > 1985 No 434), introduced in March 1985), apply certain provisions of the 1984 Act to the Acquired Immune Deficiency Syndrome (AIDS) but do not make it compulsorily notifiable. The provisions which apply to AIDS are section 35 (medical examination), section 37 (removal to hospital) (see above for both), and section 38 (detention in hospital) (see above again), but note that section 38 is modified in the case of AIDS to permit an order to be made:

"... if the Justice is satisfied that on his (the patient's) leaving hospital proper precautions to prevent the spread of that disease would not be taken by him—

(a) in his lodging or accommodation, or

(b) in other places to which he may be expected to go if not detained in the hospital."

In Scotland the statute law has been consolidated and the law is to be found in a number of statutes extending back to the Infectious Diseases (Notification) Act 1889. Sections 54 to 58 of the Public Health (Scotland) Act 1897 (as amended) contain similar provisions to sections 17, 19, 20, 37 and 38 of the 1984 English Act and in addition make it an offence to send a child to school with an infectious disease, (for notification see chapter 3.3)

The Health Services and Public Health Act 1968, sections 71 to 74, provide powers under the order of the sheriff for compulsory medical examination of individuals or groups in similar circumstances to those provided by sections 35 and 36 of the English statute.

Although AIDS is not a notifiable infectious disease in Scotland, there are powers under the Public Health (Scotland) Act 1897, sections 45 to 59, to provide for the compulsory examination of those suspected of any infectious disease and, if necessary, for their compulsory removal to hospital.

1.8 National Assistance Act 1948

Section 47 of the National Assistance Act 1948 provides that on the certificate of a community physician, the local authority can apply to the magistrates court for a removal order. The provision is intended to assist those with grave chronic disease or people who are physically incapacitated, and who are unable to look after themselves, and are not being properly cared for by other people. It must be judged that removal from home is necessary either in the person's own interests or because the person represents a health threat or serious nuisance to others. The order will authorise the person's transfer to hospital or other convenient place where he can be given care and attention. The maximum period for such an order is three months (renewable).

In many cases the person's plight will be raised by his general practitioner (GP) to the "proper officer" of the local authority, the public health physician. It can be done verbally or in writing and does not require the subject's consent, although the subject has the right to know whether his GP has initiated the procedure. It is considered prudent to discuss the situation with the subject first and, if he agrees, with the next of kin.

The National Assistance (Amendment) Act 1951 provides an additional emergency procedure where it is necessary to remove the person without delay. This is used more often than the full procedure and is invoked in cases of extreme urgency. In this case the order can be made ex parte; the community physician may make application himself, supported by a second medical opinion, and periods of notice required under section 47 can be waived.

Both of these procedures are provisions of last resort and are generally regarded as draconian and stigmatising. Consequently, some local authorities refuse to use them. This is a matter currently under consideration by the Law Commission.

1.9 Consent to research

1.9.1 *Local research ethics committee approval*

Attention is often drawn to the fact that, as a nation, we have regulated research on animals by law for over a century (since the Cruelty to Animals Act 1876 and more recently the Animals (Scientific Procedures Act) 1986), but no such specific legal provisions have traditionally been extended to humans beyond the common law concept of consent and the statutory framework for drug licensing by the Committee on the Safety of Medicines (see chapter 9.6). Now that parliament has passed the Human Fertilisation and Embryology Act 1990, research on embryos has been brought within statutory supervision, but other difficult areas such as research on children, prisoners, people with severe mental disabilities and the elderly remain unregulated by law or binding regulations.

The Department of Health issued guidelines on local research ethics committees (LRECs) in 1991. These specify that LREC approval must be obtained for any research project involving:

• NHS patients

• fetal material and in vitro fertilisation involving NHS patients

• the recently dead, in NHS premises

• access to records on past or present NHS patients

• access to NHS premises

By agreement, LRECs can also advise on studies in the private sector. There is no single national body which can centrally approve research to be carried out in different areas, although an LREC in one area may be content to accept the opinion of a research project given by an LREC elsewhere, or by the Research Ethics Committee of the Royal College of General Practitioners (RCGP), or the case of research in general practice. One of the functions of the LREC is to determine whether specific patient consent is required for the research project in question.

1.9.2 *Guidance to doctors*

Legal experts have questioned whether the Sidaway judgement (see Chapter 1.1) concerning informed consent has relevance for research. One view is that advice arising from the Sidaway case concerns circumstances in which the doctor's only intention is to treat the patient.

In the absence of statute many reputable bodies have issued guidance on the question of subject consent in the context of research. The Medical Research Council, for example, states the basic principles in a number of its policy booklets. The Council says:

"Seeking the consent of an individual to participation in research reflects the right of that individual to self-determination and also his fundamental right to be free from bodily interference whether physical or psychological. These are ethical principles recognised by English law as legal rights. We identified three elements to consent in its broadest sense) the information given, the capacity to understand it and the voluntariness of any decision taken.

At the most basic level, failure to supply information about the nature and purpose of what is proposed may lead to a claim that the interference with the research subject's body constitutes a trespass to person. Thus it should be made clear to the subject that he is being invited to participate in research even if what is proposed is part of normal treatment. If a person then freely consents that consent is real provided there has been no misrepresentation of the facts. However, additional information, for instance, on possible risks and alternatives is required in a suitable form before it can properly be said that the researcher has fully discharged his general duty to put the subject in a position to make a rational judgement about whether to participate."

Importantly, in 1991 the Medical Research Council also published a revision of its 1962 statement on consent, which had previously set the tone for research standards. It drew attention to the fact that the Council's statement had played an important part in the development of the discussion of the ethics of medical research, but that the position set out in it with respect to consent is now seriously out of line with contemporary thinking. The root of the problem lies in the part of the statement which read:

"In the case of procedures directly connected with the management of the condition in the particular individual, the relationship is essentially that between doctor and patient. Implicit in this relationship is the willingness on the part of the subject to be guided by the judgement of his medical attendant. Provided, therefore, that the medical attendant is satisfied that there are reasonable grounds for believing that a particular new procedure will contribute to the benefit of that particular patient, either by treatment, prevention on increased understanding of his case, he may assume the patient's consent to the same extent as he would were the procedure entirely established practice."

In its review the MRC said "We readily accept that trust between doctor and patient continues to be central to good clinical practice, but we suggest that it can no longer be assumed that the patient will, or indeed, should, be guided solely by the judgement of his medical attendant, or that there are any circumstances (other than some emergencies) where the doctor can assume consent.

It is now generally accepted that the doctor has a duty to explain to the patient the pros and cons of the various feasible courses of action in offering treatment or measures intended to prevent or improve a given condition. If this is so for treatment it must hold even more true for research. Those we consulted were unanimous that for most classes of research the patient must understand that he is taking part in research and give his consent to participation in that research."

1.9.3 *International standards*

The two principal sets of international ethical standards relevant to researchers are the World Medical Association's Declaration of Tokyo and the *European Commission's Guidelines on Good Clinical Practice for Trials on Medicinal Products in the European Community*. These latter guidelines have not yet entered the statute in the United Kingdom, but it is proposed to require all member states to make them part of national law within the next few years.

1.9.4 *Subjects unable to consent to research*

Participation of minors in research is discussed in chapter 7. Research on mentally incapacitated people (and others unable to give consent, such as unconscious patients) is discussed in chapter 8. The European (as yet non-statutory) guidelines seem to permit only "therapeutic" research on such groups.

Paragraph 1.13 states:

"If the subject is incapable of giving personal consent (eg, unconsciousness or severe mental illness or disability), the inclusion of such patients may be acceptable if the ethics committee is, in principle, in agreement and if the investigator is of the opinion that participation will promote the welfare and interest of the subject. The agreement of a legally valid representative that participation will promote the welfare interest of the subject should also be recorded by a dated signature. If neither signed informed consent nor witnessed signed verbal consent are possible, this fact must be documented with reasons by the investigator."

Paragraph 1.14 states:

"Consent must always be given by the signature of the subject in a non-therapeutic study, ie, when there is no direct clinical benefit to the subject."

1.9.5 *Epidemiological research*

The requirement for patient consent for disclosure of identifiable information is discussed in chapter 3.7.

1.9.6 *Embryo research*

The Human Fertilisation and Embryology Authority took over responsibility for supervising embryo research in 1991. Its power stems from the Human Fertilisation and Embryology Act 1990. Schedule 3 of the Act describes the consent that must be obtained from gamete donors for gametes or embryos used for the purposes of any project of research. Each protocol for such research must relate broadly to one of the existing categories of research aims. These are:

(a)   promoting advances in the treatment of infertility;

(b)   increasing knowledge about the causes of congenital disease (an amendment seeking to limit this to life-threatening or severely disabling conditions was withdrawn);

(c)   increasing knowledge about the causes of miscarriage;

(d)   developing more effective techniques of contraception (an amendment condemning this as "frivolous" was defeated);

(e)   developing methods for detecting the presence of gene or chromosome abnormalities in embryos before implantation;

(f)   more generally for the purpose of increasing knowledge about the creation and development of embryos and enabling such knowledge to be applied.

2 Medical malpractice

This chapter looks at the remedies which are available to a patient who is not satisfied with the medical care he has received. He may feel that he did not agree to treatment or that he was not properly informed about the risks of treatment; he may have agreed to treatment and ended up worse rather than better and seek compensation through the courts. He may want a thorough investigation and review of his case.

2.1 Battery

In chapter 1.1 it was stated that any doctor who operated on, injected, or even touched or examined a patient without that patient's consent could be sued for battery. There are important differences between an action for battery and one for negligence.

(i) In battery the patient only has to establish that the doctor touched him—he does not have to show that any loss or damage resulted from the unlawful act. In negligence the patient must prove that the doctor's negligence in touching or treating without consent caused the particular injury for which damages are sought (see section on causation in 2.2.1). This means that if a doctor decided that treatment would benefit the patient and went ahead without consent and the patient improved the patient could still sue. For example, in Devi *v* W Midlands Regional Health Authority (1981) a doctor discovered that his patient's womb was ruptured while performing minor surgery and performed a sterilisation procedure there and then, although she had not consented. Although sterilisation was in her best interests, the doctor was held liable.

(ii) In battery damages will be awarded for all direct consequences of the battery, even a freak reaction. In negligence damages can be recovered only for consequences which are reasonably foreseeable.

2.2 Negligence

2.2.1 *General principles*

If one person has behaved negligently towards another then it may be possible for that other to sue for damages in the civil courts. Not every medical mishap gives the patient the right to sue for damages. Negligence is defined in law as the breach of a duty to use reasonable care as a result of which there is damage to another. To mount such an action successfully the person aggrieved will have to establish (on the balance of probabilities) a number of elements. Firstly, a legal duty of care must be owed by the alleged wrongdoer to the victim. Secondly, the former must have been in breach of that duty—that is, his or her behaviour must have fallen short of the standard required by law, and it must have been reasonably foreseeable that the careless behaviour in question could damage the plaintiff. Thirdly, a causal link between the behaviour and the damage in question must also be proved and some damage must have been sustained. If the plaintiff fails to establish any of these elements the claim will fail.

There is no doubt that a doctor owes a duty of care to a patient he or she is treating whether privately or under the NHS. The law imposes a duty of care in any situation where one person can reasonably foresee that his or her conduct would harm another—for example, a GP accepting a patient on his or her list undertakes a duty to the patient, as does a hospital and its staff where the patient is admitted for treatment.

The judge must rule on what is the appropriate standard of care in any given situation. The standard of care required by a doctor is the standard of the reasonably skilled and experienced doctor. In the case of Bolam *v* Friern Hospital Management Committee (1957) the judge said "The test is the standard of the ordinary skilled man exercising and professing to have that special skill. A man need not possess the highest expert skill; it is well established in law that it is sufficient if he exercises the ordinary skill of the ordinary competent man exercising that particular art." The defendant will be tested against the standard of the doctor in his particular field of medicine. A doctor who professes to exercise a special skill must exercise the ordinary skill of his specialty.

In a series of cases it has been established that if a doctor treats a patient in a way that is considered acceptable at the time by one responsible body of medical opinion the doctor cannot be held to be negligent even if there is another responsible body of medical opinion which considers the treatment in question was wrong.

In the case of Bolam, for instance, a patient to whom electroconvulsant therapy was administered sustained fractures. No relaxant drugs or manual restraints were used. At the time there were two bodies of opinion within the profession, one in favour of the use of relaxant drugs and one against, and there were also two opinions as to whether in the absence of relaxants manual control should be applied. The doctor was therefore absolved from negligence. In the headnote to the case it is stated:

"(i) a doctor is not negligent, if he is acting in accordance with a practice accepted as proper by a responsible body of medical men skilled in that particular art, merely because there is a body of such opinion that takes a contrary view."

In the case of Whitehouse v Jordan (1981) 1 AER 267 damages were claimed when a baby was born with brain damage after a senior hospital registrar had pulled the baby several times with obstetric forceps. The baby was delivered eventually by caesarean section. The House of Lords upheld the Court of Appeal's rejection of the trial judge's finding of negligence, but not the Court of Appeal's conclusion that an error of clinical judgement could not in law ever amount to negligence. The headnote to the law report states (per Lord Edmund-Davies, Lord Fraser, and Lord Russell): "While some errors of clinical judgement may be completely consistent with the due exercise of professional skill, other acts or omissions in the course of exercising clinical judgement may be so glaringly below proper standards as to make a finding of negligence inevitable. The test whether a surgeon has been negligent is whether he has failed to measure up in any respect, whether in clinical judgement or otherwise, to the standard of the ordinary skilled surgeon exercising and professing to have the special skill of a surgeon." The last sentence probably states the position so far as is possible.

Accepted practice must be judged according to current practice at the date of the operation or treatment, not the date that the claim comes to trial (Roe v Ministry of Health (1954)). The doctor must keep up to date with new developments, but it is accepted that it may take some time for research findings to be made known to all doctors in a particular field. A doctor will be judged by the standard of awareness of a doctor in his or her type of practice. For example, in Crawford v Board of Governors of Charing Cross Hospital (1953) failure to read a single, recent article in the *Lancet* was not negligent. However, disregard of a series of warnings in the medical press could well be evidence of negligence.

A doctor who departs from accepted practice is not necessarily negligent but must be able to justify his action by showing special features of the case which called for a different method of treatment or by showing that the mode of treatment is at least equal to accepted practice (see Clark v MacLennan (1983)).

The court has also applied the standard of care test in situations where a patient claims that a doctor was negligent in not providing information on the risks of treatment (see Sidaway v Bethlem Royal Hospital, chapter 1.1).

A similar test applies to claims relating to negligent diagnosis. The plaintiff must prove that the doctor has failed to carry out a test that was appropriate, having regard to the patient's symptoms, or that he reached a conclusion that no competent doctor would reach. Where a diagnostic procedure is not routine and may itself carry some risk the doctor must consider whether the patient's symptoms justify it (see Maynard v West Midlands RHA (1985)).

Even where negligence is established the plaintiff still has to prove that the negligence caused his injury or unimproved condition. In Wilsher v Essex Area Health Authority the House of Lords found that the administration of excess oxygen to a premature baby was negligent. However, there was an irreconcilable difference of opinion among the experts giving evidence at the trial as to the cause of the plaintiff's injury (blindness). The plaintiff was able to prove that negligence was one of the possible causes of the injury but failed in his claim because he had not established that negligence was the actual cause or had materially contributed to the injury.

A similar point as to proof of causation was made in the complicated litigation over pertussis vaccination. In Loveday v Renton (1990), the court held that establishing a mere chance that pertussis vaccine might cause brain damage in children did not discharge the obligation on the plaintiff.

2.2.2 Proving negligence

To prove negligence a patient must prove that, on the balance of probabilities, injury resulted from the negligent act of the doctor. This means that the patient must show that it is more likely than not that the doctor was negligent and that this caused the injury.

In certain circumstances there is a shift in the burden of proof. The principle known as "res ipsa loquitur" (literally, the thing speaks for itself) applies when an accident happens which does not ordinarily happen if proper care is taken. In such circumstances the accident itself is reasonable evidence of negligence, and the defendant will be liable unless he can provide a satisfactory explanation of the accident. The doctrine does not shift the onus of proof to the defendant; what it does achieve is to give rise to an inference of negligence on the defendant's part. It is thus considerably easier for the plaintiff to succeed in a claim when res ipsa loquitur applies. This principle is generally invoked in cases which concern items of operating equipment being left inside patients after surgery. In Mahon v Osborne it was stated that the surgeon had overall responsibility to ensure that swabs were not left inside the patient and that procedures must be adopted to minimise the possibility of this occurring. However, it was accepted that it may be necessary to dispense with normal procedures in an emergency.

2.2.3 Vicarious liability

If a doctor is employed by someone else then that employer is "vicariously liable", and can also be sued, if the doctor is negligent in the course of employment. A doctor who employs staff can in turn be held legally responsible for his employee's negligent actions. In an NHS hospital if the patient can identify the person who was negligent he can sue that person and also the employer. Where a patient cannot identify a specific member of staff who was negligent, but all staff responsible for his care were employed by the health authority, then the health authority is necessarily vicariously liable for whoever may have been at fault. In Cassidy v Ministry of Health in 1951 the court found that a patient's injury was caused by negligence and that all the staff involved were employed by the NHS. Therefore, there was evidence of negligence against their common employer. A health authority can also be liable directly to the patient in that it failed to provide an adequate and safe service (see Wilsher *v* Essex Area Health Authority, chapter 2.2.6).

Under the indemnity scheme, which came into effect 1 January 1990, health authorities assumed responsibility for the handling of all negligence claims against the authority or its employees in hospital or community health services including the payment of compensation. The final decision on whether to settle a case now rests with the health authority. Where a doctor feels that his interests are distinct from those of the authority, although this may be taken into account by the authority, he has no right to contest the claim. However, with the agreement of the plaintiff, the health authority, and the court the doctor can be separately represented.

As independent practitioners GPs are not employees of the health authority. In the case of a single-handed practitioner, action would be taken against that GP alone. Where a GP is in partnership his partners are jointly liable for his negligence. A GP is not vicariously liable for the negligence of a locum or deputy because he is not an employee of the GP. However, the GP may be directly liable if he was negligent in selecting a locum or deputising service for example, if he failed to check a locum's qualifications.

2.2.4 *Time limits*

Time limits within which legal actions must be brought are set out in the Limitation Act 1980 (England and Wales only) and in the Prescription and Limitation (Scotland) Act 1984. The basic rule is that when claiming damages for personal injury or death a person must start action within three years of the episode (in cases of economic loss only the time limit is six years).

There are the following exceptions to this basic rule:

(i) *Subsequent knowledge*

If certain criteria are met a claim in respect of personal injuries may be made within three years of the claimant discovering certain facts. In Scotland if the claimant was not aware of some material fact of a decisive nature until some date after the injury was sustained then the claimant can bring the action within three years of acquiring this knowledge. In England and Wales a similar extension is allowed—"three years from the date of knowledge (if later) of the person injured". The Act spells out in some detail what the "date of knowledge" means in this context. It means the date on which the person first had knowledge (see below) of the following facts.

1   That the injury in question was "significant", defined as follows: "... if the person whose date of knowledge is in question would reasonably have considered it sufficiently serious to justify his instituting proceedings for damages against a defendant who did not dispute liability and was able to satisfy a judgement."

2   That the injury was attributable in whole or in part to the act or

omission which is alleged to constitute negligence, nuisance or breach of duty.

3   The identity of the defendant.

4   And, if it is alleged that the act or omission was that of a person other than the defendant, the identity of the person and the additional facts supporting the bringing of an action against the defendant.

Two further points must be borne in mind:

(1)   Knowledge that any acts or omissions did or did not, as a matter of law, involve negligence, nuisance, or breach of duty is irrelevant.

(2)   A person's "knowledge" is deemed to include "... knowledge which he might reasonably have been expected to acquire

   (a)   from facts observable or ascertainable by him; or

   (b)   from facts ascertainable by him with the help of medical or other appropriate expert advice which it is reasonable for him to seek."

However, if a person has taken all reasonable steps to obtain (and where appropriate act on) expert advice he shall not be deemed for these purposes to have knowledge of a fact ascertainable only with the help of expert advice.

(ii) *Court discretion*
If given leave by the court, a claimant can also be permitted to start an action outside the normal three year limit if the court considers that to give such leave would be "equitable." The English Statute lists several criteria to be taken into account. The court must consider the extent to which the plaintiff would be prejudiced if the action was not allowed to proceed out of time, and, conversely, the extent to which the defendant would be prejudiced if the court exercised discretion in favour of the plaintiff. The court must look at all the circumstances but a number of criteria are to be particularly considered:

(a)   "the length of, and the reasons for, the delay on the part of the plaintiff";

(b)   the extent to which, having regard to the delay, the evidence adduced by the plaintiff or the defendant is or is likely to be less cogent than if the action had been brought in time;

(c)   "the conduct of the defendant after the cause of action arose, including the extent (if any) to which he responded to requests reasonably made by the plaintiff for information or inspection for the purpose of ascertaining facts which were or might be relevant to the plaintiff's cause of action". (Doctors or hospitals faced with queries from dissatisfied patients should particularly note this provision and should immediately seek legal advice if appropriate.)

(d) the duration of any disability of the plaintiff arising after the date of the accrual of the action (examples of legal "disabilities" are mental illness or being under the age of 18);

(e) "the extent to which the plaintiff acted promptly and reasonably once he knew whether or not the act or omission of the defendant, to which the injury was attributable, might be capable at that time of giving rise to an action for damages";

(f) "the steps, if any, taken by the plaintiff to obtain medical, legal or other expert advice and the nature of any such advice he may have received".

Two additional exceptions, relating to minors (who have three years from the age of 18) and to mentally ill people (who have three years from recovery of sanity) are dealt with in detail in chapters 7 and 8, respectively.

Schedule 1 of the Consumer Protection Act 1987 amends both the Limitation Act 1980 and the Prescription and Limitation (Scotland) Act 1973 in respect of product liability where injury results from a defective product.

A new section 11A of the Limitation Act 1980 relating to action in respect of defective products, states:

"(1) This section shall apply to an action for damages by virtue of any provision of Part 1 of the Consumer Protection Act 1987.

(2) None of the time limits given in the preceding provisions of this Act shall apply to an action to which this section applies."

This alters the maximum period of limitation in respect of such actions to 10 years from "the relevant time", while providing for shorter time limits similar to, but not identical with, those mentioned below. (See chapter 9.6.5 for further details). A similar provision is made in the Prescription and Limitation (Scotland) Act 1973.

The net result of the above is that a doctor could be sued some years after giving treatment. The three year limit applies only to start of proceedings; once began they could drag on for many years.

2.2.5 Records

In certain circumstances the patient has a statutory right of access to records (see chapter 4.3). This right can be exercised at any time whether or not there is any real intention to begin proceedings. The right can be exercised by the patient or the patient's personal representative, or through the patient's solicitors. In the latter situation the doctor should ensure that he has the written consent of the patient before releasing the record. (The BMA has an advice leaflet on releasing records for litigation purposes).

Disclosure of records for the purpose of litigation is dealt with in England and Wales by the Supreme Court Act 1981, sections 33 and 34, and the County Court Act 1984, section 52 (2), and in Scotland by the Administration of Justice (Scotland) Act 1972. Under these statutes the court can order disclosure of all documents, including medical records, relevant to the action when legal proceedings in respect of personal injury and death have started or there is the intention to bring proceedings. Section 33 relates to disclosure where a person having custody of the record is likely to be a party to the proceedings. Section 34 covers the situation where the record is in the custody of someone not a party to the proceedings—for example, where the patient wishes to sue a hospital but also needs access to notes made by the GP.

The court will not order such disclosure unless there is a real likelihood of proceedings. It will not permit a "fishing expedition" (a look through records in the hope that negligence may come to light). The court has a discretion to restrict disclosure to the patient's legal and medical adviser, or where the patient has no legal adviser to his medical adviser alone.

Most medical reports/records must be disclosed, but certain reports are privileged and do not have to be revealed to the patient's legal advisers. A report is privileged if the sole or dominant purpose for which it was prepared was for submission to a legal adviser in anticipation of court proceedings. This would include the reports of expert witnesses. However, if it is desired to call the writer of any expert report to give oral evidence, then the court will order that the report must first be shown to the other side, unless there are special reasons for not doing so (Order 38, Rule 37 of the rules of the Supreme Court). Order 38, Rule 38 of the rules of the Supreme Court provides for a direction as appropriate for medical experts to meet and identify the main issues.

In the following paragraphs we consider the legal position (in terms of negligence claims) of junior hospital doctors and medical students doing clinical work. Also discussed is the duty of doctors who suddenly come across the scene of an accident and the duties of GPs to refer their patients to specialists (with special reference to the problems caused by NHS waiting lists).

2.2.6 *Junior Hospital Doctors*

The Court of Appeal considered the standard of care required of a junior doctor in Wilsher *v* Essex Area Health Authority [1987] 2WLR 425. A premature baby was treated and his life probably saved in a special care baby unit. He was given extra oxygen. The oxygen concentrations in his blood were not properly monitored because a junior doctor failed to insert a catheter correctly and a senior registrar who checked what the junior doctor had done failed to notice his mistake. The baby was rendered blind.

The court considered that inexperience is no defence to negligence. The law requires that in a specialist unit a doctor will possess a degree of skill and experience appropriate to the post he occupies and the tasks he undertakes. The court recognised the need for doctors to learn on the job and held that an inexperienced junior doctor would have a defence in a negligence claim if he sought and followed the advice of a more senior doctor. In Wilsher the junior doctor was held not to have been negligent, but the senior registrar was.

Conversely, a junior doctor who chose to depart from the instruction he was given by his senior could find himself vulnerable to a negligence action if anything went wrong.

The defendants, having failed in the Court of Appeal, appealed to the House of Lords. The appeal was allowed in 1988 but on the basis of causation (see 2.2.1). The opinion of most of the Court of Appeal remains legally binding on the standard of care expected of a junior doctor (see section 2.3 on criminal liability).

2.2.7 Medical students doing clinical work

The following guidance concerning the employment of medical students in hospital has been given by the government (but note that the Medical Act referred to has now been replaced by section 47 of the Medical Act 1983).

The Medical Acts 1956 and 1978: A DHSS letter to regional health authorities in September 1971 (DS 256/71) stated the following:

"4   By virtue of Section 28(1) of the Medical Act 1956 as amended by schedule 7, to the Medical Act 1978, an appointment as physician, surgeon or medical officer in a National Health Service hospital can only be held by a person registered with the GMC. Undergraduates are unable, therefore, to hold such appointments. Medical students however, are able to undertake voluntary work or when covering for an absent house officer because of holidays or sickness.

Conditions under which students do clinical work:

5   In view of the advice contained in paragraph 4 above, health authorities should ensure that when students undertake clinical work, whether as part of their clinical course or when voluntarily assisting in hospital departments, they do so under the close supervision of a registered medical practitioner. The following conditions must be observed:-

   (i)   The consultant in charge, who has an overall clinical responsibility for his patients, will be responsible for ensuring supervision by a suitable named practitioner. The named practitioner must have his responsibilities clearly explained to him by the consultant in charge. It will be for this named practitioner to determine the actual degree of supervision necessary for the various clinical procedures which may be undertaken by the student. Where a student assists with a maternity case the supervision of a certified midwife is acceptable.

(ii) A student should not initiate treatment for a patient on his own diagnosis; both the diagnosis and treatment must be confirmed by a registered practitioner.

(iii) A student must not act as or be regarded as a "locum" for an absent house officer. The responsibility for an absent house officer's job, if a locum tenens is not engaged, must at any one time devolve upon a named member of the medical staff, who may be assisted in covering the house officer's job as well as his own by a medical student. The practitioner who is standing in must at all times supervise the clinical activities of his student assistant.

(iv) A student must not, in any circumstances, prescribe.

(v) A student should not request X-rays.

(vi) Health boards must secure the consent of the Dean of the medical school or his authorised representative before allowing a medical student to act as an assistant. Health boards will wish to discuss with Deans the most convenient arrangements for this (where it is not already done)."

There do not appear to be any decided cases at present concerning negligence of a student, but any student taking on such a post should heed the observations in the Wilsher case. In that case one judge in the Court of Appeal observed "to my mind this notion of a duty tailored to the actor, rather than to the act which he elects to perform has no place in the law of tort". A student who "elected" to take on a post which should be filled by a qualified doctor would be expected to perform with the expertise of such a doctor. It is likely also that the health authority would be considered negligent for placing a student in such a post. (This too was noted in the Wilsher case.)

Consultants and others should note that improper delegation to a medical student could give rise to a finding of negligence against the delegator.

2.2.8 Coming upon the scene of an accident

A doctor who suddenly comes across the scene of an accident might be in some dilemma as to the extent of his responsibilities in such a situation. In England both the criminal and the civil law have been concerned overwhelmingly with protecting the individual from wrongful omissions. To quote one academic: "There is no general duty to act positively for the benefit of others. An adult who stands by and watches a child (to whom he stands in no special relationship) drown in a foot of water may have to answer before some higher tribunal somewhere, sometime, but he is not accountable for negligence in the English court, though he has omitted to do what most men would for others". (See Rogers WVH, ed. Winfield and Jolowicz on Tort, 12th edition. London: Sweet and Maxwell, 1984: 80.)

A person who comes across the scene of an accident and decides to do nothing to assist the victim could not therefore in general be prosecuted for the crimes of manslaughter or assault nor could he be sued in the civil courts for negligence. The person could be held responsible, however, if he had some sort of special relationship with the victim—for example, if he was the parent or guardian of the drowning child referred to above.

There is no statute or as yet decided common law case to the effect that a doctor coming across an unconscious individual with whom he has no connection whatever is by virtue of his position as a doctor under a duty to assist that person. This is a peculiarity of the common law in the United Kingdom. In virtually every other legal system, especially within the EC, it is a serious offence under the penal code not to offer assistance and is heavily penalised.

However, a general practitioner coming across an unconscious person within his own practice area might be in breach of his NHS terms of service if he did not assist. The NHS (General Medical and Pharmaceutical Services) Regulations (SI 1974 No 160) (as amended) schedule 1, part 1, states in paragraph 4 that a doctor's patients include "persons to whom he may be requested to give treatment which is immediately required owing to an accident or other emergency at any place in his practice area." There are exceptions to this requirement—for example, for elderly infirm doctors.

In Scotland the NHS (General Medical and Pharmaceutical Services) (Scotland) Regulations (SI 1974 No 506) provide as follows: paragraph 4 (1(e)) states that the persons for whose treatment a doctor is responsible include "all persons for whom he may be required in terms of sub-paragraph (3) to provide treatment which is immediately required in case of accident or other emergency."

Paragraph 4 (3) further states "if a doctor is requested to provide treatment, and is available, he shall provide treatment immediately required, by reason of accident or other emergency, by a person who is not on the list of and who has not been accepted as a temporary resident by or assigned to, any doctor practising in the locality, or who is on the list of or has been accepted as a temporary resident by or assigned to, such a doctor, but neither the said doctor nor any deputy whom he may have appointed is available."

To walk away deliberately from a seriously ill person would no doubt be unethical; for example, the English text of the *International Code of Medical*

Ethics states among other things: "A physician shall always bear in mind the obligation of preserving human life".

Once a decision is taken to intervene then the rescuer is under the usual duty to take reasonable care. "There is authority for saying that, although a person is not normally under a duty to rescue another, yet once he embarks upon the actual task of rescue he may be liable if the method of rescue, or its abandonment, leaves the other worse off than he would otherwise have been." (See Clerk JF and Lindsell WHB. *Clerk and Lindsell on Torts.* 16th edition. London: Sweet and Maxwell, 1989: 34.)

However, if the rescuer is injured while assisting then he in turn may be able to claim damages from the person responsible for the hazardous situation. (That person may, of course, be the victim himself.) For example, in one case a doctor died when going down a well full of fumes to rescue two workmen. His estate claimed successfully for damages for his death from the defendants whose defective system of work had led to the accumulation of lethal gas inside the well. (See Baker and Anor *v* T E Hopkins and Son Ltd [1959] 1 WLR, p 966).

For the issue of lack of consent see chapter 1.

2.2.9 *Referral of patients to specialists*

The legal position regarding the referral of patients to specialists needs to be considered firstly from the point of view of the GP and secondly from the point of view of the consultant and the employing authority.

Are GPs bound to refer patients to specialists? So far as NHS patients are concerned there is a clear duty to do so as and when necessary. In England and Wales the NHS (General Medical and Pharmaceutical Services) Regulations (SI 1974 No 160) (as amended) provide for GPs' terms of service to include a condition that they must give to their patients "all necessary and appropriate personal medical services of the type usually provided by general medical practitioners, including arranging for the referral of patients as necessary to any other services provided under the Health Services Acts". (Chapter 5.3 contains a discussion of a doctor's duties with regard to referring patients for termination of pregnancy.) The BMA's ethical advice is that GPs should always acquiesce in any reasonable request by a patient for a second opinion.

The GMC guidelines *Professional Conduct and Discipline: Fitness to Practise* (February 1991), state the duties general practitioners are considered to have in the area of referral of patients to specialists. "The medical profession in this country has always considered that it is in the best interests of patients for one doctor to be fully informed about and responsible for the comprehensive management of a patient's medical care, but increasing specialisation within medicine has led members of the public to an awareness of high standards of expertise and often to seek direct access to these. In this situation general practitioners have a double duty to educate their patients to an understanding of the central position of their primary role, and also to consider carefully any request by a patient for a specialist opinion even if the general practitioner is not convinced that such consultation is essential. In order to continue to fulfil their central role, general practitioners must have information about the range of specialist expertise which other doctors are qualified and available to provide, especially in their locality."

In Scotland the NHS (General Medical and Pharmaceutical Services) (Scotland) Regulations (SI 1974 No 506) (as amended) also stipulate that GPs must give their patients all proper and necessary treatment and that: "The doctor shall also give his patients such advice or assistance as he may consider appropriate to enable them to take advantage of other medical services available under the National Health Service."

Whether the patient is private or NHS, failure to refer the patient to a specialist in circumstances where such a referral ought to have been made could result in a successful claim for negligence if the patient obtained injury as a result.

In the case of NHS patients a general practitioner who charged a fee for referring these patients to a private consultant would be considered to be in breach of his terms of service (paragraph 32).

In all cases any agreement whereby the general practitioner was to receive part of the consultant's fee (as a "commission", for example) could result in disciplinary proceedings. The GMC has regarded fee-splitting arrangements "with concern."

Once a GP has decided to refer the patient to a specialist then the question of what responsibilities the GP continues to have must be considered. The general position is that the GP's duty of care towards the patient still continues. If, however, the hospital fails to give the patient an appointment to see a specialist or delays for a long time in doing so then the GP could be placed in a difficult position through no fault of his own. There are no fixed rules in either the common law or statute as to whether the general practitioner is under a legal duty to chase the hospital up and ensure that the patient is seen by a specialist within a reasonable time. That being so a GP could only be held responsible for a delay in the patient obtaining hospital treatment if the GP had been negligent, applying the usual legal criteria in this respect. The sorts of situations that could lead to trouble are, for instance, failing to make sure that the hospital was made aware that the patient's condition was serious or had become so while the patient had been waiting to be seen by a consultant.

It should be noted in this context that in 1976 the Health Service Commissioner found that maladministration had occurred when there had been a failure to secure emergency treatment from the NHS. The Ombudsman stated that if the general practitioner had approached the consultant rather than a junior he would probably have obtained a bed for his patient.

The case of Coles *v* Reading HMC (*The Times*, January 31, 1963) illustrates also that the GP is expected to find out exactly what treatment his patient has been given in circumstances where the patient has referred himself to hospital. In that case a man who had a crushed thumb went to a cottage hospital. There he was told to go to a nearby general hospital for an anti-tetanus injection. He did not do so. He was seen later by his GP, who wrongly made the assumption that as the man had been seen at a hospital he must have been given an anti-tetanus injection. The man later died and the court held that both the hospital authority and the GP had been negligent, the hospital authority because they had not adequately impressed on the man the importance of having the injection and the GP because he had failed to enquire as to whether adequate prophylactic treatment had, in fact, been given.

In England and Wales the National Health Service Act 1977, section 1, provides that the Secretary of State for Social Services is under a duty to "... continue the promotion in England and Wales of a comprehensive health service designed to secure improvement

(a)   in the physical and mental health of the people of those countries; and

(b)   in the prevention, diagnosis and treatment of illness, and for that purpose to provide or secure the effective provision of services in accordance with this Act."

The Act goes on to impose on the Secretary of State a duty to provide to such extent as he considers necessary to meet all reasonable requirements, hospital accommodation and a wide range of other services. The problems GPs may encounter when a patient referred for specialist advice is kept waiting a long time have already been mentioned. In the case of R *v* Secretary of State for Social Services ex p Hincks 1979 (unreported) QB 24.1.79 (Court of Appeal 18.3.80) orthopaedic patients who had been kept waiting longer than was medically advisable attempted to obtain legal redress against the government for the failure to treat them within a reasonable time. The action failed, the court ruling that regard had to be paid to the financial limits imposed on the Secretary of State by parliament. Later cases involving 'hole-in-the-heart" babies have gone the same way.

Although the duty to provide hospital facilities lies with the Secretary of State, as the law stands at present, if there is not sufficient money to provide treatments under the NHS as promptly as doctors consider desirable then there is no legal basis to challenge this. (The National Health Service (Scotland) Act 1978 makes similar provisions in respect of medical facilities.)

The converse situation is that where a consultant accepts a patient for treatment without being asked to do so by the GP. It is clear from the GMC guidelines in *Professional Conduct and Discipline: Fitness to Practise*, that, in general, for a specialist to accept a patient without a referral from a GP is considered to be a breach of medical ethics.

There are some areas of practice in which specialist and hospital clinics may accept patients referred by sources other than their GPs. In these cases the GMC has advised on what action should be taken to keep the patient's GP informed of what has occurred, and the duties of the specialist in these circumstances (February 1991); "... If a specialist does decide to accept a patient without such reference, the specialist has a duty immediately to inform the general practitioner of his findings and recommendations before embarking on treatment, except in emergency, unless the patient expressly withholds consent or has no general practitioner. In such cases the specialist must be responsible for the patient's subsequent care until another doctor has agreed to take over that responsibility. Doctors connected with organisations offering clinical, diagnostic or medical advisory services must therefore satisfy themselves that the organisation discourages patients from approaching it without first consulting their own general practitioners ... In expressing these views the Council recognises and accepts that in some areas of practice specialist and hospital clinics customarily accept patients referred by sources other than their general practitioners. In these circumstances the specialist still has the duty to keep the general practitioner informed."

2.2.10 Private patients

A private patient enters into a contract with the doctor for treatment. Patient and doctor are free to negotiate the terms of such a contract. However, under the Unfair Contract Terms Act 1977 the doctor cannot exclude liability for negligence. The doctor's duty of care is, therefore, usually indistinguishable from the duty owed by a doctor to an NHS patient.

It is rare for a written contract to exist between doctor and patient, rather the terms will be implied from their relationship. Unless the doctor expressly promises to cure his patient the court will not infer any term other than that the doctor will exercise all due care and skill.

2.3 Criminal liability

However serious a negligent act may be it is only a matter for the criminal law if the victim dies. Gross negligence or recklessness causing death can amount to manslaughter. The degree of negligence required to establish criminal liability is more than that required for civil liability. The doctor must have shown such disregard for the life and safety of others as to amount to a crime against the state and conduct deserving of punishment. Until recently it was almost unheard of for doctors to be convicted of manslaughter following the death of a patient under their care. However, in 1990 there were two such convictions, both of locum anaesthetists (*Lancet* 1990; **336**:

430-1). These cases represented the beginning of a new trend—namely, the criminalising of death unintentionally caused by serious medical negligence. In November 1991, after a four week trial, two junior doctors who injected a patient with leukaemia with vincristine into the spine instead of the arm were convicted of manslaughter. This fatal case is one of four recent ones in which leukaemic patients have died or been seriously injured due to bungled injections of vincristine or similar drugs. The other doctors were not prosecuted. The doctors in the recent case are currently (July 1992) appealing their conviction.

Thus doctors in England and Wales whose patients die due to their recklessness or gross negligence look increasingly likely to be at risk of a charge of manslaughter. It remains to be seen whether very serious injury caused by a doctor's gross negligence will also attract criminal prosecution.

2.4 Complaints about doctors: non-judicial remedies

A person who feels that he or she had been harmed by the action of a doctor has a number of channels for complaint which do not involve the courts.

2.4.1 Complaints to Family Health Services Authorities

The Family Health Services Authority (FHSA) is empowered to investigate allegations of breach of contract by GPs—for example, failure to respond to an out of hours call. The complaint must be put to the general manager of the FHSA no later than 13 weeks after the event. There are formal and informal procedures for dealing with complaints. In the case of an informal complaint the FHSA will appoint a lay conciliator who may interview the complainant and the doctor to clear up any misunderstanding. If this is not successful then there is a formal investigation. Formal investigations are carried out by a committee of an equal number of FHSA lay members and practitioners, with a non-professional chairman. A report is made and copies sent to the complainant and the practitioner concerned. If the complaint is proved the general practitioner may be given a warning or have pay deducted. The complainant is not entitled to compensation; for this he or she would have to sue in the courts.

2.4.2 Complaints about hospital treatment

The Hospital Complaints Procedures Act 1985 requires health authorities to make arrangements for dealing with hospital patient complaints. Arrangements include having a designated officer for complaints and adequate publicity for these arrangements.

Each district health authority has a Community Health Council (CHC) which acts as the "patient's friend" in the NHS. An important role of the

CHC is to advise on complaints procedures and where appropriate to take up cases on the patients' behalf.

2.4.3 *Complaints to the health service commissioner*

Patients who do not feel that they have received satisfaction through the hospital complaints procedures have the option of complaining to the health service commissioner. The commissioner (known as the NHS ombudsman) has a parliamentary duty to investigate complaints about maladministration, such as failure in services or poor communication. He cannot deal with matters of clinical judgement. Complaints to the commissioner must be made in writing within a year of the incident. The commissioner has considerable powers to order the production of records or documents, and to compel health authority staff to testify. The most common remedy is an apology to the complainant. The commissioner may also recommend changes in practice at the hospital concerned. He presents reports periodically to a select committee of the House of Commons who may ask health authority representatives or doctors to appear before them to discuss particular cases. The Commissioner cannot investigate complaints about GPs and other family practitioners (dentists, opticians, and pharmacists), but his jurisdiction does extend to all hospital services, ambulance services, clinics and community nursing services.

2.4.4 *Complaints to the regional medical officer*

Where a complaint is about incompetence or negligence a patient can request the regional medical officer to arrange for an independent professional review. This is a formal procedure carried out by two independent consultants from another region. The consultants are nominated by the Joint Consultants' Committee of the Royal Colleges and the BMA. They meet with the person making the complaint and compile a report for the regional health authority. The complainant does not see the report but is told of any action taken as a result of the complaint.

2.4.5 *Complaints to the General Medical Council*

The GMC has the power to discipline any doctor who is guilty of serious professional misconduct. It is not concerned with errors in diagnosis and treatment (unless they amount to serious professional misconduct) but with improper behaviour which brings the medical profession into disrepute, such as adultery, sexual advances, drunkenness, fraud, etc. The ultimate penalty is for a doctor to be struck off the register so that he or she can no longer practice; a Doctor may also be suspended for a period or simply receive a warning. Details of the disciplinary procedures of the GMC are to be found in *Professional Conduct and Discipline: Fitness to Practise*, which is periodically updated.

At the time of publication of this edition (July 1992) the GMC is considering the introduction of new disciplinary mechanisms dealing with standards of performance by doctors which consistently fall below those expected.

2.4.6 *Other disciplinary procedures*

Disciplinary procedures, for hospital medical and dental staff, and doctors in public health medicine, for misconduct which falls short of serious professional misconduct, are considered in chapter 11.

3 Confidentiality

3.1 The duty owed

There is no doubt that a doctor owes a legal duty of confidentiality to those who consult him. It is in the public interest to impose this obligation so that patients can come forward for advice and treatment knowing that they can communicate frankly with their doctor. Any breach of that duty could result in disciplinary proceedings. Whether the aggrieved patient could successfully sue in the civil courts is a matter of some debate, but any doctor who risked putting this to the test would be extremely ill advised.

At present there is no statutory right to sue another person for damages for breach of confidentiality and the legal position can only be defined from a study of decided court cases and academic comment. It is generally accepted that professional people, including doctors, owe a legal duty of confidentiality to those who consult them. Courts will generally enforce such a duty in the following circumstances:

(i) where information is not a matter of public knowledge; *and*

(ii) information is entrusted to an individual in a situation where there is an obligation not to disclose the information without consent; *and*

(iii) where protecting the confidentiality of that information is in the public interest.

An injunction could be used to restrain a breach of confidence, for in X *v* Y [1988] 2 A11 ER 648 an injunction was obtained to prevent the publication of the names, and other information which could identify them, of two doctors who had AIDS. A civil action is less effective in providing compensation after a breach of confidence has occurred. Such an action has rarely been used in medical cases because it is generally considered that it would not be possible in most cases to claim damage for mental distress, although a claim for financial loss might well succeed.

The Law Commission, in its report *Breach of Confidence* (1981–Cmnd 8388), recommended that, as the common law action for breach of confidence is ineffective, it should be replaced by a statutory offence to include "such usual confidences as arise between doctor and patient" (paragraph 6.1). In addition, it should be extended to reports passing between general practitioners and specialists. However, 11 years later there seems little likelihood of such an offence being established.

There is also doubt additionally as to what, if any, legal duty of confidentiality is owed to the dead. In its report the Law Commission was of the opinion that the deceased's executors could only sue in relation to a breach of confidence after death if the "information is of a "quasi-proprietal" character—such as information relating to "know-how"—which can be regarded as an asset of the deceased's estate."

In revised guidance on professional confidence produced in November 1991 and appended (Appendix 1) the GMC makes it clear that doctors are under a duty "not to disclose to any third party information about an individual that they learned in their professional capacity, directly from a patient or indirectly." The GMC later adds that "a patient's death does not of itself release a doctor from the obligation to maintain confidentiality," but the extent to which disclosure after death would be regarded as proper is considered. It is stated that this "cannot be specified in absolute terms and will depend on the circumstances. These include the nature of the information disclosed, the extent to which it has already appeared in published material, and the period which has elapsed since the patient's death." The GMC does not give a time limit for the latter.

There are exceptional circumstances in which a breach of the general duty of confidentiality may be justified, as detailed below. If a doctor should decide to breach confidentiality the guidance of the GMC (November 1991) must be heeded:

"A doctor who decides to disclose confidential information about an individual must be prepared to explain and justify that decision, whatever the circumstances of the disclosure."

"Doctors who are faced with the difficult decision whether to disclose information without a patient's consent must weigh up carefully the argument for and against disclosure. If in doubt, they would be wise to discuss the matter with an experienced colleague or to seek advice from a medical defence society or professional association."

The main exceptions are the following:

(1) Consent by patient to disclosure (for example, in report to employer) (see subchapter 4.3.2).

(2) Order of court to disclose (see chapter 3.2.3).

(3) Statutory duty–notifiable diseases (see chapter 3.3)

(4) Statutory duty–other drugs (see chapter 9.5.1)
   abortion (see chapter 5.3)
   births (see chapter 5.4).
   deaths (see chapter 6.4).
   accidents at work (see chapter 12.5)

(5) Disclosure to family and other third parties in the interests of the patient (see chapter 3.4).

(6) Disclosure in the public interest (see chapter 3.5).

(7) Sharing information with other health professionals for the purposes of treating the patient (see chapter 3.6).

(8) Disclosure for medical teaching and bonafide research purposes (see chapter 3.7).

(9) Disclosure to health service management (see chapter 3.8).

Three other topics should also be considered in this context:

(10) The extent to which police officers investigating a crime may be justified in seizing medical records (see chapter 3.9).

(11) Doctors employed in the prison service, armed forces, or in occupational medicine may find their duty of confidentiality to the patient conflicts with their duty to their employer (see chapter 12).

(12) Confidentiality and sexually transmitted diseases, including HIV infection (see chapter 3.10)

3.2 Court proceedings

3.2.1 *General*

There is no rule of law to the effect that a doctor cannot be ordered by a court of law to reveal confidential information obtained during the course of his work. If a doctor were to be ordered by a court to reveal such information and then did so, no legal action for breach of any duty of confidentiality could later be brought against him on that basis. The GMC would also not subject a doctor to disciplinary proceedings if the breach of confidence took place because a court of law ordered a doctor to disclose confidential information. Conversely, if a doctor decided to defy an order of the court he might later be found to be in "contempt of court," and as a result of such a finding the doctor could incur severe penalties. This situation shows how the rule of law can sometimes conflict with medical ethics.

3.2.2 *Pre-trial disclosure of documents*

For some time there has been a court rule to the effect that once a civil legal action has begun in the courts, all parties to it must, at some stage before the actual hearing, produce by each other all documents which they have in their "possession, custody or power" and which are relevant to the issues and not privileged—that is, immune—from production. Medical records are not privileged in this context and the court can order a third party not involved in the litigation to produce relevant documents. In England and Wales the litigation must have actually begun. The order may be subject to conditions and may direct that disclosure be to the claimant, or limited to his medical, legal, or other professional adviser. The subject of ownership and retention of health records is covered in chapter 4. NHS hospital records are considered to be in the custody of the relevant health authority, to whom applications for disclosure should be properly directed. NHS general practice records, although the property of the Secretary of State, would usually be in the custody of the GP. Private practice records would likewise be in the custody of the medical practitioner, and employees' health records would be in the custody of the occupational health physician.

Note also that an English court case has decided that, if on balance it would not be in the public interest to order a party to reveal a document that party can be excused from doing so. The case was D v NSPCC [1977] 1 All ER 589 at p.618A (HL). A parent started a court case against the National Society for the Prevention of Cruelty to Children (NSPCC) and applied for an order requiring the organisation to disclose confidential records to the parent. Information which proved to be unfounded had been given to the NSPCC to the effect that the parent had been mistreating her children and the parent wanted to find out who the informer was. The court declined to order disclosure on the basis that to do so would be contrary to the public interest because other informers would be deterred from passing information to the NSPCC if they could not be certain that their identities would be kept secret.

GMC advice (November 1991) states:

"Where litigation is in prospect, unless the patient has consented to disclosure, or a court order has been made, information should not be disclosed by a doctor merely in response to demands from other people such as a third party's solicitor or an official of the court."

In other words, even though the doctor is made aware that a power to order disclosure exists the doctor might still wait for a formal court order before disclosing any information in circumstances where the patient objects to the disclosure being made. (A guidance note for doctors on releasing records for litigation purposes is available from the BMA.)

3.2.3 Evidence in court

A doctor may be summoned to attend court to give evidence and to produce medical records at the same time (subpoena ad duces tecum). Any subpoena or witness summons should be accompanied by "conduct money" (to pay the witness' fares to court) and the doctor is entitled to be paid an allowance for attending (the amount of this allowance is fixed in accordance with prescribed rates which change from time to time). If a doctor were to fail to attend court when summoned this could amount to a contempt of court.

Once in the witness box, before the oath is sworn the doctor should inform the judge if he has good reason to believe that part or all of the required evidence, whether oral or written, should not be disclosed—for example, because it would reveal sensitive information about third parties unconnected with the action. The judge will then listen in camera to the doctor's objections which he may or may not accept. Similarly, when the doctor is giving evidence, if he is asked a question which he does not wish to answer on the grounds that this would breach his duty of confidentiality, then it is open to the doctor to ask the judge for permission to be excused from answering the questions on this ground. If, however, the judge orders the doctor to answer questions then the doctor legally must do so. To refuse could amount to contempt of court. In the course of one divorce case a psychiatrist who had been consulted by the wife and co-respondent was subpoenaed by the husband's legal advisors. Once in court he was asked by the husband's counsel to reveal what the wife and co-respondent had said to him during the consultation. The psychiatrist protested on the grounds of professional confidence, but the judge ruled that he must answer the questions or be committed to prison for contempt of court. Not surprisingly, he then gave evidence. (Nuttall v Nuttall and Twyman [1964] 108 Sol J 605.) The Law Reform Committee, when it reviewed the Nuttall case, stated that if the psychiatrist had refused and had appealed against the direction to disclose the evidence the Court of Appeal might have upheld him. However, that statement was queried in the D v NSPCC case (D v NSPCC [1977] 1 All ER 589 at p. 168A (HL)) (see chapter 3.2.2). This rule has been held to apply even in circumstances where a doctor is under a statutory duty to keep the information in question confidential.

The subject of privilege has been dealt with during the past 25 years by both the Law Reform Committee (16th report *Privilege in Legal Proceedings*, 1967, Cmnd 3472) and the Criminal Law Revision Committee (11th report, *Evidence–General*, 1972, Cmnd 4991).

The GMC advises (November 1991) that a doctor "may disclose information if so directed by a judge or other presiding officer of a court".

However, the advice goes on to state:
"In such circumstances the doctor should first establish the precise extent of the information which needs to be discussed, and should not hesitate to make known any objections in the proposed disclosure, particularly when the order would involve the disclosure of confidential information about third parties."

3.2.4 *Inquiries following a death*

The GMC also advises (paragraph 12) that a doctor may give information to a coroner or his nominated representative so as to enable a coroner to determine whether an inquest should be held. If summoned to appear before a procurator fiscal in Scotland under the latter's power to investigate sudden suspicious deaths, the doctor may also disclose information.

3.3 Notifiable diseases

In some cases the doctor's general duty of confidentiality is overridden by a statutory duty to notify the authorities that a patient has a particular infectious disease. In England and Wales the law on this subject is presently contained in the Public Health (Control of Disease) Act 1984 and various Regulations.

Under the Act a registered medical practitioner, who becomes aware or who suspects that a patient whom he is attending within the district of a local authority has what the Act terms a "notifiable disease" or food poisoning, must send to the proper officer of that local authority the appropriate certificate unless he has reasonable grounds for believing that some other registered medical practitioner has already done so.

The certificate must state:

(a) The name, age, sex and address of the patient;

(b) The disease from which the patient has, or is suspected of having, and the date or approximate date of its onset; and

(c) If the patient is in hospital, the day on which the patient was admitted, the address of the premises from which he came there, and whether or not, in the opinion of the person giving the certificate, the disease or poisoning was contracted in the hospital.

The certificates are available to registered medical practitioners on request, free of charge. The practitioner receives a fee on notifying the authorities.

Failure to comply with this duty could result in a criminal prosecution, the penalty being a fine.

Further powers exist under the Act in respect of those with notifiable diseases. Sections 35 and 36 provide for compulsory examination of those suspected of having or being carriers of notifiable diseases (see chapter 1.6 on Consent).

The following diseases are "notifiable" by virtue of the 1984 Act.

• Cholera

• Plague

• Relapsing fever

- Smallpox

- Typhus

Those below are "notifiable" under the Public Health (Infectious Diseases) Regulations 1968, as amended.

- Acute encephalitis
- Acute meningitis
- Acute poliomyelitis
- Amoebic dysentery
- Anthrax
- Bacillary dysentery
- Diphtheria
- Food poisoning or suspected food poisoning
- Infective jaundice
- Leprosy
- Leptospirosis
- Lassa fever

- Malaria
- Marburg virus disease
- Measles
- Ophthalmia neonatorum
- Paratyphoid fever
- Rabies
- Scarlet fever
- Tetanus

- Tuberculosis
- Typhoid fever
- Viral haemorrhagic fever
- Whooping cough
- Yellow fever

Public Health (Infectious Diseases) Regulations 1985 (SI 1985 No 434) (introduced in March 1985) apply certain provisions of the 1984 Act to the AIDS, but do not make it compulsorily notifiable (see chapter 1.6).

In Scotland the statute law has been consolidated and the law is to be found in a number of statutes extending back to the Infectious Diseases (Notification) Act 1889. Sections 54 to 58 of the Public Health (Scotland) Act 1897 (as amended) contain similar provisions to sections 17, 19, 20, 37 and 38 of the 1984 English Act and also make it an offence to send a child to school with an infectious disease. Notification is to be made by a GP who becomes aware that a patient has an infectious disease to the chief administrative medical officer of the local health board (National Health Service (Scotland) Act 1972–schedule 6).

Although AIDS is not a notifiable infectious disease in Scotland, there are powers under the Public Health (Scotland) Act 1897, sections 45 to 59, to provide for the compulsory examination of those suspected of any infectious disease and, if necessary, for their compulsory removal to hospital. The following infectious diseases are compulsorily notifiable in Scotland by regulations made by the Secretary of State for Scotland:

- Anthrax
- Cholera
- Continued fever
- Diphtheria
- Dysentery
- Erysipelas
- Lassa fever
- Leprosy
- Leptospiral jaundice
- Malaria
- Marburg virus disease
- Measles
- Membranous croup
- Meningococcal infection
- Ophthalmia neonatorum
- Paratyphoid A
- Paratyphoid B
- Plague
- Poliomyelitis, acuite, paralytic
- Poliomyelitis, acute, non-paralytic
- Puerperal fever
- Rabies
- Relapsing fever
- Scarlet fever
- Smallpox
- Tuberculosis, respiratory
- Tuberculosis, non-respiratory
- Typhoid fever
- Typhus fever
- Viral hepatitis
- Viral haemorrhagic fever
- Whooping cough
- Yellow fever

Food poisoning is notifiable under the Food and Drugs (Scotland) Act 1956.

Sexually transmitted diseases are dealt with in chapter 3.10.

3.4 Disclosure to relatives and other third parties in the interests of the patient

There may be circumstances in which it is considered undesirable, for medical reasons, to tell the patient the full implications of his condition. With regard to this the GMC guidance states:

"In exceptional circumstances a doctor may consider it undesirable, for medical reasons, to seek a patient's consent to the disclosure of confidential information. In such cases information may be disclosed to a relative or some other person but only when the doctor is satisfied that it is necessary in the patient's best medical interests to do so."

The essence of this is that a doctor should be free to speak with a relative when he judges this to be in the best interests of the patient—for example, if the doctor feels that the patient is too ill to make decisions about treatment. The doctor may be able to speak to someone other than a relative, such as a close friend. It is inferred that the patient would consent to such communication.

If a competent patient places a ban on communication with a relative or other third party then the doctor must respect the patient's wishes. The doctor may try to persuade the patient to change his mind, but if the patient refuses he still is entitled to require confidentiality to be maintained. This is particularly relevant where the patient is under the age of 16 (see chapter 7.3).

There may be difficult decisions over disclosure of information—for example, where the patient may have been sexually or physically abused. In such cases the GMC advises (November 1991) "...the patient's medical interests are paramount and they require the doctor to disclose information to an appropriate person or authority." An interesting difference of opinion has arisen between the GMC and the BMA over the responsibility of the doctor who is consulted by a girl and decides that she is too immature to form the necessary consent for contraceptive treatment so that further action cannot be taken without the parent's or guardian's consent. The BMA believes that if the doctor is unable to persuade the girl to allow her parent or guardian to be involved her confidence must be respected, otherwise, the BMA has argued, such girls will be discouraged from approaching a doctor and the opportunity to counsel them will be lost. The GMC on the other hand, advises that if the doctor is not satisfied as to a patient's maturity, (or mental capacity) to appreciate what the advice or treatment being sought may involve (November 1991):

"the doctor should attempt to persuade the patient to allow an appropriate person to be involved in the consultation. If the patient cannot understand or be persuaded, but the doctor is convinced that the disclosure of information would be essential to the patient's best medical interests, the doctor may disclose to an appropriate person or authority the fact of the consultation and the information learned from it. A doctor who decides to disclose information must be prepared to justify the decision and must inform the patient before any disclosure is made."

In other words, the responsibility of the doctor to respect the confidence of a consultation by an immature girl about contraception is regarded as absolute by the BMA and as qualified by the GMC.

3.5 Disclosure in the public interest

The patient's right to confidence is qualified, not absolute. Circumstances may occur where the public interest in maintaining confidentiality is outweighed by a stronger public interest in disclosure. The GMC states (November 1991):

"Rarely cases may arise in which disclosure in the public interest may be justified, for example a situation in which the failure to disclose appropriate information would expose the patient, or someone else, to a risk of death or serious harm."

The "public interest exception" has recently been considered by the courts in W *v* Egdell [1990] 1 All ER 835. A patient convicted of manslaughter and detained in a special hospital engaged an independent consultant psychiatrist (Dr Egdell) to report on his mental state in connection with an application to a mental health tribunal for his discharge. Dr Egdell's report did not support the application which was consequently withdrawn. The doctor felt that if the patient were released there would be a substantial risk to the public. Despite the fact that the patient's solicitors had refused permission to do so, the doctor brought his report to the attention of the hospital and the Home Office. The patient's application to prevent release of the report was refused. Although the court considered that it was in the public interest to maintain confidentiality in such cases, on balance, that duty was overridden by the public interest in protecting the public against a real risk of danger.

In the case of X *v* Y (see 3.1 above) the court found that 'the very important public interest in the freedom of the press" and an informed public debate was outweighed by the public interest in ensuring that people with AIDS should be able to come forward for treatment without fear of their identity being revealed.

Another situation which may arise and cause a doctor to give consideration to the patient's right to confidence is in the context of a patient with epilepsy or a significant visual disability who fails to inform the Driver Vehicle Licensing Centre (DVLC) and continues to drive.

In what circumstances is a doctor justified in informing the police of suspicion of criminal conduct on the part of a patient?

The general position is that it is not a criminal offence not to reveal information to the police about a crime. In England and Wales section 5(5) of the Criminal Law Act 1967 sets this out. Indeed, in the English case of Rice *v* Connolly [1966] 2 QB 414, where a man charged with the offence of obstructing the police in the execution of their duty following his refusal to give any information about himself, was found not guilty, Lord Justice Parker stated: "It seems to me quite clear that though every citizen has a moral duty or, if you like, a social duty to assist the police there is no legal duty to that effect."

In the case of most crimes the choice whether to inform the police rests with the doctor. There are, however, certain statutes which require that a person answer questions asked by the police. A doctor is not exempt from this requirement even if he considers the information to be confidential. In the case of Hunter *v* Mann [1974] QB 767 the courts found that a " doctor is not exempt from the statutory obligation, under the Road Traffic Acts, to supply information to the police about the identity of persons injured in a road accident.

3.5.1 *Treason*

It still is a common law offence in England and Wales for a person who knows, or has reasonable cause to believe, that another has committed treason to omit to disclose this information or any material part of it to the proper authority within a reasonable time.

In Scotland the offence of misprision of treason still exists. This is the failure by anyone who has any information that might lead to the arrest of a traitor to give that information to the authorities. It might also be misprision to fail to give information of a projected treason.

3.5.2 *Terrorism*

Under the Prevention of Terrorism (Temporary Provisions) Act 1984, failure to give information about certain acts of terrorism could result in prosecution. This is set out in section 11 of the Act which covers only acts of terrorism connected with Northern Irish affairs. An "act of terrorism" in this context is defined in section 14(1) as: "the use of violence for political ends, and includes any use of violence for the purpose of putting the public or any section of the public in fear."

Section 11 provides that a person can be guilty of a criminal offence in the following circumstances. Firstly, "if he has information which he knows or believes might be of material assistance.

(a) in preventing the commission by any other person of an act of terrorism; or

(b) in securing the apprehension, prosecution or conviction of any other person for an offence involving the commission, preparation or instigation of an act of terrorism."

And, secondly, if he "fails without reasonable excuse to disclose that information as soon as reasonably practicable

(i) In England and Wales to a constable;

(ii) In Scotland to a constable or the procurator fiscal; or

(iii) In Northern Ireland to a constable or a member of Her Majesty's Forces."

The penalties if a prosecution takes place in a higher court could be up to five years in prison, or a fine, or both.

3.5.3 *Repercussions of reporting a serious crime*

If a doctor decides to report details about a patient to the police in connection with a serious crime—that is, where there is a risk of consequential death or permanent disability to a third party or the patient, what repercussions might there be? Ultimately only the court can decide whether a breach of confidence is justified. The decision "must turn, not on what the doctor thinks but on what the court rules." In making its ruling the court will give "such weight to the considered judgement of a professional man as seems in all circumstances to be appropriate" (W v Egdell). The legal position regarding breach of confidentiality is, as explained, far from clear, and all that can be said is that no doctor has been sued successfully for reporting a patient for committing a crime. Furthermore, the courts can protect the identity of an informant (see D V NSPCC in chapter 3.2.2).

Another area of concern for a doctor might be the possibility of disciplinary proceedings being brought by the GMC. As stated above, the GMC points out that any breach of confidence must be justified and doctors are advised to consult their defence organisations or professional organisations when in doubt.

3.6 Sharing information with other health professionals

There may be circumstances in which a doctor wishes to disclose confidential information about a patient to other health professionals in order to provide optimal care. To what extent is a doctor justified in breaching confidence in this type of situation?

The GMC (November 1991) states:

"Most doctors in hospital and general practice are working in health care teams, some of whose members may need access to information, given or obtained in confidence about individuals, in order to perform their duties. It is for doctors who lead such teams to judge when it is appropriate for information to be disclosed for that purpose. They must leave those whom they authorise to receive such information in no doubt that it is given to them in professional confidence. The doctor also has a responsibility to ensure that arrangements exist to inform patients of the circumstances in which information about them is likely to be shared and the opportunity to state any objection to this."

Sharing of information is permissible when the doctor, as a matter of clinical judgement, perceives it to be in the patient's interests. It is necessary to draw a distinction between the situation where a doctor discloses without seeking express permission, and that where permission is sought but a patient refuses to allow disclosure.

If a patient has not specifically been asked whether he objects to his doctor passing information on to other health professionals, a court would probably infer consent, in that by submitting himself to a doctor's care, the patient implicitly accepts any steps the doctor may take in his best interests. This would not, however, justify a doctor disclosing confidential information to other health professionals at random. The criterion for disclosure must be a narrowly defined "need to know" basis—that is,only disclosure so far as is required to provide optimal care. Disclosure to someone outside that group would certainly be an unjustifiable breach. May a doctor rely on therapeutic privilege where a patient has expressly refused permission to disclose? The answer is probably not. What a doctor must do, however, is point out to the patient that unless he is able to share the information with other health professionals, his ability to treat him as comprehensively as he would like would be severely limited, and he should urge the patient to reconsider.

If the patient still adamantly refuses, the doctor must respect the patient's feelings and maintain confidentiality. He should endeavour to treat the patient medically as far as is possible without disclosure. A doctor who refuses to treat in these circumstances could be negligently failing in his duty of care towards this patient.

3.7 Disclosure for medical teaching and research

Research into health and disease may benefit existing or future patients, or lead to improvements in public health generally. This often requires access to confidential personal health information about identified patients. Normally, such information should not be used or disclosed for research without the patient's consent. However, this may not always be practicable in the case of some kinds of research (or medical audit); it could also in some cases be against the patient's own interest to ask for it.

The information should only be used or disclosed only if an LREC has satisfied itself that a sufficient case has been made for dispensing with the patient's consent and has approved the research proposal.

In this regard the Department of Health's guidance on LREC states:

"3.11 Researchers should be asked to confirm that personal health information will be kept confidential, that data will be secured against unauthorised access and that no individual will be identifiable from published results, without his or her explicit consent. All data from which an individual is identifiable should be destroyed when no longer required for the purposes of the original research. If, exceptionally, the researcher wishes to retain confidential information beyond the completion of the research, the LREC, the relevant NHS body and the research subject must first be made aware of the reasons for retaining the information and the circumstances in which this might be disclosed. The subject's consent to these arrangements must be recorded.

3.12 Epidemiological research through studies of medical records can be extremely valuable. Patients are, however, entitled to regard their medical records as confidential to the NHS and should in principle be asked if they consent to their own records being released to research workers. However, there will be occasions when a researcher would find it very difficult or impossible to obtain such consent from every individual and the LREC will need to be satisfied that the value of such a project outweighs, in the public interest, the principle that individual consent should be obtained. Where a patient has previously indicated that he or she would *not* want their records released then this request should be respected.

3.13 The LREC will need to be assured that this kind of research will be conducted in accordance with the current codes of practice and data protection legislation. Wherever possible consent should also be sought from the health professional responsible for the relevant aspect of the subject's care. Once information has been obtained from the records no approach should be made to the patient concerned without the agreement of the health professional currently responsible for his care.

3.14 Certain enquiries and surveys, involving only access to patient records, such as the national morbidity surveys and the post-marketing surveillance of drugs, which are in the public interest, do not need prior approval of an LREC."

To carry out undergraduate and postgraduate medical teaching personal information about patients, sometimes in the form of medical records, has to be shared with students or doctors. Where this occurs in a manner which does not allow individuals to be identified, no question of breach of confidentiality will arise. But, where patients are directly involved it is important that consent should be obtained from the patient and that the students or doctors understand the nature and importance of confidentiality and its preservation.

The GMC (November 1991) states:

"Where the disclosure would enable one or more individuals to be identified, the patients concerned, or those who may properly give permission on their behalf, must wherever possible be made aware of that possibility and be advised that it is open to them, at any stage, to withold their consent to disclosure."

3.8 Disclosure to health service management

With the development of an "internal market" in the NHS concerns have arisen about safeguarding the confidentiality of patient data which might appear on bills for extra-contractual referrals, etc. The Department of Health booklet *NHS Review Information Systems: Action for Managers* stated that "very strict, tightly controlled administrative and computer security arrangements will be necessary to safeguard confidentiality and to deal with subject access requests." This emphasis on such a breach of confidentiality as a very serious matter has been reinforced in NHS management executive letter EL(91) 49.

All grades of NHS staff, including clerical officers who might handle confidential bills relating to individual patients, are reminded in this letter that breach of confidence is a disciplinary offence, and arrangements for handling data containing patients" details must be agreed with an appropriate senior medical officer. Despite these guidelines pressure is mounting for a coding system on NHS bills and contracts which would ensure complete confidentiality.

3.9 Police and Criminal Evidence Act 1984

3.9.1 *Confidentiality*

While the Police and Criminal Evidence Act 1984 was progressing through parliament there was considerable debate as to whether police officers investigating alleged criminal offences should be permitted in the course of their investigations to seize a person's medical records. The resulting provisions of the Act provide that they may do so in only a very limited number of situations.

Section 8 of the Act sets out what power magistrates have to authorise police officers to enter premises and search them. The warrant may be granted only if "there are reasonable grounds for believing that a serious arrestable offence" (which includes murder, serious sex offences, terrorism, firearms offences and serious theft) "has been committed; and that there is material on the premises" which does not come within the listed categories but is likely to be relevant evidence *and* it is not practicable to communicate with the person entitled to grant entry to the premises or access to the material, *or* entry would not be granted voluntarily, *or* the purposes of the search may be frustrated or seriously prejudiced unless a constable arriving at the premises can secure immediate entry to them.

One of the three listed categories referred to above—that is, one sort of material that magistrates may not grant a warrant to search for—is what the Act terms "excluded material." This is defined in section 11 to include:

"(a) Personal records which a person has acquired or created in the course of any trade, business, profession or other occupation or for the purposes of any paid or unpaid office and which he holds in confidence."

"Personal records" are defined in section 12 to include "documentary and other records concerning an individual (whether living or dead) who can be identified from them and relating ... to his physical or mental health." The expression "holds in confidence" is also defined (see below). Also included are the following:

"(b) Human tissue or tissue fluid which has been taken for the purposes of diagnosis or medical treatment and which a person holds in confidence."

"Holds in confidence" is stated to mean being held subject to "a) an express or implied undertaking to hold it in confidence; or b) to a restriction on disclosure or an obligation of secrecy contained in any enactment."

There can be no doubt, therefore, that a patient's medical records would be classed as "excluded material" for the purposes of the Police and Criminal Evidence Act 1984.

It is next necessary to consider in what circumstances police officers could, despite this classification, obtain such records. Section 9 states that a constable may apply to a circuit judge for such an order. Schedule 1 of the Act states the criteria that must apply. The application must be on notice and the judge must be satisfied that various listed "access conditions" apply. These are:

(1) there must be reasonable grounds for believing that there is excluded material on the premises specified in the application;

(2) there must be some statutory authority passed before the Police and Criminal Evidence Act which would have authorised such a search, and;

(3) the issue of a warrant under those provisions would have been appropriate.

Medical records could only be obtained by this method, therefore if they could have been lawfully obtained by statute before the passing of the Police and Criminal Evidence Act. There were a number of statutes passed before the Police and Criminal Evidence Act which authorised the police to enter and search premises under warrant and in some cases seize documents, such as Misuse of Drugs Act 1971 and Official Secrets Act 1911.

If the order is made it will be to the effect that the person who appears to be in possession of the excluded material shall produce it to the constable for him to take away or shall give the constable access to it. In certain circumstances the judge may grant a warrant to allow the constable to enter, search, and seize excluded material. The above access conditions must be satisfied, plus one extra condition similar to those set out for magistrates- —that is, connected with difficulties in communicating with the property owner, fears that serving a notice would seriously prejudice the investigation, or that a notice has been served and disclosure of the material is feared.

There is another method by which, in theory, police could seize medical records. Section 19 provides a general power of seizure of documents, etc, to a constable who is lawfully on premises—that is, either with the consent of the owner or by virtue of a warrant. Such a constable may, once inside, seize anything he finds which he has reasonable grounds to believe:

"(a) that it has been obtained in consequence of the commission of an offence; and

(b) that it is evidence in relation to an offence which he is investigating or any other offence; and

(c) that it is necessary to seize it in order to prevent the evidence being concealed, lost, altered or destroyed."

There are also provisions requiring information held on computer to be produced. It follows from the above that a police officer who is lawfully inside premises could in theory seize medical records if he could justify doing it by virtue of the above criteria.

3.10 Confidentiality and sexually transmitted diseases

3.10.1 *HIV disease*

The care of people with HIV infection and AIDS raises some particularly sensitive issues of confidentiality. On the one hand, disclosure of a person's HIV antibody status could have a serious effect on the psychological and social well being of the patient with an impact on livelihood, accommodation, and relationships. People need to be able to come forward for testing, counselling, and treatment in the expectation that confidentiality will not be breached. On the other hand, the doctor may feel that there is a public interest argument in disclosing the patient's HIV antibody status to people who may be at risk of infection, such as a sexual partner or health care staff.

In its guidance on HIV infection and AIDS (issued in May 1988) the GMC has stated:

"When diagnosis has been made by a specialist and the patient, after appropriate counselling, still refuses permission for the general practitioner to be informed of the result, that request for privacy should be respected. The only exception would be when failure to disclose would put the health of the health care team at serious risk. All people receiving such information must consider themselves under the same obligations of confidentiality as the doctor principally responsible for the patient's care. Occasionally the doctor may wish to disclose a diagnosis to a third party other than a health care professional. The Council thinks that the only grounds for this are when there is a serious and identifiable risk to a specific person, who, if not so informed would be exposed to infection ... A doctor may consider it a duty to ensure that any sexual partner is informed regardless of the patient's own wishes."

Breach of this code of practice is not something which, of itself, entitles the patient to recover damages from a doctor in court, although it would probably form the basis for proceedings for serious professional misconduct before the GMC.

The courts have shown themselves willing to preserve the confidentiality of information relating to patients with AIDS in the case of X *v* Y [1988] 2 All ER 648 (see 3.1 and 3.5). The judge said in this case "In the long run, preservation of confidentiality is the only way of securing public health ... for unless those infected come forward they cannot be counselled."

3.10.2 *National Health Service (Venereal Diseases) Regulations 1974*
The provisions of the National Health Service (Veneral Diseases) Regulations (SI 1974 No 29) (England and Wales) impose a statutory obligation on health authorities to take steps to prevent the identification of individuals who have been treated for any sexually transmitted disease. Although the veneral diseases regulations do not technically apply to Scotland, they have always been respected in Scotland although not specifically legislated for.

Regulation 2 requires "...every regional and district health authority to take all necessary steps to secure that any information capable of identifying an individual obtained by officers of the authority with respect to persons examined or treated for any sexually transmitted disease shall not be disclosed except

(a) for the purpose of communicating that information to a medical practitioner, or to a person employed under the direction of a medical practitioner in connection with the treatment of persons suffering from such a disease or the prevention of the spread thereof, and

(b) for the purpose of such treatment or prevention."

Although HIV infection is not transmitted exclusively through sex, the general view is that the regulations apply to *all* cases of HIV infection. The regulations only apply to health authorities and not to GPs or private hospitals and clinics.

4 Medical records

Until recently the only medical records to which patients had a right of access were those held on computer. The provisions of the data protection legislation gave a right of access to health records kept on computer from November 1987 onwards. The Access to Health Records Act 1990 extended the right of access to records held in manual form but it only applies to records made after the Act came into force on November 1 1991. Control over information in records prior to these dates depends on ownership of the record. Patients also have a statutory right to see medical reports prepared for insurance and employment purposes by virtue of the Access to Medical Reports Act 1988.

4.1 Ownership of medical records

Questions of patients' access to their medical records and control over their disclosure to third parties turn on the fact of ownership.

The concept of ownership of information is very underdeveloped in England and Wales, and at common law the person who "controls" the records is the person who writes them. Therefore, private doctors who write down the information on their writing material own the medical records and control what happens to them (subject, of course, to statutory rights of access to information and ethical controls on the disclosure of confidential information). Despite the fact that the information emanates from the patient telling the doctor what the matter is, and is thus in one sense owned by the patient, the substance of the record is an interpretation of that information as a function of the doctor's skill, and is thus owned by him.

As regards NHS records, medical records written and retained by NHS general practitioners are made on forms supplied by the FHSA and are expressly stated to remain its property. Similarly, medical records written by hospital doctors are made on NHS property. But as hospital doctors are employed by a health authority, any records made by them in the course of their employment are kept by the relevant health authority, and are ultimately the property of the Secretary of State.

Occupational health records of NHS staff are retained by the relevant occupational health doctor and are not made available to the employing authority automatically.

4.2 Death of owner of medical records

England and Wales

The question of ownership of medical records has been briefly discussed above. It was pointed out that NHS records are considered to be the property of the Secretary of State. NHS hospital medical records are kept by the relevant health authorities but on the death of an NHS general practitioner records are returned to the FHSA. Medical records in private cases, however, are considered to belong to the doctor, unless some agreement to the contrary has been made between the doctor and patient. Consideration, therefore, has to be given as to what happens to the records of a private practitioner when that person dies. If the doctor has left a will then the persons named therein as the personal representatives have a duty to distribute the doctor's property in accordance with the terms of the will. If no will has been left then property devolves on the next of kin in accordance with a statutorily laid down order. Persons entitled to the estate can usually apply for letters of administration enabling them to administer that estate. The order is broadly speaking as follows:

(1)   surviving spouse;

(2)   children;

(3)   parents;

(4)   brothers and sisters of the whole blood, or their children if they have died already;

(5)   brothers and sisters of the half blood, or their children if they have died already;

(6)   Grandparents;

(7)   Uncles and aunts of the whole blood, or their children if they have died already;

(8)   Uncles and aunts of the half blood, or their children if they have died already.

If the deceased had none of the above, then property devolves first on the Crown, and the Treasury may apply for letters of administration, secondly, on the Duchy of Lancaster, whose solicitors may apply for letters of administration, and, lastly, on the Duchy of Cornwall, whose solicitors may similarly apply.

A creditor of the deceased may apply for letters of administration to administer the estate, but is not entitled to the estate itself, except to the extent of the debt owed to him.

The question is posed as to what would happen if the person entitled to ownership of the records following the death of a doctor in private practice decided to misuse them in some way—for example, by selling the contents to a newspaper. The extent to which there is a legal duty of confidentiality owed to patients is discussed under confidentiality, chapter 2.1. It is pointed out there that private patients might well have a right to sue a doctor for damages if a breach of confidentiality occurred. It is suggested that a patient could also try to sue any person in possession of the records if they were wrongfully to disclose the contents. Once the action had been launched an immediate injunction could be applied for to restrain publication. Whether such an action would succeed is a matter for speculation. Bearing in mind the difficulties that could arise doctors in private practice should be encouraged to deal with this issue in their will.

Scotland

In Scotland the order of succession to a moveable property in intestacy is (after the surviving spouse's prior rights have been satisfied):

(1)   the deceased's children and their issue;

(2)   collaterals (brothers, sisters, or their offspring);

(3)   ascendants (parents, etc).

Thereafter succession depends on whether there was a surviving spouse; at the end of the day succession ends with the Crown as ultimus haeres.

The question of confidentiality between a private patient or the person or organisation who inherits his medical advisor's records is but one aspect of what may be a growing problem as private medical care burgeons. It is, for example, desirable that whoever takes over the care of the patient has access to the previous records and that they are not destroyed or misused by the relatives. It may be that a similar rule should be applied to private medical practitioners as applies to NHS doctors.

4.3 Recommended length of retention of records

Medical records in private cases are considered to belong to the doctor, unless an agreement to the contrary has been made between doctor and patient. It is therefore up to the private practitioner to decide how long he should keep those records. NHS records are considered to be the property of the Secretary of State. In the case of NHS hospital records the responsibility for keeping same is vested in the relevant health authorities.

A GP's records are kept by the GP, who returns same to the FHSA when the patient dies, emigrates, or changes doctor.

By virtue of the Public Records Act 1958 (as amended) health authorities are under a duty to preserve such hospital records as ought to be permanently preserved, and arrange for their safe keeping.

All those who have the responsibility for keeping records need to consider, apart from the need to retain same in the interests of the patient and for research purposes, the question of retaining records in connection with possible future litigation (see chapter 2.2.2).

Department of Health circular HC(89)20 recommends to health authorities minimum periods for which hospital records should be retained as follows:

(a) Obstetric records: 25 years.

(b) Records relating to children and young people (including paediatric, vaccination and community child health service records): until the patient's 25th birthday or eight years after the last entry if longer.

(c) Records relating to mentally disordered persons within the meaning of the Mental Health Act: 20 years from the date at which, in the opinion of the doctor concerned, the disorder has ceased or diminished to the point where no further care or treatment is considered necessary.

Except that such records need only be retained for a minimum of eight years after the death of a patient, (or, in the case of obstetric records, death of the child—but not of the mother.)

(d) All other personal health records: eight years after the conclusion of the treatment.

As records could be required in litigation, virtually without limit of time, the Department recognises that inevitably records might be destroyed which subsequently are wanted for litigation. They state that if this happens any prejudice thereby occasioned should be taken into account if damages are later apportioned between the doctor and the health authority.

4.4 Access to medical records

4.4.1 *Data Protection Act 1984*

The Data Protection Act 1984 protects individuals from the misuse of personal information recorded in a form in which it can be processed by equipment operating automatically in response to instructions given for that purpose—for example, held on a computer. Anyone who controls the content and use of personal data is required to register under the Act.

Data protection principles

The principles as set out in schedule 1 of the Data Protection Act are:

The first principle: "The information to be contained in personal data shall be obtained and personal data shall be processed, fairly and lawfully."

The second principle: "Personal data should be held only for one or more specified and lawful purposes."

The third principle: "Personal data held for any purpose or purposes shall not be used to disclose in any manner incompatible with that purpose or those purposes."

The fourth principle: "Personal data held for any purpose or purposes shall be adequate, relevant and not excessive in relation to that purpose or those purposes."

The fifth principle: "Personal data shall be accurate and, where necessary, kept up to date."

The sixth principle: "Personal data held for any purpose or purposes shall not be kept for longer than is necessary for that purpose or those purposes."

The seventh principle: "An individual shall be entitled—

(a) at reasonable intervals and without undue delay or expense—

  (i) to be informed by any data user whether he holds personal data of which that individual is the subject; and

  (ii) to access to any such data held by a data user; and

(b) where appropriate, to have such data corrected or erased."

The eighth principle: "Appropriate security measures shall be taken against unauthorised access to, or alteration, disclosure or destruction of, personal data and against loss or destruction of personal data."

Registrar's duties

The data protection registrar's duties include the maintenance of a register of data users who hold personal data and of providers of bureau computer services to persons in control of personal data. He has the power to execute legal penalties against individuals in regard to a wide variety of offences connected with the Act. This includes the power to initiate legal action against any person holding or using data not covered by their registration entry, or in a manner not consistent with that entry or with the "Data Protection Principles."

As of 11 May 1986 data subjects have been entitled to compensation from data users if it can be proved that they have suffered damage because of:

(1) loss of personal data;

(2) unauthorised destruction of personal data;

(3) unauthorised disclosure of personal data;

(4) inaccurate personal data.

As of 11 November 1987 data subjects have had the right to have access to information about them contained in data. Consequently, patients have the right of access to all personal information held on them by doctors and other health professionals (that is, data users). The Data Protection Act (Subject Access Modification) (Health) Order 1987 was issued subsequently by the Home Secretary. This Order allows a doctor who believes that serious harm will result to the physical or mental health of a patient if full access were provided to prevent access to harmful data. However, no definition is given as to what constitutes serious harm.

The BMA's General Medical Services Committee has prepared guidance in the form of three booklets for GPs who need to register under the Data Protection Act 1984. The first on subject access provisions was published in December 1987, the second on registration in March 1988 and the most recent one is in the form of a code of practice for GPs.

Guidance to health authorities on modified access to personal health information was issued in health circular HC(87)14 in September 1987 prior to the issue of the Order (see above). A further health circular HC(87)25 (HC(FP)(89)9) issued in November 1987 gives advice as to the rights of children and parents under the Act.

4.4.2 Access to Medical Reports Act 1988

This Act allows individuals to see medical reports written about them for employment and insurance purposes by the doctor they usually see in a "normal" doctor/patient capacity. This means either the patient's own GP or another doctor who has been involved in the patient's clinical care. "Care" includes examination, investigation or diagnosis for the purposes of, or in connection with, any form of medical treatment. The individual has the following rights under the Act:

(1) to give or refuse consent for an employer or insurance company to seek a medical report relative to physical or mental health;

(2) to see any report after completion by the doctor;

(3) to seek amendment to the report if dissatisfied with it;

(4) to withhold permission for the doctor to send the report to the employer or insurance company.

The company (the "applicant") requesting the report must notify the individual of his rights of access to the report. The doctor must ensure that he has the written consent of the individual before any report is written. If the doctor is informed at the time that the application is made that the patient wishes to see the report he must not send it for 21 days to allow time for the patient to see it. Alternatively, after the application has been made the individual may notify the doctor that he wishes to see the report, in which case the individual has 21 days after such notification to seek access to the report. (It must be appreciated, however, that before such notification is received, the doctor may already have supplied the report to the applicant.) Once the patient has seen the report it must not then be sent on until the patient has agreed to its release. If the patient believes there are factual inaccuracies in the report he may ask for them to be corrected. The doctor is not obliged to make amendments, but if he refuses to amend the report he must agree to attach the patient's statement disputing the information. In the last resort, consent for the supply of the report can be withheld by the patient. Requests for changes to the report, or for a statement to be attached, must be made in writing.

At any time within six months of the report being sent the individual can require access to a copy of it. The doctor should ensure that an accurate, dated copy is kept for this period.

Where a copy of the report is supplied at the request of the patient, the doctor may make a reasonable charge for the costs of copying it. He should not charge the patient simply for *seeing* the report.

The doctor has a right to withhold information from an individual seeking access where its release would cause serious harm to that individual's mental or physical health or the health of any other person.

Where information in the record has been supplied by, or would reveal the identity of, someone other than the patient or a health professional, the patient has no right to see this information if it would mean that this third party could be identified, unless the third party has consented. There is no obligation in the Act to seek the consent of this third party.

There is no provision in the Access to Medical Reports Act for an application for a report to be made on behalf of someone who is mentally incapable.

Bearing in mind that time limits have been set by the Act for access to medical reports, the BMA advises doctors to mark applications for reports with the date and to ensure that correspondence sent to applicants who request such reports is also clearly dated. Reports should be written on the assumption that they will ultimately be read by the subject of the report.

The application of the Act to occupational physicians is detailed in chapter 12.5.

4.4.3 *Access to Health Records Act 1990*

This Act gives patients, and in certain circumstances other people acting on the patient's behalf, access to manually held health records made after 1 November 1991. "Health record" is defined as meaning a record of information relating to the physical or mental health of the individual and which has been made by or on behalf of a health professional in connection with the care of that person. The Act does not prevent a doctor from informally allowing a patient sight of notes when asked in surgery, if the doctor is agreeable. "Care" includes examination, investigation, diagnosis and treatment.

The Act is not confined to NHS records; it applies equally to private medicine and to records created by doctors in Crown public service (prison doctors, doctors in the armed services and Civil Service occupational physicians). Records made in connection with the investigation of a crime are excluded. In many situations—for example, in hospital—the patient's record will be compiled by many different health professionals. The Act defines "health professional" as including registered doctors; registered dentists; registered opticians; registered pharmaceutical chemists; registered nurses, midwives and health visitors; registered chiropodists, dieticians, occupational therapists, orthoptists, or physiotherapists; clinical psychologists, child psychotherapists or speech therapists; art or music therapists employed by a health service body; and scientists employed by a health service body as heads of department.

Within the NHS the duty to give a patient access to his health record is not imposed on each of the health professionals who adds to that record. The duty to give access to records is imposed on the "holder" of the record. In the case of general practice records, the GP is most likely to be asked to give access to a record as the "holder"of the record at the time of application. If the individual is not registered with a GP or is deceased the holder is the FHSA (or health board) on whose list the patient was most recently included. Where the record was made by a health professional providing services for a district health authority, a regional health authority or an NHS Trust it is that authority or trust which is the holder. The FHSA, health authority or trust is required to take advice from the appropriate health professional (the patient's GP, or previous GP, or the hospital consultant responsible for the clinical care of the patient if in hospital) before giving access. If no GP who has cared for the patient is available, an experienced GP will advise the FHSA.

The right of access to information is principally for the patient himself, if he is capable of understanding. The patient may also authorise another person, in writing, to make an application on his behalf. In certain cases other people have the right of access to the patient's records. However, this right does not extend to information given by the patient in the expectation that it would not be disclosed to the applicant. A patient can also request that a note be included in his records stating that he does not wish access to that record to be given after his death.

Where the patient is a child, the parent, or a person having parental responsibility, can have access (see chapter 7.3). The parent can apply for access only with the child's consent if the child is capable of giving consent. If the child is incapable of understanding the nature of the application but access would be in the child's best interests, the record holder can give access. Information given previously by the child in the expectation that it would be kept confidential cannot be revealed, nor can the results of investigations or examinations which the child thought were confidential at the time they were conducted.

If the applicant is a child (a person under 16 in England and Wales) or pupil (a girl under 12 or boy under 14 in Scotland) the record holder should not give access unless convinced that the young person is capable of understanding the nature of the application.

Where the patient is incapable of managing his own affairs, the person appointed by the court to manage the patient's affairs has the right of access (see chapter 8). Where the patient has died, the patient's personal representative and any person who may have a claim arising out of the patient's death, have a limited right of access to the record relevant to any such claim.

Applications for access must be made in writing to the person or body who is the holder of the record. The record holder must verify that the applicant is the individual to whom the record relates, or is somebody entitled to apply on the patient's behalf. If the record holder has insufficient information to decide this further information must be sought within 14 days of the application date. The holder must then give access to the records within 21 days of the date of the application, if the record was made within the preceding 40 days. Where the record relates to a period more than 40 days before the application, the holder has 40 days to provide the information. When additional information has been requested to verify the individual's right of access, these time limits run from the date of provision of the additional information. The Act only applies to records made after 1 November 1991 unless, in the opinion of the record holder, the accessible part of the record is unintelligible without information recorded before 1 November 1991. In that case the earlier information must be given to the applicant unless there is an overriding reason for withholding it.

Access is given by allowing the applicant either to inspect the record or to inspect an extract setting out the part of the record he or she is entitled to see.

No fee may be charged for this. If the applicant wants a copy of the record or extract this must be supplied. In this case a fee may be charged, which must not exceed the cost of making the copy and any postage for records made within 40 days. For other records the fee must not exceed the maximum set out in section 21 of the Data Protection Act 1984 (at present £10).

The applicant is entitled to an explanation of any terms which would not be intelligible to a lay person without explanation.

There are certain circumstances where access may be modified or denied:

(a) access will not be given to any part of a health record which, in the opinion of the holder, would cause serious harm to the physical or mental health of the patient or any other individual who could be identified from the information;

(b) access will not be given to any part of a health record which, in the opinion of the holder, would disclose information provided by, or relating to, an individual other than the patient (a "third party") who could be identified from that information. This protection does not extend to a health professional who has been involved in the care of the patient;

(c) where the relevant part of the health record was made before the the Act came into effect on 1 November 1991 (but see above);

(d) where an application for access is made by an individual on behalf of the patient because the patient is mentally incapable or has died, no information can be revealed which the patient gave on the understanding that it would be kept confidential. Similarly, no results of examination or investigation can be disclosed if, at the time they were carried out, the patient thought they would be confidential. No informaiton at all can be disclosed if the patient requested non-disclosure and this has been noted in the record.

If the record holder grants the applicant restricted access this will have to be in the form of an extract from the records prepared by the relevant health professional. A person who considers that any part of the health record to which he has had access is inaccurate can apply to the holder to have it corrected. The record holder may either make the necessary amendment to the record or attach a note of the matters the applicant considers inaccurate. The applicant must be supplied with a copy of the correction or note made, free of charge.

The holder is not required to give an explanation of why any part of the record has been withheld. If the holder of a health record fails to comply with the Act the applicant can apply for a court order for compliance. To make a decision the court may require a record to be made available for its own inspection.

Guidance on the implementation of the Access to Health Records Act 1990 is given in a booklet, *A Guide for the NHS*, which accompanies NHS circular HSC(91) 6. This guidance indicates that the Secretary of State proposes that NHS hospitals (directly managed units and NHS Trusts) should deal with complaints of non-compliance within the arrangements of the Hospital Complaints Procedures Act 1985. These arrangements have not yet been finalised and in the meantime complaints about non-compliance with the Access to Health Records Act 1990 can be taken direct to the courts.

5 Fertility and birth

5.1 Human Fertilisation and Embryology Act 1990

In recent years there has been increasing awareness of the value of fetal research and experimentation. At the same time, however, the real moral concerns which this raises and the need for legal regulation of this difficult area of medical science have also been recognised.

The Human Fertilisation and Embryology Act 1990 embodied this regulation in statute. The Act creates an independent body, the Human Fertilisation and Embryology Authority (HFEA), to control and license centres undertaking any of the following activities:

(i)   offering treatment using donated sperm and eggs, or involving the creation of human embryos outside the body;

(ii)   storing human sperm, eggs, or embryos;

(iii)   carrying out research on human embryos.

These activities will be illegal and subject to criminal penalties unless carried out in accordance with such a licence. A licence cannot permit storage of gametes for a period exceeding 10 years or embryos for more than five years. Experimentation on human embryos is permitted only until the 14th day following fertilisation.

The Act does not regulate artificial insemination where the husband's sperm is used to inseminate his wife (AIH), nor does it regulate "do it yourself" techniques of artificial insemination undertaken without medical assistance. GIFT (gamete intra-fallopian transfer), where eggs and sperm are placed in the woman's fallopian tubes to fertilise there, is not within the scope of the Act, but the Secretary of State has the power to make regulations to bring it within statutory control should this prove necessary.

The Authority has considerable autonomy in granting and revoking licences, and in the conditions to be attached to such licences. Opportunities to challenge decisions are limited. Appeal against decisions of the Authority's licensing committee can only be made to the court on a point of law.

The Act requires proper records to be maintained by the providers of infertility treatment and for these to be forwarded to the Authority. Records should include details of persons donating or receiving gametes or embryos and any child born as a result of treatment. The Authority is required to maintain a register of such information. A person who has reached the age of 18 or who intends to marry is entitled to receive information from the register if it shows that he or she was, or may have been born as a result of regulated infertility treatment. This information is only to be provided after proper counselling. There has been discussion about the range of information about their genetic background which might eventually be made available to children born as a result of some infertility treatments. The Authority is currently collecting a wide range of information about donors as it cannot be anticipated what details may be required by future regulations. At present, the Act specifically forbids giving information which may identify the gamete or embryo donor.

The Act also clarifies the status of children born as a result of regulated infertility treatment (but not do it yourself measures). The woman who carries the child is deemed to be the mother whatever the genetic history of the child. The woman's husband or partner is regarded as the child's father unless it is shown that he did not consent to his partner's treatment.

The Act also makes provision for children born as a result of surrogacy and amends the law on abortion (see sections 5.2 and 5.3 below).

A *Code of Practice* for licensed centres has been drawn up by the HFEA. An area of particular concern to doctors has been the transmission of information. The Act only allows information to be passed on by the patient or with the patient's explicit consent, unless the information is going to another doctor or health professional covered by the licence for the purposes of providing treatment under the licence. A model letter for licensed centres to enable them to carry out this is included in the Authority's code of practice. Unforseen consequences of the confidentiality provisions in the Act seem to include restrictions on release of identifying clinical information to legal representatives of a clinician operating in a licensed centre if sued for negligence. Satisfactory resolution of these problems might require amendment to the Act.

5.2 Surrogacy

Under the Surrogacy Arrangements Act 1985 surrogacy arrangements are not in themselves illegal. What the Act does prohibit is the making of a surrogacy arrangement on a commercial basis. However a couple may make a payment to the surrogate mother to cover expenses and the court could authorise further payments to the surrogate.

An agreement between a commissioning couple and the surrogate to transfer parental rights is not enforceable by the court (Surrogacy Arrangements Act 1985 – section 1A), as amended by section 36 of the Human Fertilisation and Embryology Act 1990. The court may make an order for a child to be treated in law as the child of a married couple where the gametes of the husband and wife are used to create an embryo and another woman carries the child through pregnancy, provided that the couple:

(i)   are resident in the United Kingdom;

(ii) are over 18 years of age;

(iii) have the child with them;

(iv) make application to the court within six months of the child's birth or within six months of the Act coming into force;

(v)   have made no payment, except with the sanction of the court, (Section 30 Human Fertilisation and Embryology Act 1990).

5.3 Abortion

Questions of abortion and sterilisation in relation to mentally incapacitated women are covered in chapter 8. The general position is that it is a criminal offence for anyone other than a registered doctor to perform an abortion. The doctor may only perform an abortion if certain criteria are adhered to.

Section 58 of the Offences Against the Person Act 1861 states: "... whosoever, with intent to procure the miscarriage of any woman, whether she be or be not with child, shall unlawfully administer to her or cause to be taken by her any poison or other noxious thing, or shall unlawfully use any instrument or other means whatsoever with the like intent ..." is guilty of an offence carrying life imprisonment.

The Infant Life (Preservation) Act 1929 (not applicable in Scotland and Northern Ireland) states in section 1(1) "... any person who, with intent to destroy the life of a child capable of being born alive, by any wilful act causes a child to die before it has an existence independent of its mother, shall be guilty of felony, to wit, of child destruction." The maximum penalty is life imprisonment. But the prosecution must prove that "... the act which caused the death of the child was not done in good faith for the purpose only of preserving the life of the mother." Section 1(2) states "evidence that a woman had at any material time been pregnant for a period of twenty-eight weeks or more shall be prima facie proof that she was at that time pregnant of a child capable of being born alive."

The Abortion Act 1967, as amended by section 37 of the Human Fertilisation and Embryology Act 1990 (not applicable in Northern Ireland), provides that no offence under the Infant Life (Preservation) Act 1929 is committed by a registered doctor who terminates a pregnancy in accordance with its provisions, provided the following conditions are observed.

67

(1) Two registered medical practitioners must be of the opinion, formed in good faith (section 1(1)):

    (a) that the pregnancy has not exceeded its twenty-fourth week and that the continuance of the pregnancy would involve risk, greater than if the pregnancy were terminated, of injury to the physical or mental health of the pregnant woman or any existing children of her family; or

    (b) that the termination is necessary to prevent grave permanent injury to the physical or mental health of the pregnant woman; or

    (c) that the continuance of the pregnancy would involve risk to the life of the pregnant woman, greater than if the pregnancy were terminated; or

    (d) that there is a substantial risk that if the child were born it would suffer from such physical or mental abnormalities as to be seriously handicapped.

See 5.3.2 for provisions concerning the certification of the medical opinions required.

(2) Section 1(3) stipulates that the abortion must be carried out in a NHS hospital (including NHS Trust hospitals) or in a place approved for the purpose by the Secretary of State. See 5.3.2 for the duty to notify that the abortion has taken place. The Secretary of State also has the power to approve places offering treatment consisting primarily of the use of specified medicines.

The Abortion Act 1967, section 5(2), as amended by the Human Fertilisation and Embryology Act 1990, also deals with the issue of selective reduction of pregnancy (the reduction of fertilised ova as part of a course of treatment for fertility). This is legal where the conditions of the Abortion Act as set out above are fulfilled—for example, where the continuation of a multiple pregnancy would involve risk of injury to the physical and mental health of the pregnant woman or existing children, or where there is a substantial risk that the child would be born seriously handicapped.

5.3.1 *Emergencies*

If there is an emergency then a doctor may perform an abortion in a place which is not authorised as above and without first getting the two opinions referred to above. The criteria are set out in section 1(4) and apply in a case where a registered doctor:

"... is of the opinion formed in good faith, that the termination is immediately necessary to save the life or to prevent grave permanent injury to the physical or mental health of the pregnant woman."

5.3.2 Certificates and duty to notify

The 1968 Abortion Regulations have now been revoked in their entirety by the Abortion Regulations 1991 (SI 1991/499) which provide the following. In non-emergency cases the opinions of the two registered doctors must be given in the form set out in the schedule to the regulations and must be obtained before the abortion is performed. In emergency cases the opinion of the doctor concerned must also be obtained in the prescribed certificate form, also before the operation, unless same is "not reasonably practicable," in which case the certificate must be signed within 24 hours. Both types of certificate must be retained by the signing doctor for a period of three years.

The doctor who performs the abortion must, within seven days of doing so, give notice of same together with other information as specified in the schedule to the regulations, to the Chief Medical Officer of the Department of Health. The information must be sent in a sealed envelope and must not be disclosed to any other person except the following:

(a)   For the purposes of carrying out their duties an officer of the Ministry of Health authorised by the Chief Medical Officer of same or the Registrar General, or authorised member of his staff;

(b)   To the Director of Public Prosecutions in relation to his duty to prosecute persons who breach the abortion laws;

(c)   To a police officer not below the rank of superintendent or authorised by same for the purpose of investigating whether an offence has been committed;

(d)   For the purposes of criminal proceedings which have already begun;

(e)   For bona fide scientific research;

(f)   To the practitioner who terminated the pregnancy;

(g)   To a practitioner with the consent in writing of the woman who had the abortion;

(h)   To the president of the GMC so that any allegation of professional misconduct can be investigated.

It is a criminal offence to breach the provision of these regulations.

5.3.3 *Conscientious objection*

Section 4 of the amended Abortion Act 1967 provides that no person is under a contractual or statutory duty to participate in any treatment authorised by the Act to which he has a conscientious objection. (The burden of proving that he has such an objection would lie on him if any legal proceedings were brought.) This does not, however, affect any duty to participate in treatment which is necessary to save the life or to prevent grave permanent injury to the physical or mental health of a pregnant woman. Although the law is not entirely clear, it is generally assumed by legal experts that the conscientious objection clause does not, however, apply to GPs. This assumption stems from the case of Janaway *v* Salford Health Authority (1988) 3 AER 1079. In that case the House of Lords decided that the issue, under section 4, was whether a person was required to "participate" in the termination. Their Lordships chose to give the word its ordinary and natural meaning—that is, that in order to claim conscientious exemption under section 4, the objector had to be required to actually take part in administering treatment in a hospital or approved centre. (The BMA has advised that registered GPs who are unwilling to sign forms for termination should promptly refer patients seeking abortion to a colleague.)

5.3.4 *Advertisements*

The Medicines (Labelling and Advertising to the Public) Regulations 1978 provide that it is a criminal offence to issue an advertisement which is likely to lead to the use except under the instructions of a doctor or dentist of any medicinal product (see glossary for the definition) or any other substance or article for the purpose of procuring the miscarriage of a woman.

5.4 Duties to notify and register births

5.4.1 *Duty to notify birth to health authorities*

In England and Wales the National Health Service Act 1977 provides a duty of notification when a birth takes place.

The duty is imposed on the father of every child born if he is residing on the premises where the birth takes place and on any person in attendance on the mother at the time of or within six hours after the birth.

The duty applies to notify regarding any child which has issued forth from its mother after the expiry of the 28th week of pregnancy, whether alive or dead.

The duty is to give notice of the birth to the prescribed medical officer (prescribed in National Health Service (Notification of Births and Deaths) Regulations 1982 (SI 1982 No 286) or to the District Health Authority for the place where the birth takes place. The notice must be given either by posting or delivering same within 36 hours after the birth. Failure to do so is a criminal offence unless the accused can satisfy the court that he believed some other person had done so.

The district health authority must supply without charge pre-paid stamped addressed envelopes together with forms of notice to any doctor or midwife residing or practising in their area who applies to them for same (Section 124, as amended).

In Scotland the Registrar sends details of the child's birth to the local area health board but there is no equivalent to section 124 in the National Health Service (Scotland) Act 1978.

5.4.2 *The duty to give particulars of live births (and stillbirths) to the Registrar of Births and Deaths*

The law about this in England and Wales is set out in the Births and Deaths Registration Act 1953, and in Scotland in the Registration of Births, Deaths and Marriages (Scotland) Act 1965. Both these Acts have been amended by the Still-Birth (Definition) Act 1992 which gained Royal Assent on 16 March 1992 and is enforced from 1 October 1992 (see 5.4.3).

In the case of every birth there is a duty to notify same to the Registrar. This duty falls primarily on the mother and father, but in the event of their death or inability the duty then falls on any other qualified informant (see below).

The duty is as follows. The informant must, within 42 days in England and Wales and 21 days in Scotland, provide the Registrar with all the required information concerning the birth and sign the register in the presence of the Registrar. The required information is set out in the schedule to the Population (Statistics) Act 1938, as substituted by the Population (Statistics) Act 1960.

Once one qualified informant has done this then all the others are relieved of any such duty.

In England and Wales if, before the 42 days have elapsed, an inquest has found that the child was stillborn the duty to notify the birth no longer applies.

The above Acts provide that certain categories of persons are qualified to give information about births. They may be referred to as "qualified informants". The categories are:

(a) the father and mother of the child;

(b) the occupier of a house where to the knowledge of that occupier a child has been born;

(c) any person present at the birth;

(d) any person having charge of the child.

If the required particulars have not been provided within the respective time limits then the Registrar is empowered by virtue of section 4 (England and Wales) and section 16 (Scotland) to serve a notice on the person who is the qualified informant requiring him to attend personally at the Registrar's office to give necessary details of the birth. It should be noted that by section 36(a) (England and Wales) and section 53(3) (Scotland) a person who is required by the statutes to give information concerning a birth and who "wilfully refuses to answer any questions put to him" by the Registrar relating to the particulars required to be registered concerning the birth, or fails to comply with any requirement made by the registrar in accordance with the statutes, can be prosecuted and fined in the criminal courts.

Section 8 (England and Wales) and section 17 (Scotland) forbid registration of a birth after three months have elapsed unless additional special procedures are followed.

5.4.3 *Duties in relation to stillbirths*

The Still-Birth (Definitions) Act 1992 (referred to in 5.4.2) amends the definition of stillbirth in certain provisions by reducing the number of weeks of pregnancy after which a child born dead is to be regarded as stillborn, from 28 to 24 weeks. The effect of the amendments is that the birth of children stillborn under the amended definition are required to be registered and that the certificate, which is required for their burial or cremation, will be available for children born dead at this earlier stage of pregnancy.

Section 41 of the interpretation section of the Births and Deaths Registration Act 1953 has been amended to state that a "stillborn child means a child which has issued forth from its mother after the twenty-fourth week of pregnancy and which did not at any time after being completely expelled from its mother breathe, or show any other signs of life, and the expression "still-birth" shall be construed accordingly." Section 12 of the Births and Deaths Registration Act 1926 (definitions) and the equivalent Scottish legislation have been similarly amended.

Under section 11(1) (England and Wales) and section 21 (Scotland) every registered doctor or certified midwife who has been present at a stillbirth or who examines the body of a stillborn child must, on being requested by a qualified informant (see above), give that informant a certificate in the prescribed form. For the form prescribed in England and Wales see the Registration of Births, Deaths and Marriages Regulations (SI 1987 No 2088).

The certificate must state that the child was not born alive and where possible must state the cause of death to the best of the knowledge and belief of the person signing it. In England and Wales the certificate must also state the estimated duration of the pregnancy, and, in Scotland, such particulars of the condition of the mother before the stillbirth as may be requested in the prescribed form.

The qualified informant must then produce the certificate to the Registrar and it is stipulated that the certificate should be requested from the doctor in preference to the midwife if there is a choice of both. If there is no doctor or midwife eligible to sign a certificate then the qualified informant must sign a declaration to that effect.

Chapter 6.4.1, on death certificates, explains the sanctions which operate if a doctor neglects to provide a certificate when under a duty to do so under these Acts, or if a certificate is provided which contains false or inaccurate particulars.

5.5 Newborns with severe mental disabilities

In the same way as premature infants of low birth weight now survive (with implications for abortion legislation), so now do babies with severe disabilities who once would have died in infancy. This calls into question the desirability of preserving the life of a newborn child with serious abnormalities.

The courts have considered this issue in two recent cases Re C and Re J. Both concerned babies between 4 and 5 months old who had sustained physical damage at birth and who were wards of court, but the decisions are equally relevant to newborns. Re C concerned a baby who was terminally ill. The court authorised the hospital to treat her to allow her life to come to an end peacefully and with dignity. It said she should be given pain relief but it was not necessary to treat her with antibiotics or to start intravenous or nasogastric feeding regimens. The decision was based on consideration for her welfare, well being, and interests. In Re J the baby was not dying but was severely brain damaged and suffered repeated fits and episodes where he stopped breathing which required ventilation. The question before the court was what was to be done if his breathing stopped again. The court concluded that it was not in J's best interests to reventilate him unless the doctors treating him considered it appropriate at the time.

General guidance was given in the judgements in Re J on this issue. Lord Donaldson stated that "The obligation to maintain life is not absolute and that a balancing exercise [is] to be performed in assessing the course to be adopted in the best interests of the child." Although there is a strong presumption in favour of prolonging life, consideration must also be given to the qualify of life and the pain and suffering which the child will experience if life is prolonged, in addition to the distress involved in the treatment itself.

"What doctors and the court have to decide is whether a particular decision as to medical treatment should be taken which as a side effect will render death more or less likely. At the other end of the age spectrum, the use of drugs to reduce pain will often be fully justified, notwithstanding that this will hasten the moment of death. What can never be justified is the use of drugs or surgical procedures with the primary purpose of doing so." (per Lord Donaldson Re J at p 938)

6 Death

6.1 Defining death

In the past death was a simple state to identify—the person would stop breathing or his heart would stop beating. Advances in our understanding of biochemistry and physiology, and advances in medical techniques and technology have called these simple definitions into question. With developments in resuscitation and life support the heart and respiratory functions can now be kept going even when there is little likelihood of an individual regaining consciousness. In open heart surgery—for example, there is deliberate cardiac arrest. Resuscitation following spontaneous cardiac arrest is also commonplace.

In addition to the traditional acceptance of cardiorespiratory death, the medical profession agrees that "brain stem death" (irreversible loss of brain function) constitutes an adequate criterion of the end of life. A code of practice for the recognition and confirmation of brain death was endorsed by the Department of Health for the benefit of all doctors. The formulation offered by the Conference of Royal Colleges and their Faculties is "the permanent functional death of the brain stem".

6.1.1 Conference of Medical Royal Colleges

The following memorandum was issued by the honorary secretary of the Conference of Medical Royal Colleges and their Faculties in the United Kingdom on 15 January 1979:

(1) In October 1976 the Conference of Royal Colleges and their Faculties (UK) published a report unanimously expressing the opinion that "brain death," when it had occurred, could be diagnosed with certainty. The report has been widely accepted. The conference was not at that time asked whether or not it believed that death itself should be presumed to occur when brain death takes place or whether it would come to some other conclusion. The present report examines this point and should be considered as an addendum to the original report.

(2) Exceptionally, as a result of massive trauma, death occurs instantaneously or near-instantaneously. Far more commonly, death is not an event: it is a process, the various organs and systems supporting the continuation of life failing and eventually ceasing altogether to function, successively and at different times.

(3) Cessation of respiration and cessation of the heart beat are examples of organic failure occurring during the process of dying, and since the moment that the heart beat ceases is usually detectable with simplicity by no more than clinical means, it has for many centuries been accepted as the moment of death itself, without any serious attempt being made to assess the validity of this assumption.

(4) It is now universally accepted, by the lay public as well as by the medical profession, that it is not possible to equate death itself with the cessation of the heart beat. Quite apart from the elective cardiac arrest of open-heart surgery, spontaneous cardiac arrest followed by successful resuscitation is today a commonplace, and although the more sensational accounts of occurrences of this kind still refer to the patient being "dead" until restoration of the heart beat, the use of the quote marks usually demonstrates that this word is not to be taken literally, for to most people the one aspect of death that is beyond debate is irreversibility.

(5) In the majority of cases in which a dying patient passes through the processes leading to the irreversible state we call death, successive organic failures eventually reach a point at which brain death occurs and this is the point of no return.

(6) In a minority of cases brain death does not occur as a result of the failure of other organs or systems but as a direct result of severe damage to the brain itself from, perhaps, a head injury or a spontaneous intracranial haemorrhage. Here the order of events is reversed; instead of the failure of such vital functions as heart beat and respiration eventually resulting in brain death, brain death results in the cessation of spontaneous respiration; this is normally followed within minutes by cardiac arrest due to hypoxia. If, however, oxygenation is maintained by artificial ventilation the heart beat can continue for some days, and haemoperfusion will for a time be adequate to maintain function in other organs, such as the liver and kidneys.

(7) Whatever the mode of its production, brain death represents the stage at which a patient becomes truly dead, because by then all functions of the brain have permanently and irreversibly ceased. It is not difficult or illogical in any way to equate this with the concept in many religions of the departure of the spirit from the body.

(8) In the majority of cases, since brain death is part of or the culmination of a failure of all vital functions, there is no necessity for a doctor specifically to identify brain death individually before concluding that

the patient is dead. In a minority of cases in which it is brain death that causes failure of other organs and the systems, the fact that these systems can be artificially maintained even after brain death has made it important to establish a diagnostic routine which will identify with certainty the existence of brain death.

Conclusion

(9) It is the conclusion of the Conference that the identification of brain death means that the patient is dead, whether or not the function of some organs, such as heart beat, is still maintained by artificial means.

There have been surprisingly few cases in English courts requiring any extensive discussion of the legal meaning of death. There have been cases where a person charged with murder claimed that he was not responsible for killing the victim but that responsibility lay with the hospital team who disconnected the life support machine. In 1981 in R *v* Malcherek and R *v* Steel the Court of Appeal dealt with two cases in which patients on life support machines had the ventilator switched off when it was found that they had irreversible brain damage. The Court of Appeal took the view that the original criminal assaults leading to hospitalisation were the causes of death, not the switching off of the life support machines. Perhaps an even more striking case was that of R *v* Blaue (1975). Blaue stabbed a woman who was a Jehovah's Witness and who refused the blood transfusion necessary to save her life. Blaue was charged with murder although he tried to argue that death occurred from a failure to treat.

There is no statutory definition of death and it is usually accepted as an issue of fact established by medical evidence. The law is content to accept the decisions of medical practitioners.

6.2 *Treatment of the terminally ill and dying*

The position in English law was set out in 1957 by J Devlin in his direction to the jury in R *v* Adams. Dr Bodkin Adams was charged with the murder of one of his patients in that he had administered unusually large doses of morphine which it was alleged he knew would kill her. The deliberate taking of life is murder and Mr Justice Devlin directed that doctors are in no special category. He also discussed, however, the example of a doctor who did or omitted to do something, because of which death occurred "at eleven o'clock instead of twelve o'clock, or even on Monday instead of Tuesday". He said:

"(N)o people of common sense would say "oh the doctor caused her death". They would say the cause of her death was the illness or injury, or whatever it was, which brought her into hospital, and the proper medical treatment that is administered and that has an incidental effect of determining the exact moment of death, or may have, is not the cause of death in any sensible use of the term." He continued that a doctor "is entitled to do all that is proper and necessary to relieve pain and suffering even if the measures he takes may incidentally shorten life . . . A doctor who is aiding the sick and dying does not have to calculate in minutes or even hours, and perhaps not even in days or weeks the effect upon a patient's life of the medicines he administers or else be in peril of a charge of murder."

In its ethical advice the BMA emphasises that it is the duty of a doctor to ensure that a patient dies with dignity and as little suffering as possible but recommends that active intervention to terminate life—that is, where drugs are given or other procedures carried out in order to cause death—even at the request of a patient, should remain illegal.

6.2.1 *Suicide*

Since the law was amended by the Suicide Act 1961 it has not been a criminal offence to attempt to commit suicide. It remains an offence, punishable by up to 14 years imprisonment, to assist someone to commit suicide. It is unclear whether a doctor who provided the means for suicide—for example, left some fatal drug by the bedside of a patient who was fully informed as to its effect—yet left to the patient the decision whether to use it would be liable under this Act. There have been no cases reported on this and it would depend on all the facts of the individual case.

6.2.2 *Refusing treatment*

The law accepts a patient's right to refuse treatment, and where a patient fully understands the consequences of refusal the doctor must respect his views and right to self determination. The position is more difficult where the patient is unconscious or otherwise lacks the capacity and understanding to give consent to or refuse treatment. The courts in Britain have considered this issue only in relation to very young children where they have considered the best interests of the child in deciding whether treatment should be given (see chapter 5).

6.2.3 *Living wills/advance directives*

The terms "living will" and "advance directive" or "advance declaration" tend to be used interchangeably, although some draw a distinction between them and this is mentioned below. Such a statement is not legally binding on doctors but it is an indication of the patient's wishes which should be accorded respect and taken into account by a doctor. The BMA strongly supports the concept of the advance directive and provides guidance on the ethical issues. The main problem is that a patient's views may change and the living will may not be sufficiently detailed to cover the particular contingency which arises.

The purpose of an advance directive is to enable a competent person to give instructions about what he wishes to be done, or who he wishes to make decisions for him, if he should subsequently lose the capacity to decide for himself. A patient can nominate a proxy decision-maker either as part of the advance directive or quite separately. In neither case can the nominee give or refuse legal consent on behalf of the patient for the patient's treatment (except in Scotland in cases where the same person is a "tutor dative"—see chapter 8). Advance directives are usually discussed in the context of medical treatment and relate mainly to the patient's right to refuse or change treatment in a disabling chronic or terminal illness. Advance directives have developed principally in the United States of America.

A living will is essentially seen as a formal declaration by a competent adult expressing the wish that, if he becomes so mentally or physically ill that there is no prospect of recovery, any procedures designed to prolong life should be withheld. The object is to rebut any presumption that the patient has consented to treatment. There are many versions of living wills and the clarity with which they give instructions varies widely. Very detailed living wills risk failing to foresee a particular turn of events; those written in very general terms may be ambiguous and require considerable interpretation by doctors. Concern has been expressed that doctors who are unhappy with the terms of a living will may be able to circumvent its operation by refusing to confirm clinically that the triggering condition, such as terminal illness, has actually occurred.

In trying to assess how the law may develop here, some have looked to Canada, where a form of advance decision making has been upheld in the courts in the case of Malette *v* Shulman. In this case damages for battery were awarded against a doctor who gave a life saving blood transfusion to an unconscious adult Jehovah's Witness despite the fact that she had a card refusing a blood transfusion. The doctor argued that there was a "shadow of doubt" regarding the patient's informed rejection of treatment, but the court regarded the card as presenting a rational and informed decision. This case may not be followed in Britain where the concept of informed consent and refusal is less well established.

6.2.4 *Comatose patients*

When is it proper to discontinue artificial ventilation of a severely brain damaged patient? As noted in 6.1 this is an issue which has not been clarified at law, but the problem has been addressed by the US Supreme Court which considered the case of Karen Quinlan, where there was "no reasonable possibility of her ever emerging from her present comatose condition." The court ruled that her death "would not be homicide but rather expiration from existing natural causes." In 1990 the US Supreme Court considered another case where there was thought to be no possibility of the patient recovering sentient life but where the patient, Nancy Cruzan, was not dependent on a ventilator. The question in this case was whether feeding could be withdrawn. On appeal, the patient's family won the right to stop the feeding and hydrating of the patient who died 12 days later. Again, this is an area unexplored in United Kingdom law.

6.3 Doctors and inquiries into a death

6.3.1 *Doctors and coroners: England and Wales*

There is no general statutory duty imposed on the doctor by virtue of his profession to report a death to the coroner, but it is accepted practice for him to do so in cases of doubt and suspicion. Such cases would generally include:

(i) sudden death where the cause is unclear and where there was non-attendance in the last illness;

(ii) accidents in any way contributing to the cause of death;

(iii) any death in custody;

(iv) chronic or acute alcoholism contributing to the death;

(v) death where an anaesthetic or surgical procedure seems to have contributed to the death, or where an operation was formed following an injury;

(vi) drug related death whether therapeutic or otherwise;

(vii) death of a foster child;

(viii) death that may be related to any industrial disease;

(ix) death where the deceased has been in receipt of a disability pension;

(x) deaths related to any forms of poisoning whether deliberate or unintentional;

(xi) stillbirths where there was any possibility of the child being born alive (see chapter 5).

Obstruction of the coroner is also a common law offence but the prosecution must prove that the defendant disposed of the body with intent to obstruct or prevent a coroner's inquest in circumstances where there would have been a duty to hold same (R *v* Pearson, 1954, unreported).

Section 8(1) of the Coroners' Act 1988 states that the coroner must hold an inquest when ". . . informed that the body of a deceased ("the deceased") person is lying within his district, and there is reasonable cause to suspect that the deceased has died (a) a violent or an unnatural death; (b) has died a sudden death of which the cause is unknown; or (c) that such person has died in prison, or in such a place or under such circumstances as to require an inquest under any other Act."

The coroner is permitted to dispense with an inquest in a case of sudden death where the cause of death is unknown, if he orders a post mortem examination and is satisfied by the outcome that death was due to natural causes (section 1a). The coroner notifies the Registrar by completing Pink Form B. This is the lower half of a composite form; the upper half of which, Pink Form A, permits the cause of death given on the doctor's death certificate to be registered—that is, in cases of death from natural causes.

Although doctors are not under a statutory duty to report any death to the coroner, they are obliged in certain circumstances to sign a death certificate and deliver same to the Registrar of Births and Deaths. See 6.4.1 for details of this duty and the duty of all persons in certain circumstances to report the fact of the death to the Registrar.

The Registrar in turn is under a statutory duty to inform the coroner of the fact of the death in certain circumstances, some of which directly relate to medical treatment or the lack of it.

The Registration of Births, Deaths and Marriages Regulations (SI 1987 No 2088) state (Regulation 33), that where the Registrar is informed of a stillbirth and has reason to believe that the child was born alive he must report that matter to the coroner.

Regulation 41 states that if a registrar is told of a death within 12 months of its occurrence the fact of the death must be reported to the coroner if the death is one:

"(a)   in respect of which the deceased was not attended during his last illness by a registered medical practitioner; or

(b)   in respect of which the registrar

   (i)   has been unable to obtain a duly completed certificate of cause of death; or

   (ii)   has received such a certificate with respect to which it appears to him, from the particulars contained in the certificate or otherwise, that the deceased was seen by the certifying medical practitioner neither after death or within fourteen days before death; or

(c)   the cause of which appears to be unknown; or

(d)   which the registrar has reason to believe to have been unnatural or to have been caused by violence or neglect or by abortion or to have been attended by suspicious circumstances; or

(e)   which appears to the registrar to have occurred during an operation or before recovery from the effect of an anaesthetic; or

(f)   which appears to the registrar from the contents of any medical certificate to have been due to industrial disease or industrial poisoning."

Note, too, that rule 19 of the Prison Rules (SI 1964 No 388) obliges prison governors to notify the coroner of any death in prison and a similar duty is imposed in relation to inmates of youth custody and detention centres.

A coroner may, of course, in practice be notified of a death by the police or by the coroner's officers.

Statute provides that medical witnesses can be summoned to give evidence at inquests and that doctors can be ordered to perform post mortem examinations. Those who disobey can be penalised.

Section 21 of the Coroners' Act 1988 enables the coroner to summon the doctor who last treated the deceased, or, if there were none, another doctor practising in the area where the death occurred.

In the case of an inquest into a death, the coroner may summon as a witness:

"(a)   any legally qualified medical practitioner appearing to him to have attended at the death of the deceased or during the last illness of the deceased; or

(b)   where it appears to him that no such practitioner so attended the deceased any legally qualified medical practitioner in actual practice in or near the place where death occurred;

and any medical witness summoned may be asked to give evidence as to how, in his opinion, the deceased came by his death."

The person so summoned can be directed also to perform a post mortem examination, but note the provisions below which in effect direct a coroner, if possible, only to select a doctor with suitable qualifications to perform post mortem examinations (section 21(2)).

If there is any allegation of negligence against a doctor that doctor should not be asked to perform a post mortem examination.

"Where a person states upon oath before the coroner that in his belief the death of the deceased was caused partly or entirely by the improper or negligent treatment of a medical practitioner or other person, such medical practitioner or other person shall not be allowed to perform or assist at the post mortem examination of the deceased" (section 21(3)).

In addition, if a coroner receives a written request from an inquest jury requesting that another doctor named by them should be summoned and further directed to perform a post mortem examination, even if one has already been done, the coroner must comply with that request (section 21(4)). The jury may make such a request if they ". . . are of the opinion that the cause of death has not been satisfactorily explained by the evidence of the medical practitioner or other witnesses brought before them."

Section 21(5) of the Coroners' Act 1988 states that any medical practitioner who fails to obey a summons of the coroner issued in pursuance of that Act can be prosecuted and fined unless he can show good sufficient cause for such disobedience.

The Act sets out additional powers in relation to the summoning of medical witnesses. Section 20 states that, in addition to the powers set out above, a coroner may at any time after he has decided to hold an inquest require any legally qualified medical practitioner to hold a post mortem examination, or examination of parts of the body, or other relevant substances or things. There is the same caveat as above against making such a request to a doctor against whom an allegation of negligence on oath has been made, but there is an additional right given to the person against whom such an allegation has been made if he so wishes to be "represented" at the post mortem examination. (section 20(3)).

The Coroners' Rules (SI 1984 No 552), Rule 6, direct a coroner to have regard to certain criteria when considering which doctor to request to perform a post mortem examination. Firstly, the post mortem examination ". . . should be made, whenever practicable, by a pathologist with suitable qualifications and experience and having access to laboratory facilities." If it seems likely that someone is to be charged with murder the coroner should consult with the police as to who should be asked to do the post mortem examination. If the deceased died in hospital the coroner should not appoint a pathologist on the staff of, or associated with, that hospital to do the post mortem examination if certain criteria apply, nor should a doctor who sits on a pneumoconiosis medical panel be asked to do so if the disease is in the category dealt with by that panel.

6.3.2 Doctors and the procurator fiscal: Scotland

There is no office of coroner in Scotland. In Scotland the procurator fiscal is charged with inquiring into all sudden suspicious, accidental, unexpected and unexplained deaths—that is:

(1) any uncertain death;

(2) any death which was caused by an accident arising out of the use of a vehicle, or which was caused by an aircraft or rail accident;

(3) any death arising out of industrial employment, by accident, industrial disease, or industrial poisoning;

(4) any death due to poisoning (coal gas, barbiturate, etc);

(5) any death where the circumstances would seem to indicate suicide;

(6) any death where there are indications that it occurred under an anaesthetic;

(7) any death resulting from an accident in the home, hospital, institution or any public place;

(8) any death following an abortion;

(9) any death apparently caused by neglect, such as malnutrition;

(10) any death occurring in prison or a police cell where deceased was in custody at the time of death;

(11) any death of a newborn child whose body is found;

(12) any death (occurring not in a house) where deceased's residence is unknown;

(13) death by drowning;

(14) death of a child from suffocation (including overlaying);

(15) where the death occurred as the result of smallpox or typhoid;

(16) any death as a result of a fire or explosion;

(17) any sudden death;

(18) any other death due to violent, suspicious or unexplained cause;

(19) deaths of foster children.

The procurator fiscal is required in terms of the Fatal Accidents and Sudden Deaths Inquiry (Scotland) Act 1976 to hold a public inquiry before the sheriff in the circumstances set out in section 1 which include, for example, all deaths in the course of employment or while in custody, or where it is considered expedient to do so on grounds that the death was sudden, suspicious, or unexplained, or gave rise to serious public concern. And the procurator fiscal must, in addition, report to the Crown office deaths occurring in a range of specified circumstances.

Such an inquiry is held in public. A doctor can be compelled to attend and give a precognition to the procurator fiscal and subsequently can be compelled to give evidence at the inquiry. He must answer all the questions (save those which might point to his being guilty of a criminal offence). The sheriff then issues a determination covering such matters as place and cause of death, the defects in any system of work resulting in death, and the reasonable precautions by which death might have been avoided. Any doctor who is involved in the circumstances which led up to the death and who is at any risk, however slight or tenuous, should have legal representation at the inquiry and even lead witnesses of his own. The transcript of the evidence at the inquiry can be used and referred to in subsequent civil proceedings.

It is worth bearing in mind that the procurator fiscal is only obliged to instruct a post mortem examination if he considers the circumstances justified. Accordingly, if a doctor, consequent on the death of a patient, considers that his treatment or diagnosis or any action is liable to be criticised then it may be advisable for him to demand a post mortem examination to determine the precise cause of death.

There is a general statutory duty in Scotland on a doctor to report to the procurator fiscal a death falling within the categories into which the latter must inquire, although clearly as a matter of public duty, any citizen and particularly a medically qualified one should report such deaths. It is doubtful whether failure to do so would be a breach of any general common law obligation.

The Registrar of Births, Marriages and Deaths is, however, statutorily obliged to inform the procurator fiscal of all deaths into which the procurator fiscal must inquire (Registration of Births, Deaths and Marriages (Scotland) Act 1965). A medical practitioner who attended the deceased in his last illness must, within seven days of death, send either to the Registrar or to any person who has an obligation to inform the Registrar (any relative of the deceased, any person present at the death, the deceased's executor or legal representative, the occupier of the premises where the deceased died) a certificate of prescribed form stating the cause of death. If no doctor was attendant during the final illness, or if the doctor present at the death cannot provide the certificate, then any medical practitioner who is able to do so may sign (section 24). (This is different from the position in England, where only the coroner or doctor in attendance during the last illness can sign the certificate.) If the doctor feels unable to sign the certificate he should contact the procurator fiscal and if the latter is satisfied that no crime or matter which might involve him are concerned he will say so and the doctor can sign the certificate.

6.4 Death certificates and notification

Another point that should be noted is that a doctor who signs a certificate containing a statement that later turns out to be untrue, misleading or otherwise improper renders himself liable to disciplinary proceedings. (See the GMC "blue book," February 1991, paragraph 45.)

In addition, many statutes which provide for the signing of medical certificates also provide for the prosecution in the criminal courts of anyone who signs such a certificate with a false statement in it.

6.4.1 *Death certificates*

See chapter 9.4 for further points concerning certificates. Details of the duty to give a certificate where a stillbirth has occurred are set out in chapter 8. In England and Wales the Births and Deaths Registration Act 1953 and in Scotland the Registration of Births, Deaths and Marriages (Scotland) Act 1965 provide that if a patient has been attended during his last illness by a registered doctor then that doctor must sign a death certificate.

In England and Wales section 22(1) of the Act provides that the certificate must be in the form prescribed by the Registration of Births, Deaths and Marriages Regulations (SI 1987 No 2088) forms 14 and 15. The latter form applies when death occurs within 28 days of birth. This now includes, among other things, a requirement to certify if death might have been caused by or contributed to by the employment of the deceased. The certificate must also contain a statement by the doctor as to the cause of death to the best of his knowledge and belief. If the doctor cannot do so then there is no obligation to sign the death certificate.

Having signed the certificate, the registered doctor must deliver same forthwith to the Registrar of Births and Deaths. The doctor must also give to a "qualified informant" (see below) notice in writing in the form prescribed by the Registration of Births, Deaths and Marriages Regulations (SI 1987 No 2088) form 16. That informant must, except where an inquest is held, deliver this notice to the Registrar.

In Scotland section 24 provides that the registered doctor must deliver the certificate either to a qualified informant (see later) or to the Registrar within seven days or such period as is prescribed by regulations (the minimum period which can be prescribed is two days). This section also provides that if there is no registered doctor available who is eligible or able to sign a certificate then such a certificate may be signed by any medical practitioner who is able to do so.

Both Acts provide that a person who is required by virtue of the legislation to give, deliver or send any certificate who fails to do so without reasonable excuse is guilty of an offence (see section 36(b) of the English statute and section 53(3)(b) of the Scottish statute).

6.4.2 *Registration of death*

There is a statutory duty under the legislation referred to above to notify the Registrar of the fact that a death has occurred. In England and Wales persons who can be obliged to report the death (referred to as "qualified informants") are as follows:

(a)   those under the primary duty are any relatives who were present at the death, or who attended the deceased in his last illness, or who live or were in the subdistrict where the death occurred;

(b)   secondly, the duty falls on any person present at the death or occupier of the house where it took place if he knew of it;

(c)   lastly, the duty falls on any inmate of the house who knew of the death or person responsible for the disposal of the body.

Note that if the person died in a place other than a house, or if a body is found and no information is available about the place of death, then there is a similar duty imposed as follows:

(a)   firstly, on any relative with knowledge of the particulars that have to be registered;

(b)   secondly, any person present at the death;

(c)   thirdly, any person finding or taking charge of the body;

(d)   lastly, any person causing the disposal of the body.

In Scotland those with a duty to report the death are any of the following:

(a)   any relative of the deceased;

(b)   any person present at the death;

(c)   the deceased's executor or other legal representative;

(d)   the current occupier of the premises where the death took place;

(e)   if none of the above, any other person with knowledge of the particulars that have to be registered.

6.5 Cremation certificates

In England and Wales a cremation cannot take place unless a certificate has been signed by a registered doctor. The law is set out in the Cremation Acts 1902 and 1952 and in various regulations.

Section 8(2) of the 1902 Act provides that any person ". . . who shall wilfully make any false . . . representation, or sign or utter any false certificate, with a view to procuring the burning of any human remains" can be prosecuted and could receive up to two years' imprisonment.

In England and Wales the Cremation Regulations SR and O.1930 No 1016 (as amended) provide the following.

Regulation 8 states that no cremation may take place unless one of five criteria has been satisfied and the medical referee has given his written authority (which he can refuse to do without giving a reason). The medical referee is a doctor attached to the cremation authority who must have not less than five years' standing and relevant experience and qualifications.

The criteria are either:

(1) A certificate in the prescribed form must have been signed by a fully registered doctor who must have attended the deceased during his last illness and must be able to certify definitely as to the cause of death. (Note the requirement that the doctor must certify "definitely": as opposed to the best of his knowledge and belief, as with a death certificate.) The form of certificate is set out in form B to the schedule to the regulations, and it should be noted that more information is required than for a certificate under the Births, Deaths, and Marriages Regulations.

A confirmatory certificate in the form prescribed (as in form C, set out in the schedule) must be given by another registered doctor who must be either the medical referee or another registered doctor of five years' standing who must not be related to the deceased, or related to, or a partner of the doctor who gave the other certificate.

A confirmatory certificate is not needed, though, if the person died in a hospital where he was an inpatient and a post mortem examination was performed by a doctor qualified as above and the registered doctor who gave the form B certificate knows the result of that examination before signing the certificate; or

(2) a post mortem examination must have been carried out by an expert in pathology appointed by the cremation authority (or the medical referee in an emergency) and a certificate must have been given by him in the form set out in form D in the schedule; or

(3) a post mortem examination must have been performed and the cause of death certified by the coroner and a certificate given by the coroner accordingly; or

(4) an inquest must have been opened and a certificate given by the coroner; or

(5) if the deceased has undergone anatomical examination then the person licensed under the relevant legislation must have given the necessary certificate.

The medical referee may permit the cremation of the remains of a stillborn child if the child has been certified to be stillborn by a registered doctor after examination of the body and the medical referee is satisfied after making any necessary enquiries that the child was stillborn. But the medical referee must still get either a certificate of registration of the death or a certificate from the coroner regarding any inquest held.

The BMA booklet *Deaths in the Community*, prepared by the BMA's forensic medicine subcommittee in 1986, gives guidance on the eight forms—that is, Forms A, B, C, D, E, F, G and H, which must be completed for different aspects of cremation under the Cremation Act Regulations (as amended in 1985). The booklet reflects the situation in England and Wales relating to medical certification, notification to the coroner, interference with the body, stillbirths, the coroner's role and duties, together with disposal of the dead.

Before cremation can take place in Scotland, a certificate must be signed by the doctor who attended the deceased during his last illness and who can definitely certify the cause of death. A confirmatory certificate by a doctor of five years' standing must also be given, except where the death took place while an inpatient in hospital, and if a post mortem examination has taken place. (For details see The Cremation (Amendment) (Scotland) Regulations (SI 1985 No 820)). If the certificate is not obtainable then a post mortem examination is carried out by an expert pathologist appointed by the cremation authority, and the procurator fiscal has to be informed of any suspicious circumstances, or if there is reason to suspect that the death occurred under anaesthetic, or if there are any suspicious circumstances surrounding a stillbirth. In general terms, if there is any doubt of the cause of death the procurator fiscal should order a post mortem examination, particularly where a cremation is envisaged.

7 Children

7.1 Children and parents

Under the Family Law Reform Act 1969 young people in England and Wales become adults at the age of 18. In Scotland the Age of Legal Capacity (Scotland) Act 1991 establishes the age of legal capacity as 16 years (see 7.2.1). For the purposes of medical treatment, however, all young people achieve this status at 16. At the age of 16, a young person can give valid consent to treatment, choose his own doctor, and seek voluntary admission to a mental hospital without consulting his parents.

In the case of Gillick v West Norfolk and Wisbech Area Health Authority the House of Lords considered the relationship between parents and children. Lord Scarman stated that "Parental rights clearly do exist and they do not wholly disappear with the age of majority ... Parental rights exist only so long as they are needed for the protection of the person and property of the child ... Parental rights yield to the child's right to make his own decisions when he reaches a sufficient understanding and intelligence to be capable of making up his own mind on the matter requiring decision." The effect of the case was to establish that if a young person has achieved sufficient understanding and intelligence to appreciate the implications of what is proposed and is capable of forming a decision, then that individual can give valid consent. A parent's right to make decisions for his or her child is a right which the courts will hesitate to enforce against the wishes of the child, the more so the older the child becomes.

The Children Act 1989 introduces the concept of "parental responsibility" which includes all the rights, duties, powers, responsibilities and authority which, by law, a parent has in relation to the child and his property. Under the Act both parents, if married to each other, or the mother if she is single, automatically have parental responsibility. This responsibility continues to exist even if a court makes an order giving parental responsibility to someone else: thus more than one person can have parental responsibility for the same child at the same time (section 2(5)). When a care order is made, parental responsibility continues but is shared with the local authority.

7.1.1 *The Children Act 1989*

The Children Act 1989 came into force on 14 October 1991. The Act has a number of implications for doctors and patients:

Section 27 requires health authorities to collaborate with social services departments in providing support for children and families.

Section 85 requires health authorities to tell social services departments when they provide, or intend to provide, a child with accommodation for three months or more. This provision also applies to any residential care home, nursing home, or mental nursing home.

Social services departments have a statutory duty when drawing up a care plan for a child to ensure that the child is provided with health care. They are required to ensure that arrangements are made for a child to be examined by a registered medical practitioner, and for the practitioner to make a written assessment of the child's state of health. Health authorities and GPs are required to be notified of each child placement.

Under the Children Act 1989, courts have new powers in relation to medical examinations connected with care orders and supervision orders. The court may prohibit such examinations, or direct that they are subject to the court's specific approval. Where medical evidence has been obtained during proceedings without the approval of the court, the court may refuse to consider it. These powers allow the court to ensure that children are not subjected to repeated examinations for evidential purposes, and that examinations take place in a sensitive way, in a suitable environment, and by suitably trained personnel. It must be noted, however, that these powers of the court are enabling but may not be decisive in the absence of consent by a competent child. An order by the court that the child be medically or psychiatrically examined (or treated pursuant to a full supervision order) is subject to that child's consent (sections 38(6), 43(8), 44(7) and paragraphs 4(4)(a) and 5(5)(a) of schedule 3 to the Children Act). These provisions allow a competent child to refuse to submit to examination, assessment, or treatment ordered by the court.

Guidance on producing court reports in such cases is given in *Diagnosis of Child Sexual Abuse: Guidance for Doctors*, issued by the Standing Medical Advisory Committee in July 1988 (London: HMSO, ISBN 0-11-321155-4). Implications for professional practice are discussed in *Working Together under the Children Act 1989: A Guide to Arrangements for Inter-agency Co-operation for the Protection of Children from Abuse* (London: HMSO, 1991: ISBN 0-11-321472-3).

7.2 Consent

7.2.1 *Young people over 16*

As discussed in chapter 1, competence and ability to understand in general terms the nature and implications of treatment is seen as the key to valid consent. In England and Wales the Family Law Reform Act 1969, section 8, provides that people who have reached the age of 16 (who are presumed to be competent to understand the issues) may validly consent to surgical, medical, and dental treatment, and that such consent is to have the same effect as if the individuals were of full age. The section also applies to procedures undertaken for the purpose of diagnosis and those, like administration of anaesthetic, which are ancillary to treatment. It means that if a competent young person who is aged 16 or over agrees to treatment then the parents cannot override the young person's decision, whatever their views. In cases, however, where treatment includes proposals for research, the position is less defined regarding consent of young people over 16 and under 18 years. Notwithstanding the competence of young people of 16 and 17, it is considered advisable to obtain parental consent in addition to the patient's consent for participation in research projects (see 7.2.4).

If the young person is not competent section 8(3) of the Family Law Reform Act preserves the parents' capacity to consent on the patient's behalf until the young person reaches the age of 18. The courts can override parental consent in such cases if they consider the proposed treatment is not in the patient's best interest (see sterilisation of the mentally incompetent patient in chapter 8.4).

In Scotland the Age of Legal Capacity (Scotland) Act 1991 recognises the legal capacity of 16 year olds to enter into all manner of transactions and to consent to medical treatment.

7.2.2 Children under 16

Scottish law exemplifies the growing recognition that competent young people do have a certain right to selfdetermination and it codifies the implications of the Gillick judgment, which are discussed further below. The Age of Legal Capacity (Scotland) Act 1991 assigns various legal rights to children over the age of 12 but sets no minimum age for legal capacity to consent to medical treatment. It recognises the capacity for understanding rather than chronological age as the criterion for providing valid consent to treatment. The Act (section 2(4)) states that "a person under the age of 16 shall have legal capacity to consent on his own behalf to any surgical, medical or dental procedure or treatment where, in the opinion of a qualified medical practitioner attending him, he is capable of understanding the nature and possible consequences of the procedure of treatment."

In England and Wales, if a child is under 16 the parents' consent will normally be required for any treatment. It must be noted, however, that although children under 16 do not have an automatic right to consent to treatment, this does not mean that such a child cannot consent to treatment if he has sufficient understanding to give consent. Such consent would be recognised as valid even if the parent objected (see the discussion of the Gillick case below). The age at which any particular child can give consent will depend on the nature of the treatment and the understanding of the child in question. A younger child may be able to consent to minor or routine treatment, but consent for elective surgery or contraception requires a higher degree of understanding, which, generally, only older children possess.

For a young child who is incapable of giving consent it is the parent or other person in whom parental responsibility is vested, who can give valid consent to medical treatment. Only in exceptional circumstances, such as an emergency or when a person with parental responsibility cannot be found, is a doctor justified in treating such a child without parental knowledge and consent.

A decision by a parent to consent on behalf of a minor to treatment which is considered controversial can be overridden by the courts in wardship proceedings. The official solicitor, in a practice note of 1990, for example, advises that the sterilisation of a minor will, in virtually all cases, require the prior sanction of the court, whatever the parents' wishes (see chapter 8.4). The practice note does not have the force of law but embodies good practice. The young person can be made a ward of court and the court will decide whether to sanction or refuse the specific treatment on the basis of what is in his or her best interests. In Re D (a minor) Wardship: Sterilisation, the court directed that an operation for sterilisation, which had been agreed by the mother of an 11 year old girl, should not be carried out. In another recent case, Re R (1991) the Court of Appeal overruled the wishes of a minor even though she was competent at the time of expressing them. In this case the Master of the Rolls, Lord Donaldson, explored the concept of "Gillick competence" and in his judgment made a clear distinction between giving and refusing consent to treatment (see 7.2.3).

The Children Act 1989 allows any person with an interest in the minor to apply to the court for a specific issue order which allows the court to settle a particular issue in dispute such as medical treatment.

In Scotland local authorities have powers under the Social Work (Scotland) Act 1968 (as amended) to take children into care and in prescribed circumstances to assume parental rights by authority of the court, but these procedures take time.

7.2.3 Refusing treatment

In the case of Re R, there was held to be a significant difference between consenting and withholding consent to treatment. Lord Donaldson interpreted what had been said in the Gillick judgment. He took the view that competent minors and young people between 16 and 18 have powers to consent to treatment, but that these powers are concurrent with parental powers to give consent. Consent by either party permits the child's treatment, but that this is not the same thing as the right to *determine* treatment. He pointed out that if the parents disagree with each other about the child's treatment there is no legal problem as long as one authorised person consents. Similarly, if the child and parents disagree about treatment the doctor still only requires the consent of one authorised person, competent child, or parent for treatment to be legally provided. Therefore, if a competent child consents to treatment provision of that treatment is lawful whether the parent consents or refuses, but the doctor is not *obliged* to treat. The doctor must exercise clinical judgment. Conversely where the child refuses treatment but the parent consents, that parental consent allows the treatment to be undertaken lawfully. Lord Donaldson stated his belief that when a child becomes competent to make his own decisions, this does not terminate the parents' decision making powers. Many feel that this view contradicts that enunciated by Lord Scarman in the Gillick case, quoted in 7.1, despite the distinction drawn between enabling and determinative consent.

The case concerned a girl of 15 whose mental health had deteriorated but who, while lucid, refused drug treatment for her condition. She was a ward of court and the court had to consider whether it could overrule her decision and authorise the use of drugs against her will. As her mental capacity was subject to fluctuation, the court decided that she could not be regarded as "Gillick competent" and could not therefore make her own decisions about treatment.

Lord Donaldson also said that the wardship powers of the court are greater than those of parents and even if a child is "Gillick competent", the court in wardship can overrule his decision to refuse treatment if it considered treatment to be in the child's best interest. He stated that this would also apply to a minor over 16 who could give consent by virtue of the Family Law Reform Act 1969.

The status of Lord Donaldson's remarks is difficult to weigh up. They appear to run counter to the spirit of the Children Act. Because his comments were "obiter" that is, not part of the decision—and neither of the other two judges affirmed them, legal experts have reasoned that they do not cast the specific provisions of the Children Act into question. Some have expressed concern that Lord Donaldson's views might be taken into account in any future cases, with a possible reduction in children's rights in treatment decisions but this remains to be seen.

If a child, who is too immature to consent, needs a life saving procedure, and the parents refuse consent or no other valid consent can be obtained, then doctors and hospitals can go ahead and treat the child, notwithstanding the lack of consent. NHS circular HSC (GEN) 81 1975 states that it is inappropriate to take court proceedings in such circumstances and advises that "The decision whether or not to provide a blood transfusion or to operate to save the life of a child, despite the wishes of the child's parents, should be taken by the consultant concerned on the basis of his clinical judgement and after a full discussion with the parents. A consultant would run little risk in a court of law if, in acting according to his conscience, he obtained:

(a)   the written supporting opinion of a medical colleague that the patient's life would be in danger if the treatment were withheld; and

(b)   an acknowledgement from the parents, preferably in writing or before a witness, that the danger had been explained to them and that their consent was still withheld."

Unfortunately, there have been instances where Jehovah's Witness parents have rejected their child following a transfusion of blood given against their wishes. Doctors should bear this possibility in mind when considering the sort of treatment to be given.

7.2.4 Research

The conduct of research on human subjects in Britain is not regulated by statute but various bodies have produced guidance for good practice. In the absence of a specific statutory framework commentators refer to principles of common law. In its publication *The Ethical Conduct of Research on Children* (1991) the Medical Research Council refers to the individual's rights of selfdetermination and freedom from bodily interference as "ethical principles recognised by English law as legal rights." Failure to supply information about the procedure and seek voluntary consent to it may lead to a claim that the research involves a trespass to the person of the research subject.

The published guidelines by bodies including the Department of Health, Medical Research Council, and Royal College of Physicians differentiate between procedures which are intended to benefit the subject (therapeutic research) and those not of direct benefit to the individual but which add to medical knowledge and may benefit others (non-therapeutic research). The participation of children in the former is held to be covered by the general rules of consent to treatment because procedures intended to benefit the child constitute "treatment"—that is, minors with sufficient understanding and intelligence can legally make their own decisions and parental consent is necessary in other cases. Nevertheless, it is widely advised that, even for therapeutic research on a competent minor who has consented, parental consent should also be sought. The Department of Health recommends that parental consent should be sought up to the point where the young person attains adult status (age 18) "unless it is clearly in the child's interests that the parents should not be informed" (Department of Health guidance on *Local Research Ethics Committees 1991*).

Participation of minors in non-therapeutic research poses ethical and legal questions. In particular, the Medical Research Council states in *The Ethical Conduct of Research on Children* (1991) that "in the strict view of the law parents and guardians of minors cannot give consent on their behalf to any procedures which are of no particular benefit to them and which may carry some risk of harm." The same point is made by the Department of Health which advises ethics committees that "those acting for the child can only legally give their consent provided that the intervention is for the benefit of the child. If they are responsible for allowing the child to be subjected to any risk (other than one so insignificant as to be negligible) which is not for the benefit of that child, it could be said they were acting illegally. It should also be noted that the giving of consent by a parent or guardian cannot override the refusal of consent by a child who is competent to make that decision" (Department of Health guidance on *Local Research Ethics Committees 1991*).

In 1990 the European Commission issued guidelines on *Good Clinical Practice for Trials on Medicinal Products in the European Community* which had been prepared by the Committee for Proprietary Medicinal Products (III/3976/88—EN Final). As yet these guidelines do not have statutory force in the United Kingdom, although it is intended that they will eventually be incorporated into the national law of all member states. The guidelines do not refer specifically to children, but some of their provisions have clear implications for research on children, especially in the context of non-therapeutic research. The guidelines state that it may be acceptable to include patients who are unable to consent, with the agreement of an ethics committee, if the research is believed to promote the welfare and interest of the subject (paragraph 1.13). When there is no direct clinical benefit to the subject, the latter must personally give signed consent (1.14).

7.2.5 Transplantation

Where the potential donor is a live adult, full, free, and informed consent for the removal of human tissue must be formally obtained as for all surgical procedures. In the case of minors, in the absence of any specific statutory authority or case precedents, it has been suggested that the general rules about consent also apply. (See Mason JK, McCall Smith RA *Law and Medical Ethics* 3rd Edition, London: Butterworths, 1991: 303). These and other writers also query whether parents can ever validly consent to medical treatment which is not in the interests of their child. Doctors would therefore be best advised to consult their defence organisation before accepting a child as a donor. In the White Paper *Advice from the Advisory Group on Transplantation Problems*, dealing with the question of amending the Human Tissue Act 1961 (London: HMSO, 1969 Cmnd 4106) it is stated that: "The propriety of using a live donor is a matter of ethical judgement of the doctor in the circumstances governing each individual case." It is possible, however, that the court would consider it to be in the best interests of a minor that the life of a close relative should be saved.

Some authorities (including the British Medical Association and the World Health Organisation) argue that a distinction should be drawn between transplantation of a regenerative organ (such as bone marrow) and of a non-regenerative organ (such as a kidney). In the former case there is minimal risk to a child donor and transplantation is ethically acceptable. In the latter case it is ethically unacceptable for a child to be used as a donor.

7.3 Confidentiality

A minor capable of consenting to treatment is also entitled to confidentiality.

The relevance of the Access to Health Records Act 1990 to children's health records and applications for access to them by children or by parents is discussed in chapter 4.3.3.

7.3.1 *Contraception*

This issue was considered in the Gillick case previously mentioned in chapter 7.2. Mrs Gillick, who had five daughters, sought an assurance from her local area health authority that it would not give advice and treatment concerning contraception to her daughters while they were under the age of 16, without her prior knowledge or consent. Failing to receive such an assurance, she applied to the court for, among other things, a declaration that the authority could not lawfully give such advice or treatment because it was against the law relating to parental rights. The case eventually reached the House of Lords where the decision on this point was that parental rights were recognised by law only as long as they were needed for the protection of the child, and such rights yielded to the child's right to his own decisions when reaching sufficient understanding and intelligence so as to be capable of making up his own mind. Therefore, a girl under 16 did not by virtue of her age lack legal capacity to consent to contraceptive advice and treatment by a doctor. The doctor has a discretion to give contraceptive advice or treatment without the parents' knowledge and consent to a girl under 16, provided the girl has reached an age where she has a sufficient understanding and intelligence to enable her to understand fully what is proposed, that being a question of a fact in each case.

The GMC's advice, revised in November 1991, is as follows:

"Difficulties may arise when a doctor believes that a patient, by reason of immaturity, does not have sufficient understanding to appreciate what the treatment or advice being sought may involve. Similar problems may arise where a patient lacks understanding because of illness or mental incapacity. In all such cases, the doctor should attempt to persuade the patient to allow an appropriate person to be involved in the consultation. if the patient cannot understand or be persuaded, but the doctor is convinced that the disclosure of information would be essential to the patient's best medical interests, the doctor may disclose to an appropriate person or authority the fact of the consultation and the information learned in it. A doctor who decides to disclose information must be prepared to justify that decision and must inform the patient before any disclosure is made."

The BMA gives the following advice to doctors where a girl under the age of 16 requests contraception but refuses to allow her parents to be informed:

(a) Attempt to convince the girl of the advisability of involving her parents in this decision. This should be part of the counselling extended over a number of interviews, where appropriate. In many cases the doctor will gain consent to involve a parent or a person in loco parentis.

(b) If he is unsuccessful the doctor must then decide whether the girl has the mental maturity to understand his advice and the possible consequences of her action. If she has not, then her consent is not informed and so invalid. The doctor cannot provide treatment in these circumstances but should keep confidential the fact and content of the consultation.

(c) If he is satisfied that she can consent he makes a clinical decision as to whether the provision of contraception is in the best interests of the patient.

(d) A decision not to prescribe does not absolve him from keeping the interview confidential.

It is only in those cases, therefore, where the under age patient does not have the necessary capacity to understand that the doctor may be justified in telling her parents what has occurred at the consultation. However, the doctor must tell the patient what he proposed to do and must also consider the patient's best medical interests and the trust that was placed in him. Where the doctor decides to tell the under age patient's parents, he must be prepared to justify his actions.

7.3.2 Child abuse

A doctor would be justified in breaching the confidence of a child patient where he suspects child abuse and he can report his suspicions to the appropriate authority. On this matter the GMC states in its 1991 advice on confidentiality:

"Deciding whether or not to disclose information is particularly difficult in cases where a patient cannot be judged capable of giving or withholding consent to disclosure. One such situation may arise where a doctor believes that a patient may be the victim of physical or sexual abuse. In such circumstances the patient's medical interests are paramount and may require the doctor to disclose information to an appropriate person or authority."

7.4 Right to sue for pre-natal injury

Under the Congenital Disabilities (Civil Liability) Act 1976 (not applicable in Scotland) a person may sue for injuries received while in the womb or for an occurrence prior to conception which leads to disability if these result from the negligent actions of a person other than his mother (unless injured by mother's negligent driving at a time when she knew or should reasonably have known she was pregnant). The normal rules of negligence law apply—that is, someone must be at fault—the negligent act must be the direct cause of the damage to the child. Additionally, section I (5) provides that:

"The defendant is not answerable to the child, for anything he did or omitted to do when responsible in a professional capacity for treating or advising the parent, if he took reasonable care having due regard to then received professional opinion applicable to the particular class of case; but this does not mean that he is answerable only because he departed from received opinion."

The Act was amended by the Human Fertilisation and Embryology Act 1990 to give similar rights to a child born as a result of infertility treatment to sue if the child sustains a disability resulting from "an act or omission in the course of the selection, or the keeping or use outside the body of the embryo carried by her or of the gametes used to bring about the creation of the embryo."

7.5 Actions by children

A child or young person under 18 has to act through an adult called the "next friend" in order to bring an action in the courts.

7.5.1 Time limits

The time limits within which actions must be brought (as set out in chapter 2.2.4) are modified in the case of minors. In England and Wales a person who wishes to claim damages for a personal injury allegedly sustained while he was under the age of 18 has the right to start a legal action in respect of that injury within three years of reaching the age of 18. In Scotland no account is to be taken in computing the periods within which an action has to be raised or any time during which the injured person was under a legal disability by reason of non-age.

If a child does not have knowledge of all the matters set out in 2.2.2 (that the injury was significant and attributable to a practical act and the identity of the defendant) he or she has a further three years from the date of acquiring such knowledge within which to start proceedings.

7.5.2 Legal aid

Children under 18 can apply in their own right to take civil actions—for example, for personal injury as a result of medical negligence. The child's means will be assessed to decide eligibility—no account will be taken of the parents' means.

8 Mental health

8.1 Consent to treatment

As stated in chapter 1, a doctor cannot normally treat a patient without having obtained prior consent from the patient. Difficulties arise with mentally disordered or handicapped people because they may not have sufficient understanding to give true consent. Whether a person has the capacity to consent to the particular procedure depends on the individual's ability to comprehend the nature and purpose of that procedure and its risks and benefits.

The law in England, Wales, and Northern Ireland is that noone, not even the next of kin, can give consent on behalf of another adult (see 8.4.2). The English Law Commission is currently looking into decision making procedures on behalf of mentally incapacitated adults.

In Scotland the law makes provision for a court to appoint a "tutor dative" who is given powers to consent on behalf of an adult. As far as the law is concerned, the mentally incapacitated adult is then in the same position as a minor. In cases where a "tutor dative" has been appointed, the extent of his authority depends on the scope of the court decree. If the powers are sufficiently broad to allow the "tutor dative" to give consent, he must assess where the patient's best interests lie and must therefore be fully informed about the treatment. This should be given against the background of part IV of the code of practice issued under the Mental Health (Scotland) Act 1984 (see 8.2). The Scottish Law Commission is also reviewing questions of consent and mental incapacity with a view to clarifying the law.

In England and Wales the Mental Health Act 1983 makes provision for treatment to be given for the patient's mental condition without the consent of the patient, subject to certain limitations. Similar legislation exists in Scotland and Northern Ireland. The courts have considered the issue of treatment without consent where the treatment is not for the patient's mental disorder and this is also considered below (8.4.2).

8.2 Admission to a psychiatric hospital

The legislation is different in Scotland and Northern Ireland from that in England and Wales. Details of the law in England and Wales are given with reference to relevant differences in Scotland and Northern Ireland.

The Mental Health Act 1983 (not applicable in Scotland and Northern Ireland) sets out the basis on which a mentally disordered person may be lawfully detained and treated in a psychiatric hospital without his consent. The Act also provides for the reception of mentally disordered patients into guardianship (see 8.1.6 below for details of what this involves).

The situation in Scotland is governed by the Mental Health (Scotland) Act 1984. This is similar in many respects but there are important differences. The English Mental Health Act Commission, originally established under section 11 of the National Health Service Act 1977 and continued under section 121 of the Mental Health Act 1983 as a special health authority, is based on the well established Scottish Mental Welfare Commission. The equivalent legislation in Northern Ireland is the Mental Health (Northern Ireland) Order 1986. The Mental Health Act Commission in Northern Ireland, established under article 85 of the Order, also fulfils a similar function to that in England, Wales, and Scotland.

The function of all Commissions is to keep under review the care and treatment of patients who are detained under the Mental Health Acts. The English Mental Health Act Commission visits and interviews detained patients and investigates complaints by patients and others on behalf of the patient. The Commission can also inspect records relating to the patient and under direction of the Secretary of State appoint doctors and review treatment under part IV of the (English) Mental Health Act 1983. The Scottish Commission also has powers to order the release of patients.

Section 1 of the English Act contains definitions which are relevant to a number of procedures under the Act:

- "Mental disorder" is stated to mean "mental illness, arrested or incomplete development of mind, psychopathic disorder and other disorder or disability of mind."

- "Severe mental impairment" is stated to mean "a state of arrested or incomplete development of mind which includes severe impairment of intelligence and social functioning and is associated with abnormally aggressive or seriously irresponsible conduct on the part of the person concerned."

- "Mental impairment" is similarly defined to include significant impairment of intelligence and social functioning.

- "Psychopathic disorder" is defined as a persistent disorder or disability of mind (whether or not including a significant impairment of intelligence) which results in abnormally aggressive or seriously irresponsible conduct on the part of the person concerned (section 1 (subsection 2) Mental Health Act 1983).

No person may be deemed to be "suffering from mental disorder by reason only of promiscuity, immoral conduct, sexual deviancy, or dependence on alcohol or drugs." The Act specifically excludes these persons (section 1 (subsection 3)).

In section 1 of the Scottish Act "mental illness" is defined as "mental illness or handicap however caused or manifested." Mental impairment and severe mental impairment are defined in the same terms as in the English Act above. There is no category of psychopathic disorder in the Mental Health (Scotland) Act 1984.

The Northern Ireland Act defines "mental disorder" as "mental illness, mental handicap and any other disorder or disability of mind." There is no category of "mental impairment" but "mental illness" (a state of mind which affects a person's thinking, perceiving, emotion or judgment to the extent that he requires care of medical treatment in his own interests or the interests of others) and "mental handicap" (a state of arrested or incomplete development of mind which includes significant impairment of intelligence and social functioning) are defined. "Severe mental impairment" is defined in Northern Ireland in the same way as in the English/Welsh Act and, in common with Scotland, there is no category of psychopathic disorder in the Northern Ireland Act.

There are a number of different routes by which a patient can be lawfully detained in hospital and, in addition, the procedures are different in the case of a person accused of a criminal offence.

Police officers have the right to remove a person they have reasonable ground to believe is mentally ill from a public place to a place of safety under section 136 of the Mental Health Act 1983, and from a private home on the basis of a warrant issued by a magistrate under section 135 of the Mental Health Act 1983. (The Scottish Act provides for this in sections 117 and 118 and the Northern Ireland Order in articles 130 and 129.)

All other compulsory admissions to psychiatric hospitals and receptions into guardianship must be backed by two medical recommendations except in the case of an application under section for a 72 hour admission which requires one medical recommendation. This must be coupled with an application by an approved social worker or a nearest relative. This process is called sectioning.

8.2.1 *Voluntary patients (section 5)*

Medical treatment for mental disorder is provided on either a voluntary or involuntary basis. Most of patients (95%) are voluntary patients—that is, not detained under a formal section of the various Mental Health Acts. Section 131 of the Mental Health Act 1983 (section 17 subsection 2 in Scotland and article 127 in Northern Ireland) provides that a patient may enter hospital for psychiatric treatment without any order being made. In these circumstances the patient has the same rights as any other hospital patient. The patient must consent to treatment, can accept or refuse treatment, and is free to discharge himself. Emergency treatment can be given under common law where the patient is unable to consent to it and is in a life threatening or deteriorating condition.

In England, under section 5 (subsections 1 and 2) the doctor in charge of the treatment of a voluntary inpatient can compulsorily detain the patient for up to 72 hours on the grounds that an application ought to be made for compulsory admission. Where it is not practicable to secure the immediate attendance of the doctor in charge, a nurse can have a voluntary patient prevented from leaving for up to six hours, or until the doctor in charge can attend, if such detention is immediately necessary (section 5 subsection 4 Mental Health Act 1983). In the Scottish Act section 25 makes similar provisions, except that the maximum period for detention arranged by a nurse is only two hours. In Northern Ireland a patient can be detained on the doctor's assessment for 48 hours and, as in England and Wales, a nurse can detain the patient for six hours.

8.2.2 *Emergency admission (section 4)*

Emergency admission to a psychiatric hospital can be effected under section 4 of the Mental Health Act 1983 (section 24 in Scotland). This is justified by reason of "urgent necessity," for example, in the case of violent or suicidal patients, and one medical recommendation is required. The doctor need not be a specialist in mental health but should, if practicable, have known the patient before and have seen him in the previous 24 hours. An application can be made by an approved social worker and need not have the consent of the nearest relative. The patient can be detained for a maximum of 72 hours which may be converted to admission for 28 days if a second opinion from a specialist in mental health is obtained. There is no right of appeal in the first 72 hours.

8.2.3 *Admission for assessment (section 2)*

A patient can be admitted compulsorily under section 2 if he has a mental disorder (defined as in 8.2 above) of a nature or degree which warrants detention in hospital for assessment for a limited period, and detention in hospital is "in the interests of his own health or safety or with a view to protection of other persons." (This provision is article 4 in the Northern Ireland Order.)

Application must be made by the patient's nearest relative (or a person authorised by the relative, or by the court to act on his behalf), or by an approved social worker. The applicant must have seen the patient within the past 14 days. The application must be supported by two registered medical practitioners, one of whom must be qualified in psychiatry. (In Northern Ireland, application may be made by the same categories of people, but the patient must have been seen in the previous two days by the applicant and also by a doctor.)

The patient may be detained for up to 28 days. This is not renewable and application for admission under section 3 would have to be made to extend the period. The patient has a right to information about his legal position and can apply to the mental health review tribunal during the first 14 days of detention. The patient will then have the right to a mental health review tribunal hearing within seven days of the date of application. (In Northern Ireland the patient can be detained for up to seven days after a report on him has been made by the responsible medical officer or a doctor appointed by the Commission, but only for 48 hours if the report is provided by any other hospital doctor.)

In Scotland short term detention is achieved by emergency admission under section 24, followed by an extension for 28 days on similar grounds to those set out above. The patient has a right to appeal to the sheriff for his discharge during the 28 day period.

8.2.4 *Admission for treatment (section 3)*

This section provides for the long term detention of patients for treatment. The grounds for admission are that the patient is:

(1) Suffering from mental illness, severe mental impairment, psychopathic disorder or mental impairment and that his mental disorder is of a nature or degree which makes it appropriate for him to receive medical treatment in a hospital; and

(2) it is necessary for the health and safety of the patient or for the protection of other persons that he should receive such treatment; and

(3) in the case of psychopathic disorder or mental impairment, such treatment is likely to alleviate or prevent deterioration in his condition.

The procedure for application is similar to application under section 2, but under section 3, the nearest relative must be consulted when the applicant is a social worker. If the relative objects an application to the county court can be made to displace the nearest relative.

Initially detention is for up to six months. This can be renewed for a further six months and then for periods of one year at a time, provided that the responsible medical officer applying for renewal believes that further treatment is likely to alleviate or prevent deterioration in the patient's condition, or that the patient would be unable to care for himself, or would be liable to serious exploitation if detention did not continue. The patient has a right of appeal to a mental health review tribunal once during the first six months of detention, once during the next six months, and once during every year after that. If the patient detained under section 3 or received into guardianship under section 7 does not himself apply for a tribunal hearing within the time scale the hospital managers must, at the expiration of the period of detention, refer the case to a mental health review tribunal. The Secretary of State can also refer the patient's case to a Mental Health Review Tribunal at any time.

Similar provisions exist in Northern Ireland by virtue of articles 12 and 13 of the order.

Similar provisions for Scotland are contained in sections 17 to 21 of the 1984 Act. In Scotland, however, the application must be approved by the sheriff, who may make such inquiries and hear such person as he thinks fit, including the patient. He cannot refuse an application without first hearing the applicant and any witnesses he wishes to call. The patient has a right of appeal to the sheriff at any time during any renewal period of detention.

8.2.5 *Reception into guardianship (section 7)*

Section 7 (section 37 in Scotland, article 22 in Northern Ireland) deals with reception into guardianship; maximum duration of six months; renewable for a further six months, then from year to year. The effect of such reception is that the patient's guardian has the right to require the patient to reside at a particular place and to attend at specified places for the purposes of medical treatment, occupation, education or training. The guardian also has power to require access to the patient to be given at his place of residence to a registered doctor, approved social worker, or other specified person.

The grounds are that the patient is mentally ill, mentally impaired, or severely mentally impaired, or has a psychopathic disorder of a nature or degree that warrants his reception into guardianship, in the interests of the welfare of the patient or for the protection of others. (In Scotland and Northern Ireland the category of psychopathic disorder is not included). Application is as in section 2 above. The guardian must be the local Social Services Department or a person accepted by them.

8.2.6 *Admission via the criminal court*

The various sections which give the English courts the power to admit mentally ill offenders (or in some cases those accused only of criminal offences) to hospital are as follows.

Section 35 enables the court to remand an accused person to a psychiatric hospital to obtain a report on his mental condition. The person can be so remanded for up to 28 days at a time and not exceeding 12 weeks in all. The court must receive written or oral evidence from a registered doctor. A person remanded under this section is not subject to the consent to treatment provisions of the Mental Health Act 1983 (part IV). Treatment can only be given with the patient's consent.

Section 36 allows a person awaiting trial (who might otherwise be remanded in custody) to be remanded to a psychiatric hospital for treatment. The time limits are the same as above, as is the requirement for medical evidence. Only the Crown Court may make such an order. Section 37 enables the court to make hospital or guardianship orders in respect of mentally disordered offenders. The effect is the same as if the person had been admitted for treatment or received into guardianship as above. The court must have written or oral evidence from two doctors. Section 38 states that the court may make interim hospital orders for up to 12 weeks (28 day extensions can then be obtained for an overall maximum period of six months).

Section 41 gives the Crown Court power to add to a hospital order, a restriction order with or without limit of time. The effect of this is that while the restriction order lasts the patient cannot be given leave of absence, discharged from hospital or transferred without the permission of the Secretary of State. Written or oral evidence to the court of two doctors is required for a Section 37 sentence to be imposed. In all cases at least one of the doctors who give evidence to the court must be approved as having special experience in the diagnosis or treatment of mental disorder. (These provisions are reflected in articles 42, 43, and 47 of the Northern Ireland Order.)

8.2.7 Criminal Procedure (Insanity and Unfitness to Plead) Act 1991

The Criminal Procedure (Insanity and Unfitness to Plead) Act 1991 abolishes automatic detention for an indefinite period for defendants found unfit to plead. Previously, those considered unfit to plead were detained in hospital without any finding as to whether they had or had not committed the offence. Written or oral evidence of two or more doctors, one of whom is approved, is required where:

the jury returns a "special" verdict under the Trial of Lunatics Act 1883; or

a jury makes a determination on fitness to be tried, replacing section 4 of the Criminal Procedure (Insanity) Act 1964;

the Court of Appeal believes the proper verdict would have been one of not guilty by reason of insanity or that the case is not one where the verdict should have been acquittal, but he should have been found to have a disability and that he "did the act or made the omission charged against him"; this amends sections 6 and 14 of the Criminal Appeal Act 1968;

where the Court of Appeal substitutes a verdict of acquittal and believes that the appellant is suffering from mental disorder which warrants his detention in a hospital for assessment and that he ought to be detained in the interest of his own or others health or safety, applying to section 13 of the Criminal Appeal Act.

Schedule 2 deals with supervision orders (by a social worker or probation officer) and treatment orders (by doctors) and explains that such orders must include a requirement that the supervised person be treated by a doctor, with a view to an improvement in his mental condition. It also deals with arrangements for continuation of treatment beyond the period of the supervision and treatment order.

In Scotland admission via the criminal court is governed by sections 175 and 376, and 178 and 379 (restriction orders) of the Criminal Procedures (Scotland) Act.

8.3 Discharge

A voluntary (non detained) patient can leave hospital whenever he chooses. A patient who has been compulsorily detained under a civil section or through the court with no restriction order can only be discharged by the responsible medical officer, the hospital managers or a Mental Health Review Tribunal. (Similar provisions exist under article 14 of the Northern Ireland Order.) In the case of a patient detained under section 2 or 3, the nearest relative can write to the hospital ordering the patient's discharge. The manager has three days to consider the request and the responsible medical officer can recommend that the patient is not ready to be discharged. If the request is refused the relative can appeal to the Mental Health Review Tribunal within 28 days. Hospital managers also have a duty to refer to a tribunal the case of any patient who has not had a hearing within the first six months of his detention or within the last three years. Where a patient is detained by the criminal courts with a restriction order he can only be discharged by the Home Secretary or a mental health review tribunal. A mental health review tribunal comprises a lawyer, a psychiatrist, and a lay person. The members hear evidence from the patient, his representative, the doctors and others caring for him and any other relevant witnesses. The tribunal can then decide whether a patient should be discharged immediately or at some future date on the evidence presented on that day. The Tribunal can also order that the patient be granted leave of absence or transfer. The patient can be legally represented and legal aid is available within the financial eligibility limits.

In Scotland a compulsory patient will cease to be detained if an order in writing discharging him is made by the responsible medical officer or by the Mental Welfare Commission, or where there has been a successful appeal to the sheriff. The patient should either not be suffering from a mental disorder of a degree which makes detention for treatment appropriate, or it is not necessary for the health or safety of the patient or for the protection of others that he should receive such treatment.

8.4 Treatment of mental condition

Section 63 of the Mental Health Act 1983 (sections 97 and 98 in Scotland and article 69 in Northern Ireland) states that medical treatments for mental disorder can be given lawfully without the consent of the patient provided that they are given by, or under the direction of, the responsible medical officer. Sections 57 and 58 impose limitations in the case of certain treatments. By virtue of section 58 of the Act (section 98 in Scotland) hazardous treatments (defined as electroconvulsive therapy (ECT) and drug treatment for a period of three months or more) can only be given if the following conditions are satisfied:

(a) The patient has consented *and* either his responsible medical officer or a registered medical practitioner appointed by the Secretary of State for these purposes has stated in writing that the patient is capable of understanding the nature, purpose, and likely effects of the treatment and has consented to it;

(b) The specially appointed doctor, who must not be the doctor in charge of the patient's treatment, must certify in writing that the patient is not capable of understanding the nature, purpose, and likely effects of the treatment or has not consented to it, but that having regard to the likelihood of the treatment alleviating or preventing a deterioration of his condition, the treatment should be given. The doctor must consult with two other persons, professionally concerned with the patient's care one of whom must be a nurse and the other must not be a nurse or a doctor.

Section 57 (section 97 in Scotland) applies to irreversible procedures which include: any surgical operation for destroying brain tissue or the functioning of brain tissue and any other treatment specified in statutory regulations. (Similar provision is made in articles 63 and 64 of the Northern Ireland Order.) The only such treatment specified at the moment (in The Mental Health (Hospital, Guardianship and Consent to Treatment) Regulations (SI 1983 No 893)) is the surgical implantation of hormones for the purpose of reducing male sexual drive.

Such treatment cannot be given without the patient's consent and this consent must be verified and certified under section 58 by an appointed doctor and two non-medical witnesses who have also been specially appointed by the Secretary of State for that purpose. The appointed doctor must also certify in writing that, having regard to the likelihood of the treatment alleviating or preventing a deterioration of the patient's condition, the treatment should be given. The practitioner must consult with two other persons professionally concerned with the patient's care, one of whom must be a nurse and the other must not be a nurse or a doctor.

The fact and results of irreversible treatments must be notified to the Mental Health Commission who may withdraw the certificate issued by the appointed doctor. The patient may withdraw his consent to treatment under sections 57 and 58 at any time.

The above provisions of sections 57 and 58 do not apply in emergency situations defined in section 62 as follows—that is, to any treatment which:

(a) is immediately necessary to save the patient's life; or

(b) (not being irreversible) is immediately necessary to prevent a serious deterioration in the patient's condition; or

(c) (not being irreversible or hazardous) is immediately necessary to alleviate serious suffering by the patient; or

(d) (not being irreversible or hazardous) is immediately necessary to prevent the patient from behaving violently or being a danger to himself or others.

In such cases treatment can be given without the formalities set out above.

8.4.1 *Treatment of mental condition outwith Mental Health Acts*

In some exceptional circumstances medical treatment for mental disorder can be authorised by a court, contrary to the patient's wish and outwith the terms of the mental health acts. In "Re R (a minor) (wardship: medical treatment) (1991)," the Court of Appeal authorised administration of treatment including sedation, for a 15 year old ward of court. Since R's competence was held to fluctuate, Lord Donaldson ruled that she was incompetent to decide the question of treatment even in periods of lucidity but that medication could be authorised in her "best interests" by the court exercising its wardship jurisdiction. If fluctuating competence is held to constitute legal incapacity in this case some have queried whether this might also apply to adults whose ability to understand fluctuates but this remains to be clarified. (The case of R is discussed further in chapter 7.)

8.4.2 *Treatment other than for mental conditions*

There is no provision in the Mental Health Act 1983 or elsewhere for an appropriate person, such as the nearest relative, to consent to such treatment on behalf of an adult patient who does not have the mental capacity to consent. As is discussed in the chapter on children, parents or guardians can consent to the provision of treatment to minors who are incapable of consenting. Courts acting in wardship can also authorise treatment for minors. Certain forms of treatment of minors falls within a "special category," which includes sterilisation to prevent pregnancy and inter vivos organ donation for transplant. If such treatment is proposed for a minor, an application should be made to the courts within the wardship jurisdiction for leave to carry it out.

Where the patient is adult (over 18), neither the court nor any other person can consent to treatment, but application can be made to the court for a declaration that the proposed treatment would not be unlawful. In the case of Re F (F *v* West Berkshire Health Authority and Another (Mental Health Act Commission intervening) 1989), which concerned the sterilisation of an adult with arrested mental development, the House of Lords ruled that the common law allows a doctor to give medical or surgical treatment to an adult patient who is incapable of consenting when it is in the "best interests" of the patient to do so. Treatment is in the best interests of a patient if it is carried out to prevent deterioration or ensure improvement in the patient's physical or mental health. The court further considered that it may well be the duty of a doctor to treat an adult with a mental disability who was detained in hospital.

This decision allows doctors to treat patients who are incapable of giving consent without recourse to the court in most circumstances. However, where the treatment proposed is sterilisation for non-therapeutic purposes, it is recommended that an application to the court should be made for a declaration that the operation is not unlawful and is in the patient's best interest.

8.4.3   *The official solicitor's practice note*

The official solicitor produced a practice note detailing a recommended, commended procedure. The text of the practice note is as follows:

Practice note (official solicitor: sterilisation)

Amended pursuant to the Judgement of Mr Justice Thorpe in Re C, *The Times*, 13 February, 1990

(1)   The sterilisation of a minor or a mentally incompetent adult ("the patient") will in virtually all cases require the prior sanction of a High Court Judge: Re B (a minor) (wardship: sterilisation) [1988] AC 199; Re F [1989] 2 WLR 1025.

(2)   Applications in respect of a minor should be made within wardship proceedings in the Family Division of the High Court which, if the minor is not already a ward, should be begun for the purpose. The originating summons or notice of application should seek an order in the following or a broadly similar form:

"It is ordered that there be leave to perform an operation of sterilisation on the minor [x] [if it is desired to specify the precise method of carrying out the operation add, eg, by the occlusion of her fallopian tubes] and to carry out such post-operative treatment and care as may be necessary in her best interests."

109

(3) Applications in respect of an adult should be by way of originating summons issuing out of the Family Division of the High Court for an order in the following or a broadly similar form:

"It is declared that the operation of sterilisation proposed to be performed on [x] [if it is desired to specify the precise method of carrying out the operation, add eg, by the occlusion of her fallopian tubes] being in the existing circumstances in her best interests can lawfully be performed on her despite her inability to consent to it.

It is ordered that in the event of a material change in the existing circumstances occurring before the said operation has been performed any party shall have liberty to apply for such further or other declaration or order as may be just."

(4) The plaintiff or applicant should normally be a parent, or one of those responsible for the care of the patient, or those intending to carry out the proposed operation. The patient must always be a party and should normally be a defendant or respondent. In cases in which the patient is a defendant or respondent the patient's guardian ad litem should normally be the official solicitor. In any case in which the official solicitor is not either the next friend or the guardian ad litem of the patient or a plaintiff or applicant he shall be a defendant or respondent.

(5) Prior to the substantive hearing of the application there will in every case be a summons for directions which will be heard by a High Court judge. The Principal Registry will fix a date for directions before a judge of the Family Division on the first open date after the passage of eight weeks when asked to do so at the issue of the originating summons.

(6) The purpose of the proceedings is to establish whether or not the proposed sterilisation is in the best interests of the patient. The judge will require to be satisfied that those proposing sterilisation are seeking it in good faith and that their paramount concern is for the best interests of the patient rather than their own or the public's convenience. The proceedings will normally involve a thorough adversarial investigation of all possible viewpoints and any possible alternatives to sterilisation. Nevertheless, straightforward cases proceedings without dissent may be disposed of at the hearing for directions without oral evidence.

(7) The official solicitor will act as either an independent and disinterested guardian representing the interests of the patient, or as an ex officio defendant. In whichever capacity he acts, he will carry out his own investigations, call his own witnesses, and take whatever other steps

appear to him to be necessary in order to ensure that all relevant matters are thoroughly aired before the judge, including cross-examining the expert and other witnesses called in support of the proposed operation and presenting all reasonable arguments against sterilisation. The official solicitor will require to meet and interview the patient in private in all cases where he or she is able to express any views (however limited) about the legal proceedings, the prospect of sterilisation, parenthood, other means of contraception or other relevant matters.

(8)   The official solicitor anticipates that the judge will expect to receive comprehensive medical, psychological, and social evaluations of the patient from appropriately qualified experts. Without in any way attempting either to define or to limit the factors which may require to be taken into account in any particular case the official solicitor anticipates that the judge will normally require evidence clearly establishing:

(1)   That (a) the patient is incapable of making his or her own decision about sterilisation and (b) the patient is unlikely to develop sufficiently to make an informed judgement about sterilisation in the foreseeable future. (In this connection, it must be borne in mind (i) that the fact that a person is legally incompetent for some purposes does not mean that he or she necessarily lacks the capacity to make a decision about sterilisation and (ii) that in the case of a minor his or her youth and potential for development may make it difficult or impossible to make the relevant finding of incapacity.)

(2)   That the condition which it is sought to avoid will in fact occur—for example, in the case of a contraceptive sterilisation that there is a need for contraception because (a) the patient is physically capable of procreation and (b) the patient is likely to engage in sexual activity, at the present or in the near future, under circumstances where there is a real danger, as opposed to mere chance, that pregnancy is likely to result.

(3)   That the patient will experience substantial trauma or psychological damage if the condition which it is sought to avoid should arise—for example, in the case of a contraceptive sterilisation that (a) the patient (if a woman) is likely, if she becomes pregnant or gives birth, to experience substantial trauma or psychological damage greater than that resulting from the sterilisation itself and (b) the patient is permanently incapable of caring for a child even with reasonable assistance—for example, from a future spouse in a case where the patient has or may have the capacity to marry.

111

(4) That there is no practicable, less intrusive, alternative means of solving the anticipated problem than immediate sterilisation, in other words that (a) sterilisation is advisable at the time of the application rather than in the future; (b) the proposed method of sterilisation entails the least invasion of the patient's body; (c) sterilisation will not itself cause physical or psychological damage greater than the intended beneficial effects; (d) the current state of scientific and medical knowledge does not suggest either (i) that a reversible sterilisation procedure or other less drastic solutions to the problem sought to be avoided—for example, some other contraceptive method will shortly be available, or (ii) that science is on the threshold of an advance in the treatment of the patient's disability; and (e) in the case of a contraceptive sterilisation all less drastic contraceptive methods, including supervision, education, and training, have proved unworkable or inapplicable.

In cases where a "therapeutic" sterilisation operation is proposed no application to court is necessary. The High Court has made it clear that it is not necessary to seek a declaration before carrying out termination of pregnancy for a mentally handicapped woman (Re G (Mental patient: termination of pregnancy) 1990), as abortion is closely regulated by statute.

8.5 Actions by mentally disordered patients

A patient who wishes to sue or start criminal proceedings against an individual in respect of any act purporting to be done in pursuance of the Act or Regulations requires the leave of the High Court for a civil action on the consent of the Director of Public Prosecution for criminal proceedings. The patient will only be granted such consent if he can show that the individual acted in bad faith or without reasonable care (Mental Health Act 1983 S139).

In England and Wales a person who allegedly sustained personal injuries at a time when he was of unsound mind may sue for damages within three years of recovering his sanity. A person of "unsound mind" is someone who by reason of mental disorder, as defined in the Mental Health Act 1983, is incapable of managing or administering his property and affairs. Such incapacity is assumed if the patient is being compulsorily detained or is subject to guardianship under the Act or if, following such detention or guardianship, the patient is continuing to receive voluntary inpatient treatment.

8.6 Research on the mentally incapacitated

8.6.1 *Consent*

In July 1990 the European Commission issued guidelines prepared by the Committee for Proprietary Medicinal Products, on *Good Clinical Practice for*

Trials on Medicinal Products in the European Community. These guidelines do not have statutory force in the United Kingdom, but it is proposed to require all member states to make them part of national law.

Paragraph 1.13 states:

"If the subject is incapable of giving personal consent (eg, unconsciousness or severe mental illness or disability), the inclusion of such patients may be acceptable if the ethics committee is, in principle, in agreement and if the investigator is of the opinion that participation will promote the welfare and interest of the subject."

Paragraph 1.14 states:

"Consent must always be given by the signature of the subject in a non-therapeutic study, ie, when there is no direct clinical benefit to the subject."

The Royal College of Physicians (RCP) 1990 report *Research involving Patients* also emphasises that, with some exceptions, such as observational research which carries no risk and is not intrusive, patients should know that they are taking part in research and that this should only be carried out with their consent.

The RCP report emphasises that many patients with severe learning disabilities and those who are mentally ill will be able to give consent. It continues:

"A strong ethical case can be made out for non-therapeutic research (involving only minimal risk) in mentally handicapped patients because only through better understanding of their condition can care for such patients be improved. We think that the best guidance under these circumstances might be that there should be agreement by the close relatives or guardians and that the mentally handicapped individual seems to agree to the procedure."

It should be noted, however, that notwithstanding the college's advice, there is no provision in English law for anyone to give consent on behalf of another adult. The Department of Health's 1991 guidance on LRECs states:

"Some research proposals will draw their subjects from groups of people who may find it difficult or impossible to give their consent, for example the unconscious, the very elderly, the mentally disordered or some other vulnerable group. In considering these proposals the LREC should seek appropriate specialist advice and they will need to examine the proposal with particular care to satisfy themselves that proceeding without valid consent is ethically acceptable." (paragraph 3.9)

and the guidance later states:

"Proposals for research where capacity to consent is impaired will need particularly careful consideration by the LREC, with regard to its accept-

113

ability in terms of the balance of benefits, discomforts and risks for the individual patient and the need to advance knowledge so that people with mental disorder may benefit."

In Scotland a court can appoint a "tutor dative" who may be given powers to consent on behalf of an adult to participation in therapeutic research. In the absence of a "tutor dative" with appropriate powers legal consent cannot be obtained for an incapacitated adult to participate in research which is non-therapeutic.

8.6.2 *Safeguards*

In its 1991 summary of the ethical and legal position regarding research on the mentally incapacitated, the Medical Research Council comments:

There is a strong case for allowing those unable to consent to participate in medical research, provided safeguards are observed. We recommend that an individual unable to consent should be included in research only:

If it relates to his condition and the relevant knowledge could not be gained by research in persons able to consent

- it is approved by the appropriate LREC(s)

- he does not object or appear to object in either words or action

- an informed, independent person acceptable to the LREC agrees that the individual's welfare and interests have been properly safeguarded and

- in the case of therapeutic research, weighing the likely benefits and the possible risk of harm to the individual concerned, participation is in that individual's best interests

- in the case of non-therapeutic research, that participation would place the individual at no more than negligible risk of harm and is not against that individual's interests.

8.7 Court of Protection

The Court of Protection's work is governed by part VII of the Mental Health Act 1983 (SI 1984/2035). Its function is to safeguard the financial and legal interests of anyone found "incapable by reason of mental disorder of managing and administering his property and affairs" and who has some assets other than state benefits. Invoking the jurisdiction of the Court of Protection in respect of the property and affairs of a patient has the effect of suspending his ability to act for himself in all areas within its jurisdiction, even if he has varying capacity to do so. Medical evidence from a single doctor of the patient's mental disorder must be provided to the Court, which has limited decision making power on behalf of the patient. Rule 70 of the Court of Protection Rules 1984 empowers the court to require the necessary medical evidence. The Court can then do whatever is necessary for the maintenance or benefit of the patient, his family, and dependants, and it has been argued that "benefit" should not be confined to financial or material matters but, in effect, those are the only areas it deals with. It is often invoked to manage the award of damages in cases of personal injury or medical negligence. In Scotland the same function can be fulfilled by the curator bonis. Explanatory leaflets about the procedures of the Court of Protection can be obtained from the Public Trust Office, Steward House, 24 Kingsway, London, WC2B 6JX, or from the Accountant of the Court, Parliament House, Parliament Square, Edinburgh, for the Scottish equivalent.

9 Drugs

9.1 Introduction

The law relating to drugs is complex and far reaching. This chapter deals with those aspects of the law which seem most likely to affect doctors in relation to the prescribing, possession, supply and sale, and import and export of drugs.

When considering the legal position it is always necessary to know how the term "drug" is defined in terms of the problem being considered. Some substances—for example, heroin, cocaine and LSD—are defined as "controlled drugs." Stringent restrictions exist stipulating who may and may not possess, supply, import and export controlled drugs. There are other substances which, although they may not be listed as controlled drugs, would be covered by the legal controls relating to what are termed "medicinal products." The legal definitions of a "controlled drug" and a "medicinal product" are listed in the glossary. Also set out is the legal definition of the term "medicinal purpose" as it is necessary to know what this is to know what is meant by a "medicinal product."

As far as issues relating to import, export, and commercial supply of drugs are concerned, special provisions exist in relation to "clinical trials." The legal definition of a clinical trial is also given in the glossary.

Consideration of legislation relating to drugs is further complicated by the ever increasing amount of pharmaceutical legislation emanating from the European Community. The Community has practically completed the harmonisation process for national pharmaceutical legislation and regulation in respect of the health and safety aspects.

The following paragraphs detail firstly national law relating to possession, supply, and prescription of controlled drugs (see 9.2–9.5). The controls that exist in relation to medical products are next considered, in particular the complicated exceptions that exist in relation to the blanket prohibition against the sale on a commercial basis of such substances (see 9.6 and 9.7). The law relating to the import and export of drugs is set out (see 9.8) and finally a summary of European Community legislation is presented (see 9.9).

9.2 Possession and supply of controlled drugs: the criminal law

The Misuse of Drugs Act 1971 provides that it is a criminal offence to manufacture, possess, or supply to others "controlled" drugs. However, the

Act also provides for regulations to be made exempting certain persons from prosecution under these provisions. A licence is required for the possession of certain categories of drugs.

The penalties applicable to offences involving the different drugs are graded broadly according to the harmfulness attributable to a drug when it is misused, and for this purpose the drugs are defined in the following three classes:

Class A includes: alfentanil, cocaine, dextromoramide, diamorphine (heroin), dipipanone, lysergide (LSD), methadone, morphine, opium, pethidine, phencyclidine, and class B substances when prepared for injection.

Class B includes: oral amphetamines, barbiturates, cannabis, cannabis resin, codeine, ethylmorphine, glutethimide, pentazocine, phenmetrazine, and pholcodine.

Class C includes: certain drugs related to the amphetamines such as benzphetamine and chlorphentermine, buprenorphine, diethylpropion, mazindol, meprobamate, pemoline, pipradrol, and most benzodiazepines

The Misuse of Drugs Regulations (SI 1985 No 2066) define the classes of person who are authorised to supply and possess controlled drugs while acting in their professional capacities, and lay down the conditions under which these activities may be carried out. In the regulations drugs are divided into five schedules each specifying the requirements governing such activities as import, export, production, supply, possession, prescribing, and record keeping which apply to them.

Schedule 1 includes drugs such as cannabis and lysergide which are not used medicinally. Possession and supply are prohibited except in accordance with Home Office authority.

Schedule 2 includes drugs such as diamorphine (heroin), morphine, pethidine, quinalbarbitone, glutethimide, amphetamine, and cocaine and subject to the full controlled drug requirements relating to prescriptions, safe custody, the need to keep registers, etc (unless exempted in schedule 5).

Schedule 3 includes barbiturates (except quinalbarbitone, now schedule 2), buprenorphine, diethylpropion, mazindol, meprobamate, pentazocine, and phentermine. They are subject to the special prescription requirements (except for phenobarbitone) but not to the safe custody requirements (except for buprenorphine and diethylpropion) nor to the need to keep registers (although there are requirements for the retention of invoices for two years).

Schedule 4 includes 34 benzodiazepines and pemoline which are subject to minimal control. In particular, controlled drug prescription requirements do not apply and they are not subject to safe custody.

Schedule 5 includes those preparations which, because of their strength, are exempt from virtually all controlled drug requirements other than retention of invoices for two years.

Regulations 8 and 9 of the Misuse of Drugs Regulations 1985, provide that a "practitioner" (this expression includes doctors who are registered medical practitioners) may while acting in his capacity as such, "manufacture or compound" and "supply or offer to supply any drug specified in schedules 2, 3,4 or 5 to any person who may lawfully have that drug in his possession" notwithstanding the general prohibition in the Misuse of Drugs Act 1971.

Regulation 7 provides that "a doctor" (this again means registered doctor) "or dentist may administer to a patient any drug specified in schedules 2, 3, or 4 to the Regulations." Any person may administer to another any drug specified in schedule 5.

Under regulation 10 a "practitioner" may, for the purpose of acting in "his capacity as such," lawfully possess the drugs listed in schedules 2 and 3. In the case of R *v* Dunbar [1982] 1 AER 188 it was held that a doctor bona fide treating himself is acting "in his capacity as a doctor" for these purposes even though he is receiving the benefit of the drug himself. Anyone may possess the drugs listed in schedule 5.

9.3 Prescribing controlled drugs

The same regulations specify what details must be contained in prescriptions for "controlled" drugs. The Misuse of Drugs Act 1971 provides that breach of these regulations is a criminal offence.

Under regulation 16 prescriptions for controlled drugs which are subject to the prescription requirements—that is, those listed in schedules 2 and 3 to the regulations—must satisfy the following criteria.

(1) The prescription must be in ink or otherwise so as to be indelible and must be signed by the person issuing same with his usual signature and dated by him. A prescription is valid for 13 weeks from the date stated thereon. (The date can be in the form of a stamp, if a doctor usually uses one, but a computer generated date is not acceptable. A computer generated date need not be deleted but the date must also be added by the prescriber.)

(2) The prescription must, except in the case of health (NHS) prescriptions, specify the address of the person issuing same.

(3) The prescription must specify in the doctor's own handwriting (the

latter requirement does not apply, though, to prescriptions containing no controlled drugs other than phenobarbitone or phenobarbitone sodium) the following:

(i)   name and address of the patient

(ii) in the case of a prescription containing a controlled drug which is a preparation, the form and, where appropriate, the strength of the preparation

(iii) the total quantity (in both words and figures) of the preparation or the number (in both words and figures) of dosage units, as appropriate, to be supplied, or in any other case the total quantity (in words and figures) of the controlled drug to be supplied.

(iv) the dose to be taken

(4) If the prescription is for a total quantity intended to be supplied by instalments it must contain a direction specifying the amount of the instalments of the total amount which may be supplied and the intervals to be observed when supplying. A special form, FP10 (HP) (Ad), in Scotland HBP (A), is available to doctors in NHS drug treatment centres for prescribing cocaine, dextromoramide, diamorphine, dipipanone, methadone, morphine, or pethidine by instalments to addicts. In Scotland GPs can prescribe by instalments on form GP10. In England and Wales forms FP10 and FP10 (HP) are not suitable but form FP10 (MDA) is available. In the case of prescription on forms FP10 (HP) (Ad) and FP10 (MDA) the prescription should only cover a maximum 14 day period, and the instructions for dispensing must be strictly adhered to. On prescription forms FP10 (MDA) the prescription must specify the number of instalments as well as the interval between instalments. For other forms an interval between instalments must be stated.

9.4 Loss of the right to prescribe and possess controlled drugs

The Misuse of Drugs Act 1971 also provides that doctors may, as a result of misconduct, be debarred from prescribing and in some circumstances from possessing controlled drugs. Section 12 of the Act states that if a doctor has been convicted of an offence under the Act then the Secretary of State may give a direction "prohibiting him from having in his possession, prescribing, administering, manufacturing, compounding and supplying and from authorising the administration and supply of such controlled drugs as may be specified in the direction."

A copy of the direction must be served on the doctor and notice of it published in the London, Edinburgh, and Belfast gazettes.

Other provisions in the Act provide that doctors who can be shown to have contravened regulations made or licences granted under the Act's provisions, or who have been prescribing controlled drugs in an irresponsible manner, can also be made subject to a direction, in these cases prohibiting them from "prescribing, administering and supplying and from authorising the administration and supply of such controlled drugs as may be specified in the direction."

Before such a direction can be given and take effect the allegation must first be referred by the Secretary of State to, and be considered by, a tribunal and in some cases also an advisory body, both of which must be constituted in accordance with the Act. Details of the provisions are as follows.

9.4.1 *Grounds for reference to the tribunal*

There are three such:

(i) Contravention of Misuse of Drugs Act 1971 Regulations.

See section 13(1). The regulations in question are those made under paragraphs (h) and (i) of section 10(2) of the Act—that is, regulations which require doctors to give to the relevant authorities details of any patient whom they reasonably suspect to be addicted to controlled drugs and those which prohibit doctors from supplying such persons with controlled drugs except in accordance with a licence granted by virtue of the Act. (The Misuse of Drugs (Notification of, and Supply to Addicts) Regulations (SI 1973 No 799), as amended, referred to in chapter 3.5 were passed under these provisions.)

(ii) Contravention of terms of a Misuse of Drugs Act licence.

(iii) Irresponsible prescribing.

See section 13(2). If the Secretary of State is of the opinion that a doctor has been: "prescribing, administering or supplying or authorising the administration or supply of any controlled drugs in an irresponsible manner" then the matter can be referred to the tribunal.

Section 16 of the Act states that the constitution and procedure of the tribunal are governed by the provisions of schedule 3 of the Act. This provides, among other things, that the tribunal must have five members. One must be a lawyer of at least seven years' standing appointed by the Lord Chancellor and the other four are appointed by the Secretary of State and will be members of the medical profession who have been nominated by any of various listed bodies which include the GMC, the BMA, and certain Royal Colleges.

The tribunal may decide that either there has been no contravention or misconduct, or that there has been such but that they do not recommend that any direction be given. If so, the Secretary of State must serve a notice to that effect on the doctor (section 14(3)).

If the tribunal decides that there has been a contravention or misconduct and that a direction should be given then the tribunal makes a recommendation to that effect and specifies which controlled drugs should be covered (section 14(4)). In that event the Secretary of State must then serve a notice on the doctor, stating whether or not he intends to give the recommended direction and, if so, stating the proposed terms of it. The doctor must also be informed of his right to make representations in writing to the Secretary of State within 28 days (section 14(5)).

If the Secretary of State receives any representations from the doctor within the 28 day period then he must refer same to an "advisory body" which must advise the Secretary of State concerning whether or not a direction should be given (section 14(6)). The constitution and procedures of this body are also set out in schedule 3. If the 28 days have expired or the Secretary of State has considered the advice of the advisory body then he may either give a direction, refer the matter back to the tribunal, or order that no further proceedings be taken (section 14(7)). If a direction is given a copy of it must be served on the doctor and it must also be published in the London, Edinburgh, and Belfast gazettes. Contravention of a direction given under either these provisions or those referred to about (under section 12) is a criminal offence.

9.4.2 *Temporary directions*

Section 15 provides that where the Secretary of State considers that there are grounds for giving a direction in respect of irresponsible prescribing (see (iii) above) and that "the circumstances of the case require such a direction to be given with the minimum of delay" then a different procedure may be adopted and a six week temporary direction made, pending the resolution of the matter by a tribunal. (The period may be extended by 28 day periods provided the tribunal consents.) The temporary six week direction may not be made until the matter has been referred to a "professional panel" (once again governed by schedule 3) and until such a panel has reported that "the information before it appears to it to afford reasonable grounds" for thinking that irresponsible prescribing has occurred.

The provision of section 17 of the Misuse of Drugs Act 1971 should also be noted. This comes into play in the following circumstances:

"... if it appears to the Secretary of State that there exists in any area in Great Britain a social problem caused by the extensive misuse of dangerous or otherwise harmful drugs in that area ..." then a notice may be served, inter alia, on any doctor practising in that area to "require him to furnish to the Secretary of State, with respect to any such drugs specified in the notice and as regards any period so specified, such particulars as may be specified relating to the quantities in which and the number and frequency of the occasions on which those drugs – (a) in the case of a doctor, were prescribed, administered or supplied by him;..."

It should be noted that pharmacists on whom similar notice may also be served under this section can be required, among other things, to give "the names and addresses of doctors on whose prescriptions any dangerous or otherwise harmful drugs to which the notice relates were supplied." It is criminal offence to fail without reasonable excuse to give the required particulars or knowingly or recklessly to supply false information.

9.5 Notification of and supply to drug addicts

The law concerning these issues is contained in the Misuse of Drugs (Notification of, and Supply to Addicts) Regulations (SI 1973 No 799), as amended.

9.5.1 Notification

Regulation 3 concerns notification and requires that any doctor who attends a person who the doctor considers, or has reasonable grounds to suspect, is addicted to any drug shall within seven days of the attendance, furnish in writing to the Chief Medical Officer at the Home Office particulars of that person. The particulars to be notified are the name, address, sex, date of birth and NHS number of that person, the date of the attendance and the name of the drug or drugs concerned, and whether the person injects any drugs (whether or not notifiable). Only the details of which the doctor has knowledge need to be notified immediately; the remainder may be notified at a later date. Notification must be confirmed annually in writing if the patient is still being treated by the practitioner. Hospital doctors and GPs may obtain from HSA 2/1 (rev) for notification of drug addicts from their regional health services authority database administrator. Private doctors, police surgeons, and prison medical officers may obtain form HSA 2/1 (rev) for notification from their FHSA.

The doctor need not make such a notification if:

(1) He "is of the opinion, formed in good faith, that the continued administration of the drug or drugs concerned is required for the purpose of treating organic disease or injury; or"

(2) If the required particulars have been supplied during the last 12 months

by either

(a)   the doctor, or

(b)   where the doctor is a partner of or employed by a firm of general practitioners a partner or employed doctor in that firm, or

(c)   where the attendance is on behalf of another doctor (whether for payment, or not) by that other doctor, or

(d)   if the attendance is at hospital by a doctor on the staff of that hospital.

9.5.2 *Supply*

Regulation 4 states that a doctor shall not administer or supply (or authorise others to do so) to a person who the doctor considers, or has reasonable grounds to suspect, is addicted to any drugs (see below), the following substances: cocaine, diamorphine, or salts, and any preparations or products containing same except:

(a)   for the purpose of treating organic disease or injury;

(b)   under and in accordance with a licence issued by the Secretary of State; or

(c)   under the authority of a doctor who has such a licence.

The term drug in both the above contexts is defined to mean the following controlled drugs listed in the schedule below:

- Cocaine
- Dextromoramide
- Diamorphine
- Dipipanone
- Hydrocodone
- Hydromorphone
- Levorphanol
- Methadone
- Morphine
- Opium
- Oxycodone
- Pethidine
- Phenazocine
- Piritramide

Also included are the stereoisomeric forms of the above (but not dextrorphan) and ester or ether forms of the substances (but not one on part II schedule 2 of the Misuse of Drugs Act 1971) and any salt or preparation or product containing same.

Nota Bene: Prescribing of controlled drugs of dependence otherwise than in the course of bona fide treatment could result in disciplinary proceedings. (See *Professional Conduct and Discipline: Fitness to Practise* from the GMC).

9.6 Possession and supply of medicinal products

9.6.1 *Introduction*

It is not a criminal offence for a member of the public to possess a medicinal product but restrictions are placed on the selling of some products. Section 7 of the Medicines Act 1968 prohibits persons acting in the course of business—that is commercially—from selling, supplying, or manufacturing for sale any "medicinal product" (see glossary for definition). Contravention of this provision is a criminal offence. There are various exemptions to this rule, some of which are dealt with below. Many of these relate to situations where a clinical trial is involved. There is one exemption which relates specifically to doctors (see below), and there are also provisions which relate to situations where a doctor has prescribed the medicinal product in question.

9.6.2 *Supply of medicinal products for use in a clinical trial*

The provisions regarding clinical trials start off in section 31(2) by prohibiting the commercial sale or supply (or acts leading to same) of any medicinal product for the purposes of a clinical trial. Contravention of this prohibition is a criminal offence. The Act then goes on to list a number of situations where a criminal offence would not, in fact, be committed and many of these exemptions relate to the involvement of doctors in the clinical trial in question. The Act defines the expression "clinical trial" (see glossary).

Exemptions

1 *Holding a product licence*

If a person holds a product licence "which authorises the clinical trial in question" (or is acting under the instructions of the holder of same), and acts in accordance with the terms of the licence then the prohibition does not apply (section 31(3)(a)).

2 *Existence of a clinical trial certificate*

If the certificate is in force and states that the licensing authority has consented to the clinical trial in question and the trial is to be carried out in accordance with that certificate then the prohibition does not apply (section 31(3)(b)).

3 *Sale or supply by doctor*

If a doctor (a) sells, supplies (or procures the sale or supply) of a medicinal product; or (b) procures the manufacture or assembly of a medicinal product specially prepared to his order; or (c) if he is to be (or he is acting at the request of) the doctor (or dentist) by whom, or under whose direction, the product is to be administered then the prohibition does not apply. See section 31(5), but also note the provisions of section 31(6). This provides that the exemption provided by section 31(5) is not applicable if the "clinical trial in question is to be carried out under arrangements made by, or at the request of, a third party (that is to say, a person who is not the doctor or dentist, or one of the doctors or dentists, by whom, or under whose direction, one or more medicinal products are to be administered in that trial)."

4 *Sales in hospitals, pharmacies, and health centres*

Section 31(7) states the prohibition does not apply to "... anything which is done in a registered pharmacy, a hospital or a health centre and is done there by or under the supervision of a pharmacist in accordance with a prescription given by a doctor or dentist; and those restrictions do not apply to anything done by or under the supervision of a pharmacist which consists of procuring the preparation or dispensing of a medicinal product in accordance with a prescription given by a doctor or dentist, or of procuring the assembly of a medicinal product."

5 *Manufacture of medicinal product to order of doctor*

The prohibition does not cover the commercial manufacture or assembly of a medicinal product if a doctor has stated "... that it is required for administration to a patient of his or is required, at the request of another doctor, or dentist, for administration to a patient of that other doctor or dentist." Nor does it apply where done to the order of a pharmacist in accordance with a doctor's prescription (section 31(8)).

6 *Notification to licensing authority of proposed trial*

The Medicines (Exemption from Licences) (Special Cases and Miscellaneous Provisions) Order 1972 (SI 1972 No 1200), as amended, provides in rule 4 that the prohibition will not apply if all the following conditions are satisfied:

(a) the seller is selling the product exclusively for the purposes of use in a clinical trial (or to the extent that the product is to be used for some other purpose that use is authorised by a licence, certificate, or other authority);

(b) the clinical trial is not to be carried out under arrangements made by or on behalf of the manufacturer or person responsible for composition or the seller, unless such person is the doctor or dentist or one of same by whom or by whose direction the medicinal product is to be administered in that trial;

(c)   the doctor or dentist must notify the licensing authority of the proposed holding of the trial, specifying the product that is to be administered and the use of same and the name and address of the supplier;

(d)   the licensing authority must not within 21 days (a longer period may be stipulated) have directed that this exemption is not to apply.

The Act provides that other exemptions may be stipulated by Order—for example, The Medicines (Exemption from Licences) (Clinical Trials) Order 1974 (SI 1974 No 498) provides that certain products which might not, strictly speaking, be covered by a product licence, but only because of a change in manufacturing procedures or a difference in shape or lack of distinctive marks, can they be exempted. Similarly exempted are products defined as being for control purposes only and licensed products surrounded by inert substances.

The Medicines (Exemption from Licences) (Clinical Trials) Order 1981 (SI 1981 No 164) additionally provides that the prohibition will not apply if certain conditions are observed. The conditions are set out in article 4 of the order and are as follows:

(a)   "the supplier has given or sent to the licensing authority a notice which states his intention to sell or supply, or procure the sale, supply, manufacture or assembly of medicinal products of the description in question for the purposes of a clinical trial and which is accompanied by

     (i)   the particulars and summaries specified in schedule 1 to this order;

     (ii)   A certificate signed by a doctor listing his medical and scientific qualifications who works within the UK and which states both that he is a medical adviser in the employment of, or consultant to, the supplier and that he has satisfied himself as to the accuracy of the summaries specified at paragraph 13 of schedule 1 to this order and that, having regard to the contents of those summaries, he is of the opinion that it is reasonable for the proposed clinical trial to be undertaken."

The "summaries" in paragraph 13 are "summaries of reports and evaluations of any experimental and biological studies and of other preclinical, clinical or laboratory studies carried out with each medicinal product, or its constituents, which in the view of the supplier are relevant to the assessment of the safety, quality or efficacy of the

126

medicinal product together with references to relevant publications or other clinical trials."

(b) The licensing authority must not have within a specific period (35 days from getting the notice although this can be extended by 28 days) have sent the supplier a notice stating that the exemption is not to apply.

(c) Lastly, the supplier must give an undertaking to the licensing authority that he will inform them of:
  "(i) any adverse reactions or effects associated with the administration of the medicinal product,

  (ii) any other matter coming to his attention which might reasonably cause the licensing authority to think that the medicinal product could no longer be regarded as a product which could safely be administered for the purposes of the clinical trial or as a product which was of satisfactory quality for those purposes,

  (iii) any change in respect of any of the matters specified in schedule 2 to this order, and

  (iv) any refusal to approve the clinical trial by a committee established or recognised by a health authority constituted under the National Health Service Act 1977 ... or by the Medical Research Council ..."

The exemption can last for up to three years if the stipulated conditions continue to be fulfilled unless the licensing authority terminates the right to take advantage of it.

Nota Bene: schedules 1 and 2 of The Medicines (Exemption from Licences) Clinical Trials Order 1974 are not covered above in their entirety.

9.6.3 *Supply of medicinal products by doctors*

Section 9 of the Medicines Act 1968 provides some exemption from the general prohibition in section 7 for doctors, dentists, and veterinary surgeons. In the case of doctors this means doctors who are registered medical practitioners.

Section 9 states that the restrictions in section 7 (which prohibit commercial supply or sale of medicinal products without a product licence) do not apply to anything done by a doctor which:

"(a) relates to a medicinal product specifically prepared, or specially imported by him or to his order, for administration to a particular patient of his, and consists of manufacturing or assembling, or procuring the manufacture or assembly of, the product, or of selling or supplying, or procuring the sale or supply of, the product to that patient or to a person under whose care that patient is, or"

(b) when the doctor does likewise at the request of another doctor or dentist for administration to a patient of their own.

9.6.4 *Prescribing medicinal products*

Section 58(2)(a) of the Medicines Act 1968 provides that certain medicinal products may only be sold in accordance with a "prescription given by an appropriate practitioner."

The question of what products are covered, who is an "appropriate practitioner" for these purposes and what must be contained in the prescription are dealt with in The Medicines (Products other Veterinary Drugs) (Prescriptions Only) Order 1983 (SI 1983 No 1212), as amended by The Medicines (Products other than Veterinary Drugs) (General Sales List) Order 1984 (SI 1984 No 756). The list of medicinal products controlled in this way is too long to reproduce here. It is contained in the schedule to the regulations and is amended from time to time. The phrase "appropriate practitioner" includes doctors who are registered medical practitioners. The prescription must:

(a) be signed in ink with his own name by the practitioner giving it; and

(b) be written in ink or otherwise indelible (there is an exception for "health"—that is, NHS prescriptions which are not for controlled drugs specified in Schedules to the Misuse of Drugs Regulations: these can be written by means of carbon paper or similar material) and

(c) include the following particulars:

  (i) the address of the practitioner

  (ii) the date

  (iii) the category of practitioner—for example, registered medical practitioner

  (iv) in the case of doctors' prescriptions the name, address and age (if under 12) of the patient.

The prescription is not to be dispensed if it is more than six months old unless it is a repeat prescription, in which case the first dispensing is not to take place more than six months after the date of the prescription. If a repeatable prescription does not specify how many times it is to be dispensed there can only be two dispensings of it except in the case of oral contraceptives which may be dispensed up to six times before the six months are up.

In an emergency prescription only drugs which are not "controlled" may be dispensed without a prescription if a doctor request same and undertakes to supply a prescription within 72 hours.

9.6.5 *Prescription by nurses*

The main purpose of the Medicinal Products: Prescription by Nurses, etc, Act 1992 is to enable retail pharmacists to dispense certain medicinal products from prescriptions issued by certain categories of nurses, midwives, and health visitors. The Act specifies that registered nurses, midwives, and health visitors are "appropriate practitioners" for the purpose of prescribing "prescription only medicines" under section 58 of the Medicines Act 1968. It gives powers to ministers to limit the categories of nurses, midwives, and health visitors who may prescribe by references to necessary qualifications and training. The Act also gives power to prohibit an "appropriate practitioner" who is a nurse, midwife, or health visitor from delegating the administration parenterally of prescription only medicinal products.

As well as England, Wales and Scotland the Act extends to Northern Ireland and contains provisions to extend the duty of FHSA (and health boards) to arrange for the provision of pharmaceutical services to cover the provision of drugs, medicines, and appliances) which are contained in a Secretary of State's list and prescribed by certain nurses.

The *Nurse Prescribers' Formulary* will be included as an appendix to the *British National Formulary*, alternating with the *Dental Formulary*. In practice, the legislation will extend limited prescribing rights to a large number of nurses working in the community. The bulk of the drugs to be included on the Secretary of State's list will be over-the-counter preparation with few prescription only medicines included. The financial effect of the Act will be an increase in prescribing and dispensing under the NHS, but it is expected to be offset by some time saving by nurses, midwives, health visitors and GPs.

9.7 Product liability

The product liability provisions of part I of the Consumer Protection Act 1987 came into force on 1 March 1988, implementing an EC directive to make producers of defective products strictly liable. The effect will be that if a person suffers damage as a result of a defective product, it will no longer be necessary to prove negligence, but only that the product was defective and that the damage was as a result of the defective product. By virtue of the Act "suppliers" will also become liable unless they can identify the "producer"—that is, the manufacturer. Products for the purpose of the Act refers to goods, their raw materials and their component parts, including drugs, medical appliances, and equipment. As potential suppliers of products there will be a considerable burden on doctors to keep accurate records which identify the sources of products, to avoid liability.

Doctors may become liable either by acting as a supplier, by dispensing drugs, by giving patients or fitting appliances, or by undertaking treatment in the consulting room; or by becoming producers themselves, by modifying drugs or appliances, or mixing medicines before supplying them to the patient. By modifying the product the doctor himself could well become liable. Strict liability will also attach to anyone who presents himself as the producer—for example, by putting "own brand" labels on the product. Where hospital doctors within the NHS supply drugs or appliances the hospital authority will be the supplier. The hospital owners of private hospitals will almost certainly be the supplier where doctors practise in private hospitals, or the hospital authority where doctors undertake private practice with an NHS hospital. However, those doctors practising privately from their own consulting rooms should observe the general guidance in this and the following section. Both doctors and health authorities fall within the scope of the Act and must consequently be aware of the provisions affecting them.

The intention of the Act is to facilitate injured consumers obtaining a remedy against manufacturers of defective products by requiring proof only that the product was defective. A duty of care and breach of duty need not be established and thus the plaintiff does not have to attribute negligence to a specific person or persons. Responsibility falls primarily on the manufacturer as producer, but if he cannot be identified it will rest with any supplier who cannot identify someone further up the chain. As many doctors and health care personnel are the last link in the chain of supply of medicines from manufacturer to patient, particular care must be taken to record the sources of all suppliers of goods. Records relating to the origin of any drug supplied to a patient must be kept for an eleven year period.

According to section 3 of the Act, a defect exists "... if the safety of the product is not such as persons generally are entitled to expect." Safety is defined in the context of risk of death or personal injury as well as risk of damage to property. The Act takes into account what people should reasonably expect the producer to have considered when the product was marketed and will cover warnings stated and instructions issued by the producer at the time the product was supplied.

The government has chosen to allow a substantial "development risk" defence (sometimes called the "state of the art" defence) which would mean producers—for example, of drugs—could escape liability if they could prove that the state of scientific and technical knowledge was such that the existence of a defect could not be discovered. Liability under the Act ceases 10 years after the product was supplied, but plaintiffs must bring their actions within three years of the discovery of the defect, the damage, and the party responsible. The right of a consumer to sue in contract is unaffected, and a victim of a defective product may still be able to bring any action in negligence if he wishes, irrespective of the Act.

Increasingly, drugs are being dispensed in the manufacturer's original packaging. This helps to make medicines tamper proof, protects them from the environment, and makes them harder to counterfeit (all important issues in product liability). The patient also receives the drug in the condition in which it was packaged, with its batch number and expiry. As well as protecting the legal position of manufacturers, original pack dispensing also makes it possible for all drug packages to include information leaflets for patients. European Community Directive 89/341 makes compulsory the inclusion, from 1992, of a patient information leaflet in the original packaging of all medicinal products, unless all the information can be given on the outside of the pack itself. Leaflets should be in "clear, understandable language" and give the reasons for the use of the drug, contraindications, instructions for use, possible side effects, storage and expiry date (see 9.9).

9.7.1 *General practice*

Advice for GPs from the BMA's General Medical Services Committee, issued in May 1988 and prepared following consultation with the then DHSS and legal advisers, is that doctors supplying medicines are unlikely to be at risk if they:

"(a) *Adhere strictly to the labelling regulations which apply to all dispensed medicines*

These regulations apply to all supplies of medicines including those given in an emergency or "out of the bag." They require the containers of all medicines prepared or dispensed by a doctor, or prepared or dispensed in accordance with a prescription given by a doctor, to be labelled with:

(i)   The name of the person to whom the medicinal product is to be administered;

(ii) The name and address of the supplying doctor (or chemist);

(iii) The date the medicines are dispensed;

(iv) The words "keep out of reach of children" or words of similar meaning.

In addition, though at the doctor's discretion, if the doctor has prescribed the medicine, the label should also indicate the name of the product, directions for use and precautions relating to use of the product in question.

(b) *Ensure that every instance of supply is recorded in the patient's clinical record*

This includes medicines supplied in an emergency or "out of the bag."

(i) Doctors supplying drugs in a proprietary form need only record the brand name of the drug supplied as this identifies the manufacturer.

(ii) The generic name of a drug does not identify the manufacturer and doctors supplying generic products should record the name of the manufacturer or their own supplier.

(iii) The recording of batch numbers for products other than those supplied in accordance with paragraph 8 of this note should not generally be required.

(iv) Records should be made of the manufacturer or supplier of products [such as dressing, appliances and injections] which are supplied or loaned to patients without a label.

(c) *Keep accurate records (invoices, etc) of their source of supply of all products and retain them for a period of 11 years."*

The guidance notes state that where a patient is no longer registered with a GP and records have been returned to the FHSA, the latter will provide for the safekeeping. However, FHSA will not provide for the safekeeping of additional papers which deal only with product liability information.

It concludes:

"(7) General practitioners who supply medicines should be aware that they may be considered to be the manufacturer of—

(i) medicines they make up and dispense themselves, ie extemporaneously dispensed medicines.

(ii) products which they dilute other than in accordance with the instructions on the data sheet.

and in these cases particular care should be exercised in maintaining accurate records.

(8) The medical defence bodies have indicated that if a member were sued under the legislation they would be indemnified in the usual way provided that the goods were supplied in connection with the doctor's professional practice. The defence bodies have advised their members to

note on a patient's clinical record the dosage, batch number, manufacturer and supplier of any fee drug samples which they give to patients."

9.7.2 *Health authorities*

Circular HN(88)3 (HN(FP)(88)5 on *Procurement Product Liability* issued in March 1988 "draws attention to the main implications for health authorities of part I of the Consumer Protection Act 1987 and offers guidance to help minimise NHS liability for defective products."

On record keeping the circular states:

"It will be apparent from the above guidance that in most instances the capacity to avoid liability or defend an action brought under Part I of the Act will depend substantially on the maintenance of clear, accurate and comprehensive records relating to the procurement, use, modification and supply of products. And, since an obligation arising from liability is extinguished only after a period of 10 years and up to one year is allowed for the serving of a writ, such records should be retained for a period of 11 years.... The Department does, however, recognise that local circumstances may make it very difficult or impracticable to record in equal or sufficient detail all products/actions to link a potentially defective product with a potential claimant. If the introduction and maintenance of new or more sophisticated systems will add substantially to an authority's costs, or disrupt patient service, the authority may wish to make its own judgement in balancing the effects of additional record keeping against the likelihood of claims. In this respect authorities should note that any increase in costs arising from a tightening up of procedures to minimise the possibility of litigation, will need to be met by health authorities from existing resources. The price of any affected product marketed for sale by the NHS should allow for recovery of an appropriate proportion of these costs. The general rule that the Crown bears its own risks precludes the option of insurance cover against the increased risk of claims for damages. The cost of successful claims would be a direct health authority liability."

On medicinal products the guidance states:

"It is recognised that particular problems may arise from the supply of medicinal preparations by hospital pharmacies as a result of the sheer volume of transactions and the extended chain by which a medicine can pass from producer to patient. In addition hospital pharmacies which make up preparations from ingredients will be regarded as producers for purposes of the Act. Liability for a defective product arising from the functions of a hospital pharmacy would, however, rest with the health authority and not the member of staff concerned. This liability could of course be avoided if the authority was not the producer within the meaning of the Act and either the authority's own supplier or the producer could be identified. This would require records to be kept along the lines indicated in paragraph 3. No detailed central guidance can be given to provide traceability of medicines along the supply chain but Regional Pharmaceutical Officers should consider the extent to which existing record keeping needs to be altered to meet the essential requirements of a system to link unambiguously the producer of the product, or its ingredients, with the end user...."

In conclusion, the circular points out that while the guidance relates principally to medical supplies, "very few products are excluded from the provisions of the Act and authorities should recognise that they may be affected as suppliers, keepers and producers of non-medical items which may give rise to claims". It advises that authorities should "view the potential implications against the background of their existing liability in tort in the event of claims for damages."

9.8 Import and export of drugs

So far as this country is concerned the legal controls over import and export of drugs depend on whether the substance in question is classified as a "medicinal product" under the Medicines Act 1968 or as a "controlled drug" under the Misuse of Drugs Act 1971. Doctors are given special exemptions when it comes to the import and export of medicinal products but the same does not apply where controlled drugs are concerned.

9.8.1 *Medicinal products*

The Medicines Act 1968 provides in section 7(2) that "medicinal products" (see glossary) must not be exported in the course of business unless a "product licence" is first obtained. Section 7(3) prohibits the importation of medicinal products except in accordance with a product licence. Breach of this section is a criminal offence. To these general rules there are various exceptions. (See chapters 9.6.2 and 9.6.3 for the special exemption for doctors, dentists, and veterinary surgeons set out in section 9 of the Act).

9.8.2 *Clinical trials*

The general prohibition contained in section 7 is also subject to some exceptions which relate to the importation of medicinal products for use in clinical trials.

Section 31(4) sets out the general position, which is that the importation of medicinal products for use in clinical trials is forbidden, but there are exceptions to this in respect of persons holding product licences or clinical trial certificates and, under section 31(5), in certain circumstances, doctors and dentists.

The exemption for product licence holders is as follows: section 31(4) states after setting out the general position that this restriction does not apply to someone who holds a product licence, authorising such clinical trials and imports a product in accordance with that licence or imports a product to the order of a person who holds such a licence.

If a clinical trial certificate has been issued the prohibition against importation does not apply. This is provided the licensing authority has consented to the clinical trial in question, the certificate is in force, and the trial is to be carried out in accordance with the licence. See section 35(1).

The exemption for doctors and dentists is set out in section 31(5). This states that section 31(4) does not apply to a doctor or dentist "... specially importing a medicinal product, where (in any such case) he is, or acts at the request of, the doctor or dentist by whom, or under whose direction, the product is to be administered."

Nota Bene: This is also subject to the provisions of section 31(6) (see 9.6.2.1).

9.8.3 Travelling abroad and controlled drugs

Patients are permitted to take limited amounts of controlled drugs overseas for their own use. The Home Office publishes a list of controlled drugs with the permitted amounts. Larger amounts and drugs which are not for personal use require a licence, as above.

Many countries have their own restrictions on the drugs which can be brought into the country. These may include drugs available on prescription or even over the counter in the United Kingdom (for example, codeine cannot be brought into Greece). Travellers should contact the relevant embassy or their travel agent for advice. Any drugs posted overseas are subject to customs labelling and postage regulations.

Section 3 of the Misuse of Drugs Act 1971 prohibits the import and export of controlled drugs (see glossary as to which drugs are controlled). Anyone who contravenes this provision could be prosecuted under legislation relating to Customs and Excise. A person would not be prosecuted, however, if he was exempted by any regulation passed by virtue of section 7 of the Act. Doctors as such are not exempted from the provisions. The Misuse of Drugs Regulations (SI 1985 No 2066) provide that section 3 does not apply to controlled drugs listed in schedules 4 and 5 to those regulations. This exemption applies to everyone, not just doctors.

Also exempted from prosecution would be those who had obtained a licence to import and export controlled drugs and who acted in accordance with same.

It follows from the above that anyone wishing to take a controlled drug out of the country must apply for a licence before doing so. This applies, for example, to GPs wishing to take emergency supplies out of the country, as well as to those currently receiving a controlled drug on prescription (but see below). To consider licence applications from individuals, written confirmation is required from the prescribing doctor of the name, form, strength and quality of drug(s) involved. Applications should be made at least two weeks before departure date and the days of departure and return must be stated. Anyone who wishes to apply for such a licence should apply to the Drugs

Branch of the Home Office, Queen Anne's Gate, London SW1H 9AT. Special arrangements exist for doctors wishing to accompany groups of pilgrims in Lourdes in the capacity of medical officer. A standard form, number MD 50 A, is available on request from the Home Office on which such doctors may apply for the necessary licence, and these arrangements have been approved by the French authorities.

The Home Office is not prepared to issue licences to doctors who wish to take controlled drugs abroad solely in case an emergency may arise. However, sympathetic consideration would be given to applications from doctors who were, for example, accompanying hazardous expeditions.

Both doctors and patients wishing to take drugs abroad *must* comply not just with the laws of this country but also with the law of the country to which they wish to take the substance in question. The Home Office will expect the person applying for the export licence to have first obtained an import licence from the country to which it is wished to take drugs.

The licence authorises the holder to carry the controlled drugs specified on the licence out of the United Kingdom under the conditions stated on the licence and to bring back any residue.

An open general licence (OGL) for the import or export of small quantities of drugs was introduced on 1 March 1987. It provides a general authority for: an ordinary traveller carrying controlled drugs for medical reasons, either for himself or for a member of his household who is unable to administer the drug himself; or a doctor accompanying a patient who requires treatment during a journey from or to the United Kingdom. A schedule sets out the controlled drugs and the maximum quantity allowed.

Such a licence does not apply "(a) to any controlled drug which is not contained in a medicinal product within the meaning of the Medicines Act 1968; (b) unless the controlled drug is under the direct personal supervision of the personal importing or exporting it; (c) to the exportation of any controlled drug by a person who is not lawfully in possession of the drug." (See glossary for definition of medicinal product.)

It should be noted that as in the case of individual licences the OGL does not have any standing outside the United Kingdom. Travellers should always obtain clearance from the representatives of the country of destination in the United Kingdom—that is, embassy or consulate, for the import of the drug into that country prior to departure from the United Kingdom.

9.8.4 *Medicinal tests on animals*

(The term "medicinal tests on animals" is defined in section 32(6) which is fully set out in chapter 13.3 on animal experiments.)

Section 32(2) sets out the general position which is that the importation of medicinal products for the purposes of medicinal tests on animals is forbidden, but there are exceptions to this if a product licence has been obtained or an animal test certificate has been issued (see glossary). The criteria by which product licences in this context and animal test certificates are considered valid for these purposes are similarly expressed as for product licences and clinical trial certificates respectively as set out above. (See chapter 13.3.1 for the exact text.) Section 32 may also be modified by an order made under section 35(8).

It should be noted that all the exceptions are subject to the fact that the government has the power to prohibit the importation of certain medicinal products. This is stated in section 62 pursuant to which for instance the following orders have been made:

The Medicines (Phenacetin Prohibition) Order 1979 (SI 1979 No 1181) and the Medicines (Bal Jivan Chamcho Prohibition) (No 2) Order 1979 (SI 1979 No 670).

Conversely, section 15 provides that the government may order that exemptions to the general prohibitions in section 7 also be made. Numerous orders have been made.

Under section 13, any person may import without a licence a medicinal product for administration to himself or any other member of his household. Also permitted under this section is the importation of a medicinal product specially imported by, or to the order of, a doctor (or dentist) for administration to a particular patient of his.

There are various other exemptions in the Act, but there is not space to detail them all.

9.9 EC pharmaceutical legislation

9.9.1 *Background*

The EC will be the major influence on the evolution of medicines regulation in the 1990s. The fullest compilation of Community legislation and regulation on pharmaceuticals has been published by the Commission under the title: *The rules governing medicinal products in the European Community*, containing:

Volume I   The rules governing medicinal products for human use in the European Community.

Volume II   Notice to applicants for marketing authorisations for medicinal products for human use in the member states of the European Communities.

Volume III   Guidelines on the quality, safety, and efficacy of medicinal products for human use.

Volume IV   Guide to good manufacturing practice for the manufacture of medicinal products.

TABLE 1
Council Directives, recommendations and decisions governing
human medicines in the european community

The framework

65/65/EEC	Sets out scope and definitions. Requires member states to grant market authorisations for new medicines on the grounds of safety, quality, and efficacy. Elaborates the summary of product characteristics.
75/319/EEC	Further definition of the general framework, particularly with regard to manufacturing. Establishes the CPMP, and the multistate procedure (first phase). [Revised by 78/420/EEC, which was subsequently repealed].
75/320/EEC	Council decision to establish the Pharmaceutical Committee.
78/25/EEC	Permitted colourings for medicines (amended by 81/464/EEC)
83/570/EEC	Amends 65/65/EEC, 75/318/EEC with regard to data requirements, and 75/319/EEC with regard to the CPMP procedure (introducing second phase).
89/341/EEC	Amends 65/65/EEC, 75/318/EEC, and 75/319/EEC to extend the scope to cover all medicinal products, and other technical changes, including requirements for patient information and export certification.
89/342, 343 and 381/EEC	Three directives introducing special provisions for biologicals (vaccines, sera, and allergens), radio-pharmaceuticals, blood and plasma products.
87/21/EEC	Amends 65/65 EEC with regard to protection against a second applicant.

Data requirements

75/318/EEC	Data requirements for physio-chemical, pharmaceutical, pharmacotoxicological and clinical testing.
91/207/EEC	Updates the annex to 75/318/EEC (as amended by 83/570/EEC).
83/571/EEC	Council recommendation introducing guidelines for safety and efficacy testing.
87/19/EEC	Amends 75/318/EEC and introduces the regulatory committee procedure to enable rapid update of guidelines and data requirements to take into account technical progress.
87/176/EEC	Council recommendation with further guidelines

Procedures

75/319/EEC	Multistate procedure (first phase).
83/570/EEC	Multistate procedure (second phase).
87/22/EEC	Concertation procedure for biotechnology and high technology products.
87/21/EEC	Amends 65/65/EEC with regard to protection against the second applicant for biotechnology products (concertation procedure), and high technology products.
91/356/EEC	Laying down guidelines for good manufacturing practice (GMP).

Transparency

89/105/EEC	Regulates the way in which member states control pricing and reimbursement of medicines.

Volume V   The rules governing medicinal products for veterinary use in the European Community.

Volumes in this series can be obtained from the Office for Official Publications of the European Community, or from HMSO.

The directives concerning medicines are all based on article 100/100A of the Treaty of Rome. The measures relating to pharmaceuticals adopted to date are listed in table 1.

The principal objective of the EC rules on pharmaceuticals is to ensure the highest possible degree of protection of public health and to promote the free movement of medicinal products in an internal market without barriers. The

138

TABLE 2
Proposed EC legislation concerning medicinal products for
human use as of April 1992

Draft directive COM (89)607: SYN 229	(a)	Procedures governing the wholesale distribution of medicinal products in the Community.
Draft directive COM (89)607: SYN 230	(a)	Legal status for the supply of medicinal products (ie the conditions under which a medicinal product may be supplied to the public).
Draft directive COM (89)607: SYN 231	(a)	Labelling of medicinal products and package leaflets.
Draft directive COM (90)212: SYN 273	(a)	Advertising of medicinal products to health professionals and the general public, extending 84/450 to encourage rational use and prevent misleading advertising.
Draft directive COM (91)313: SYN 251	(b)	Manufacture, control, inspection and marketing of homeopathic medicinal products. Extends many of the provisions of 75/319/EEC to cover homeopathic medicines.
Draft regulation COM (90)101: SYN 255	(b)	Creation of a supplementary protection certificate for patent term restoration (protection for 15 years).
Draft regulation and directives COM (90)283: SYN 309-312 Draft directive COM (90)283	(c)	Future procedures for authorisation and supervision of medicinal products, and creation of a European Medicines Agency. Amendments to 65/65/EEC, 75/318/EEC and 75/319/EEC in respect of future procedures for authorisation of medicines.

Footnote
(a) Common position agreed November 1991. Final approval in April/May 1992. Implementation on 1 January 1993 (except labelling and package leaflets on 1 January 1994).
(b) Common position agreed December 1991.
(c) Agreement on common position unlikely before 1994.

protection of public health is the motive for the progressive harmonisation within Europe of the criteria on which a marketing authorisation application is assessed—mainly safety, quality and efficacy. This harmonisation is continuing.

9.9.2 *Committee for Proprietary Medicinal Products and the "bio/high-tech" procedure*

As Community legislation on pharmaceutical products evolved, it was intended that the increasing level of harmonisation should make it easier for national licensing authorities to recognise each other's decisions. The existing EC directives were promulgated to further this process (75/319/EEC and 87/22/EEC) by setting up the CPMP Multistate application procedure and the "prior concertation" or "bio/high-tech" procedure (which is now also referred to as the "special concertation procedure").

In order to assist in this an EC committee of representatives of the national registration authorities, the Committee for Proprietary Medicinal Products (CPMP), was established in accordance with Directive 75/319/EEC in 1976. Under the aegis of this committee, a procedure to enable rapid partial mutual recognition of a licensing authorisation granted by one member state to some or all of the other member states was established. This multistate procedure was subsequently modified to make if more effective, and to enable direct representation by companies to the CPMP.

Recent developments in the area of biotechnology have resulted in a new range of pharmaceutical products, in relation to which all member states are facing new problems of evaluation. The Community therefore established, under Directive 87/22/EEC, a mechanism whereby the CPMP considers applications for new products of biotechnology prior to their evaluation and grant of a marketing authorisation by a member state. This "bio/high-tech" concertation procedure was intended to lead to even greater harmonisation of decision making processes within the EC.

9.9.3 New pharmaceutical products

The EC rules cover new and existing pharmaceutical products. Products such as vaccines, toxins and sera, allergens, blood products, homeopathic medicines and radiopharmaceuticals were initially exempted from the provisions of the EC rules, but (with the exception of homoeopathics, for which a directive has been introduced) they have since been incorporated (89/341/EEC, 89/342/EEC, 89/343/EEC and 89/381/EEC. Commission proposals are expected for the necessary adaptations of EC technical standards to cover these products.

9.9.4 The transparency directive

Primary pharmaceutical regulation within the EC sets out the mechanism for granting a marketing authorisation, requirements for labelling and information to be available to health professionals, and criteria and normal protocols for the assessment of safety, quality, and efficacy. It also introduces controls over manufacturing licences and good manufacturing practices, introduces requirements for good laboratory practice (quality assurance of licensing data generated in studies involving laboratory animals), and requirements for qualified person status, and further steps are under way to enable the Community to become a party to the European Pharmacopoeia Convention.

The Community recognises the importance of a unified Community market for pharmaceutical products. Apart from harmonisation of the grant of marketing authorisations, the pricing and reimbursement of medicines are important elements in the achievement of free circulation. For this reason, the EC Council of Ministers adopted the directive on the transparency of national pricing control systems for human medicines and their inclusion in the scope of the national health insurance systems (89/105/EEC). This directive, which came into force in the member states on 31 December, 1989, should permit the clarification of the criteria used and of the procedures followed by the competent national health authorities as regards the pricing and reimbursement of medicines.

9.9.5 *Future developments*

In the light of the 1992 deadline for the completion of the internal market, the Commission has, since late 1989, submitted a range of proposals for further legislation in the pharmaceutical sector (table 2).

The various proposals will be examined within the Community consultation process and decisions are expected to be reached on them during the period 1992-1994.

10 Medical practice

Doctors may practise medicine alone, or in partnership with others, and medical practices may take on NHS work, or private work, or both. A number of legal implications arise as a result of this business activity. To what extent, if any, may the existence of the practice or the attributes of the doctors be advertised? Is it legal for a doctor to sell the goodwill of his practice? May partners in a medical practice bind each other to an agreement that if one of them leaves that person will not set up a rival practice nearby? (The legal expression for this is a "restrictive covenant".) What legal obligations is the doctor under to members of the public and to his staff?

10.1 Advertising

Certain types of advertising in relation to medical treatment would contravene the criminal law. For instance, no person is allowed to advertise treatments for cancer. See Cancer Act 1939 which provides in section 4 that: "No person shall take part in the publication of any advertisement:

(a) containing an offer to treat any person for cancer, or to prescribe any remedy therefor, or to give any advice in connection with the treatment thereof."

It is not, however, a criminal offence in this context to advertise, so far as is reasonably necessary, to bring the article in question to the notice of registered medical practitioners, nurses, and pharmacists, etc, or if the advertisement is published only in a technical journal circulated within the medical profession.

Secondly, the Venereal Disease Act 1917 provides in section 2(1) that "a person shall not by any advertisement or any public notice or announcement treat or offer to treat any person for venereal disease, or prescribe or offer to prescribe any remedy therefor, or offer to give or give any advice in connection with the treatment thereof."

This restriction does not apply to any advertisement by a local or public authority, published with the sanction of the Secretary of State, or in any publication sent only to duly qualified medical practitioners, or wholesale or retail chemists for the purposes of their business.

There are also restrictions against the advertisement of medicinal products if those advertisements are likely to lead to their use, except under the instruction of a doctor or a dentist.

In *Professional Conduct and Discipline: Fitness to Practise* the GMC provides guidance about the advertising of doctors services. It reminds doctors that there is a general requirement that all advertisements should be "legal, decent, honest and truthful" and should conform with the other requirements of the British Code of Advertising Practice. Doctors must be aware that patients are vulnerable and need protection from misleading advertisements and that the provision of medical services is not to be treated as a purely commercial activity. Every doctor is personally responsible for ensuring that information about him and the way it is distributed complies with this guidance whether the doctor arranges its publication or merely allows another to publish it.

10.1.1 *Practice leaflets*

The GMC distinguishes between the advertising of GP services and specialist services. GPs are encouraged to provide factual information to the public about the services they offer so that patients can make an informed choice about a family doctor.

Under their new terms of service NHS GPs must provide members of the public with information about their services in the form of a practice leaflet (see 10.7). There are no specific restrictions as to the size of leaflet, type of paper used in its production, or layout of text. Information provided within the leaflet of NHS practitioners must include the following items. Private practitioners are not obliged to adopt the same content for any leaflet they choose to produce but may find it useful.

Personal and professional details of the doctor
  (1) Full name
  (2) Sex
  (3) Medical qualifications registered by the GMC
  (4) Date and place of first registration as a medical practitioner

Practice information
  (5) The times during which the doctor is available for consultation by patients at the practice premises
  (6) Whether an appointment system is operated by the doctor for consultations at the practice premises
  (7) If there is an appointment system, the method of obtaining a non-urgent appointment and the method of obtaining an urgent appointment
  (8) The method of obtaining a non-urgent domiciliary visit and the method of obtaining an urgent domiciliary visit
  (9) The doctor's arrangements for providing personal medical services when he is not available

(10) The method by which patients are to obtain repeat prescriptions from the doctor

(11) If the doctor's practice is a dispensing practice, the arrangements for dispensing prescriptions

(12) If the doctor provides clinics for his patients, their frequency, duration and purpose

(13) The number of staff, other than doctors, assisting the doctor in the practice, and a description of their roles

(14) Whether the doctor provides (1) maternity medical services, (2) contraceptive services, (3) child health surveillance services, and (4) minor surgery services

(15) Whether the doctor works single-handed, in partnership, part-time or on a job share basis, or within a group practice

(16) The nature of any arrangements whereby the doctor or his staff receive patients' comments on the provision of general medical services

(17) The geographical boundary of the practice area by reference to a map

(18) Whether the doctor's practice premises have suitable access for all disabled patients and, if not, the reasons why they are unsuitable for particular forms of disability

(19) If an assistant is employed, details for him as specified in paragraphs 1-4

(20) If the practice is either a GP training practice for the purpose of the NHS (Vocational Training Regulations 1979) or undertakes the teaching of undergraduate medical students, the nature of arrangements for drawing this to the attention of patients.

Supplementary to the requirements of the NHS terms of service, doctors may also feature:

• Particular interests of the partners such as women's health, or expertise, or qualifications in treatments such as acupuncture or hypnotherapy

• A general statement about the practice approach to health care

• Photographs of the premises and doctors

The BMA has also produced advice to doctors on advertising and sponsorship which is reproduced in Appendix 2

10.2 Sale of goodwill

Statute provides, in effect, that it is a criminal offence to buy or sell the goodwill of an NHS practice. The relevant legislation is contained in the National Health Service Act 1977 (as amended) (England and Wales only) and the National Health Service (Scotland) Act 1978. Certain dispositions would be deemed for these purposes to constitute the sale of goodwill, but doctors who are in doubt as to whether any particular transaction could amount to a sale of goodwill may clarify the position with the Medical Practices Committee, and thus may have a good defence to any prosecution later brought. Details of the provisions are as follows.

Section 54 of the English statute and section 35 of the Scottish statute provide that where the name of any medical practitioner is or has been at any time entered on any list of medical practitioners undertaking to provide general medical services, it shall be unlawful subsequently to sell the goodwill or any part of the goodwill of the medical practice of that medical practitioner. However, there are two situations where this general prohibition does not apply:

"Where a medical practitioner whose name has ceased to be entered on any list of medical practitioners undertaking to provide general medical services practises in the locality of a Family Health Services Authority without his name ever having been entered on a list of medical practitioners undertaking to provide general medical services" then the sale of the goodwill of his practice (or any part of it) in that locality is not unlawful. Such a sale would also not be unlawful if the sale is by a medical practitioner "whose name has never been entered on a list of medical practitioners, undertaking to provide general medical services there, notwithstanding that any part of the goodwill to be sold is attributable to such a practice previously carried on by a person whose name was entered on such a list."

In this context "general medical services" is defined as services provided pursuant to the provisions of part II of the National Health Service Act 1977 by arrangement with the FHSA.

Schedule 10 of the English statute and schedule 9 of the Scottish statute provide that anyone who buys or sells the goodwill of a medical practice in contravention of the above provisions is guilty of a criminal offence, although in England and Wales no such prosecution can take place without the consent of the Director of Public Prosecutions.

In case there should be any attempt to avoid these provisions by disguising the sale of goodwill the schedules set out circumstances in which a sale of goodwill will be deemed to have taken place. For example, disposing of the premises will be assumed to be the sale of goodwill if the price is "substantially in excess of the consideration which might reasonably have been expected if the premises had not previously been used for the purposes of medical practice."

Similarly, if in pursuance of a partnership agreement a partner pays a "valuable consideration" (that is, anything of value, not just money) to enter a partnership or is given the same to leave it then this too may be assumed to amount to the sale of goodwill. The same assumption may be made if an assistant works for a cheap rate and is later accepted into the partnership or if a person agrees for a valuable consideration to do or not to do anything to facilitate his entry to the partnership, or if the person pays such a consideration for such entry.

It might be difficult for doctors to know when any particular transaction might land them in the criminal courts. Therefore, the schedules provide that any medical practitioner or his personal representative may apply to the Medical Practices Committee for the latter's opinion as to whether a proposed transaction would involve the unlawful sale of goodwill. The committee must consider any such application and, if satisfied that the transaction would not have such an effect, they must issue a certificate to that effect. The certificate must set out "all the material circumstances disclosed to the committee." Production of such a certificate will provide a good defence to any subsequent criminal proceedings unless it becomes obvious that there was a failure to disclose a relevant factor.

Apart from the statutory prohibition referred to above, there is no law against the sale of medical goodwill. Private practitioners should be careful, however, before selling their goodwill, to ensure that they are not breaking the law by virtue of the present or past appearance of their name on the list of practitioners willing to provide general medical services.

10.3 Restrictive covenants and partnership agreements

It is common for partnership deeds to provide that if a partner leaves he may not set up a rival business nearby. There has been a great deal of litigation on this subject when partners seek to enforce such a provision against an ex-partner. The latter may argue that the provision should not be enforced. In the case of private medical practice as with other businesses, to be enforceable such a restriction must go no further than is reasonable for the protection of the goodwill.

At one time such agreements were not considered to be enforceable in the case of NHS practices because of the prohibition against the sale of goodwill. However, in the case of Kerr v Morris [1986] 3 AER 217 the court decided that a restrictive covenant could be enforced against a doctor quitting an NHS partnership as the covenant protected the livelihood of the doctors and did not amount to such a sale.

The question of whether or not a particular restrictive covenant in a partnership agreement is or is not reasonable is a matter for the particular circumstances of each case. Factors such as the geographical breadth of the restriction and the length of time the restriction will last must be considered as well as the general public interest when weighed against the interests of the parties. A partnership agreement normally also regulates the financial arrangements between the partners, and in the case of a medical practice may have to cater for matters such as the use and ownership of the surgery. In general it is advisable that all partners take legal/accountancy advice when drawing up or entering into a partnership agreement. Consideration needs to be given to the possibility of dissolution of the partnership and the practical issues which would arise such as the separation of patient lists. (The General Medical Services Committee of the BMA has drawn up a basic framework for a medical partnership agreement which covers such matters as the provisions of the Sex Discrimination Act 1975 (see 10.6.13).)

10.4 Responsibilities imposed by the Occupiers' Liability Act

If a member of the public had an accident while on the doctor's premises could the doctor be sued for damages? The Occupiers' Liability Acts 1957 and 1984 (not applicable in Scotland and Northern Ireland) stipulate what responsibilities are owed to members of the public by occupiers of premises.

First, it is necessary to consider what is meant by the term "occupier." This is not defined in the Acts and so the original common law rules still apply. In Wheat *v* E Lacon and Co Ltd, the House of Lords held that "in order to be an occupier exclusive occupation is not required, and the test is whether a person has some degree of control associated with, and arising from, his presence in, and use of, or activity in, the premises." It follows that doctors who are partners in a medical practice would be regarded as occupiers of the premises where the practice was situate for the purposes of being responsible under this legislation.

The responsibility owed depends on whether the member of the public in question was on the one hand, invited or permitted to be on the premises by the doctors—for example, a patient—or had not been so invited or permitted, either expressly or impliedly—for example, a trespasser.

Responsibility for the first category of person, referred to as visitors from now on, is dealt with in the Occupiers' Liability Act 1957. A "duty of care" is owed to all visitors and is defined in section 2(2) as follows:

"The common duty of care is a duty to take such care as in all the circumstances of the case is reasonable to see that the visitor will be reasonably safe in using the premises for the purposes for which he is invited or permitted by the occupier to be there."

In this context the Act states that an occupier must be prepared for children to be less careful than adults. The Act anticipates and does not forbid the contracting out by the occupier of his responsibilities by, for example, a disclaimer notice, but a later piece of legislation, the Unfair Contract Terms Act 1977, puts considerable limits on the extent to which businesses may evade their obligations to visitors to their premises by such methods. That Act states in section 2(1):

"A person cannot by reference to any contract term or to a notice given to persons generally or to particular persons exclude or restrict his liability for death or personal injury resulting from negligence."

The above only deals with liability for death or injury responsibility which the occupier cannot avoid. The Act goes on to state that liability for other loss or damage, such as damage to property, can only be contracted out of if the term or notice in question is reasonable. (The Act gives guidance on that point in a later section.) Section 2(4)(a) of the Occupiers' Liability Act 1957 also states that even if the occupier warns of the existence of the danger this does not necessarily absolve him of all responsibility unless in all the circumstances the warning "was enough to enable the visitor to be reasonably safe."

Section 2(5) of the Occupiers' Liability Act 1957 does state, however, that the occupier is under no obligation to a visitor in respect of risks willingly accepted by that visitor.

There are special provisions in respect of "independent contractors" on the premises, such as builders, plumbers, etc. The Act states (section 2(3)(b)) that an occupier is entitled to expect that a person in the exercise of his calling will appreciate and guard against any special risks ordinarily incidental to it (so far as the occupier leaves him free to do so). In the case of Roles v Nathan, Roles v Carney [1963] 2 AER 908 CA two chimney sweeps were killed by carbon monoxide fumes while sealing up a sweephole. Evidence was given to the effect that they had been warned of the danger on numerous occasions by an expert employed by the occupier. It was held that the occupier was not responsible for their deaths. Not only had sufficient warning been given for purposes of section 2(4)(a) (see above) but the danger was a special risk ordinarily incident to the exercise of their calling against which the occupier might expect them to guard. Section 2(4)(b) of the Act also stipulates that if the visitor is damaged as a result of faulty work done by an independent contractor then the occupier is not to be automatically liable for what occurred, provided, that is, that the occupier acted reasonably in entrusting the work to the contractor by taking reasonable steps to satisfy himself that the contractor was competent to perform it and that the work had been done properly.

Following the passing of the Occupiers' Liability Act 1957 there were several cases concerning the responsibility of occupiers to persons other than visitors—for example, children straying on to railway lines. This led to the passing of the Occupiers' Liability Act 1984 which codifies the law on this question. First, it should be noted that the 1984 Act does not impose any liability for loss of, or damage to, property. The duty is firstly owed in respect of any risk of a person other than a visitor suffering injury on the premises by reason of any damage due to the state of the premises or to things done or omitted to be done on them. The occupier is, however, still only liable for any injury sustained by persons other than his visitors if a number of criteria apply:

(1) if the occupier is aware of the danger or has reasonable grounds to believe that it exists; and

(2) if he knows or has reasonable grounds to believe that the person is in the vicinity of the danger concerned or that he may come into the vicinity of the danger; and

(3) if the risk is one against which in all the circumstances of the case he may reasonably be expected to offer the other some protection.

If all the above exist then there is a duty of care, and the extent of it is to take such care as is reasonable in all the circumstances to see that a person other than a visitor is not injured on the premises because of the danger concerned. The occupier may absolve himself from the duty by taking such steps as are reasonable in all the circumstances to give warning of the danger concerned or to discourage the person from incurring the risk. Note, too, that if the person willingly accepts the risk in question no duty is owed than by virtue of the Act.

It is obvious from what is said above that it is highly desirable to be insured against any claim under the occupier's liability legislation.

10.5 Responsibilities imposed by health and safety at work legislation

10.5.1 Health and Safety at Work Act, etc, 1974

This legislation which relates to occupiers' liability provides that members of the public who have an accident on the premises may be able to sue the person in control of those premises for damages in the civil courts. The Health and Safety at Work etc. Act 1974 additionally imposes obligations on employers, the self-employed, business occupiers and workers, breach of which could result in criminal prosecution. Doctors, therefore, who employ others or who are self employed, or who are employed should take note of these provisions. An amendment to the Act in 1987 removed Crown immunity from NHS premises.

The aims of the Act are stated to be, among other things, to secure the health, safety, and welfare of persons at work and to protect members of the public from risks that might be created by the work activities of others. In this context the meaning of work has been extended to include any activity involving genetic manipulation (Health and Safety (Genetic Manipulation) Regulations (SI 1978 No 752) or the keeping or handling of certain pathogens (Health and Safety (Dangerous Pathogens) Regulations (SI 1981 No 1011)).

The Act sets out a number of statutory duties owed by various persons to various categories of people and although, as stated, a breach of these obligations could result in a criminal prosecution the Act states that breach of any of them does not of itself confer a right on the aggrieved person to sue in the civil courts.

Section 2 of the acts sets out what general duties are owed by employers to their employees as follows:

"It shall be the duty of every employer to ensure, so far as is reasonably practicable, the health, safety and welfare at work of all his employees. This duty is stated to include in particular:

(a) the provision and maintenance of plant and systems of work that are, so far as is reasonably practicable, safe and without risks to health;

(b) arrangements for ensuring, so far as is reasonably practicable, safety and absence of risks to health in connection with the use, handling, storage and transport of articles and substances;

(c) the provision of such information, instruction, training and supervision as is necessary to ensure, so far as is reasonably practicable, the health and safety at work of his employees;

(d) so far as is reasonably practicable as regards any place of work under the employer's control, the maintenance of it in a condition that is safe and without risks to health and the provision and maintenance of means of access to and egress from it that are safe and without such risks;

(e) the provision and maintenance of a working environment for his employees that is, so far as is reasonably practicable, safe without risks to health and adequate as regards facilities and arrangements for their welfare at work."

Except in "prescribed" cases (one of which is employers who employ fewer than five persons) each employer must prepare a written statement of his general policy regarding the health and safety at work of his employees and the organisation and arrangements currently in force for carrying out that policy. This statement has to be brought to the notice of all employees.

Employers must also note the provision of the Employers' Liability (Compulsory Insurance) Act 1969 (not applicable in Northern Ireland). This provides that every employer carrying on any business (later defined to include a profession) in Great Britain must insure and maintain insurance under an approved policy and with an authorised insurer "against liability for bodily injury or disease sustained by his employees, and arising out of and in the course of their employment in Great Britain in that business." Failure to insure as above is a criminal offence. There is no obligation to insure against injuries or diseases suffered or contracted outside Great Britain. Section 2 also lists various relatives who do not need to be covered. The certificate of insurance must be displayed and the employers' liability (compulsory insurance) general regulations (SI 1971 No 11/17) prohibit the inclusion of certain conditions in the insurance policy and fix the amount of cover required.

Section 3 of the Health and Safety at Work etc. Act 1974 sets out the general duties owed by employers and self-employed persons to members of the public other than their employees. The duty owed in both cases is to conduct their undertakings in such a way as to ensure, so far as is reasonably practicable, that persons not in their employment who may be affected thereby are not thereby exposed to risks to their health and safety.

Section 4 deals with the duties owed by persons concerned with premises (that is, each person who has, to any extent, control of the premises) to persons who are not their employees but who "use non-domestic premises made available to them as a place of work or as a place where they may use plant or substances provided for their use there." The duty owed is "to take such measures as it is reasonable for a person in his position to take to ensure, as far as is reasonably practicable, that the premises, all means of access thereto or egress therefrom available for use by persons using the premises, and any plant or substance in the premises or, as the case may be, provided for use there, is or are safe and without risks to health."

The duties owed by employees are set out in section 7: "it shall be the duty of every employee while at work:

(a)   to take reasonable care for the health and safety of himself and other persons who may be affected by his acts or omissions at work; and

(b)   as regards any duty or requirement imposed on his employer or any other person by or under any of the relevant statutory provisions, to co-operate with him so far as is necessary to enable that duty or requirement to be performed or complied with."

It is a criminal offence to fail to discharge any of the above duties. It is also a criminal offence to disregard any provision laid down in regulations made under the Act.

One such set of regulations is the Reporting of Injuries, Diseases and Dangerous Occurrences Regulations (SI 1985 No 2023). These provide for the compulsory reporting of certain mishaps at work to the enforcing authority. The following must be reported: any death resulting from an accident at work; any injury or "condition" arising as above, the categories of same being listed. They include various fractures, amputations, eye injuries, burns, loss of consciousness from lack of oxygen and "either acute illness requiring medical treatment, or loss of consciousness, resulting in either case from absorption of any substance by inhalation, ingestion or through the skin." Also "acute illness requiring medical treatment where there is reason to believe that this resulted from exposure to a pathogen or infected material; and any other injury which results in ..." immediate hospital admission for more than 24 hours.

There is also a duty to report the fact that a person has been incapacitated for more than three consecutive days as a result of an accident at work, and if an employee has had a notifiable condition and then dies from it within one year that death must be reported. If a person at work has one of the diseases listed in the Schedule to the regulations and if he has been engaged in the activity listed opposite that disease that fact must be reported if the condition has been diagnosed.

Certain dangerous occurrences must also be reported. These, too, are listed in article 10. The obligations above do not apply "to a patient when undergoing treatment in a hospital or in the surgery of a doctor or dentist."

The relevant medical authority under the Health and Safety at Work etc. Act 1974 is the Employment Medical Advisory Service (EMAS).

10.5.2 *Control of Substances Hazardous to Health Regulations 1988*

Complementary to the Health and Safety at Work etc. Act, the control of substances hazardous to health regulations (COSHH) expand and clarify the duties of employers in respect of hazardous substances at work to which employees and others may be exposed. Clinical waste falls within the scope of these regulations. COSHH specifically requires that risk assessments are made of all hazardous substances likely to be encountered as a result of a work activity.

Waste can be categorised into groups, that is groups A to E. The actual level of hazard will vary both within and between the groups, but to ensure that clinical waste does not present a risk to staff and others suitable control measures must be adopted. It is therefore essential that a written health and safety policy which includes safe handling and disposal of clinical waste should be prepared for the particular work place.

Training

All employees who are required to handle and move clinical waste should be adequately trained in safe procedures and in dealing with spillages or other incidents for their area of work. In general practice, the principals will be responsible for ensuring that general practice ancillary staff and nursing staff are suitably trained and protected. The employer's clinical waste policy and COSHH assessments will have identified any need for personal protective equipment, and the employer has a further duty under COSHH to ensure that items are provided, used, and maintained.

The domestic waste collection service should not be used for clinical waste. Options for disposal include local authority special collection and disposal service, independent contractors to the local hospital or practitioners may arrange to take waste by arrangement to the local hospital incinerator. All contaminated sharps and needles should be placed in a sharps container made to current British standard and all clinical waste must be clearly identified before it is removed from sight for disposal. Clinical waste generated in a patient's own home as a result of treatment by practitioners or their employees should be dealt with by the person providing the treatment. (The Environmental Protection Act 1990 (EPA) is the principal Act and replaces much of the Control of Pollution Act 1974. EPA places a duty of care on those whose import, produce, carry, keep, treat or dispose of "controlled waste" to take all such measures applicable to them in that capacity as are reasonable in the circumstances to prevent unlawful depositing, the escape of waste from their control, and to ensure that waste is only transferred to an authorised transporter. Controlled waste includes waste from hospitals, nursing homes, surgeries and blood transfusion units). It is essential that GPs ensure that all staff who handle clinical waste, contaminated sharps, or blood are trained in the appropriate techniques to ensure their safety and compliance with the Health and Safety at Work etc, Act, COSHH, and EPA. The BMA has produced two codes of practice which may be used as training manuals by GPs for their staff to ensure basic awareness and compliance with the legislation. (*Sterilisation of Instruments* (1989) and *The Safe Use and Disposal of Sharps* (1990)).

10.6 Responsibilities imposed on employers

Doctors in general practice will probably be employing others. In their position as employers those doctors should be aware that employed persons have a considerable number of rights, violation of which could lead to an award against the employer in the industrial tribunal or in the civil courts. Doctors who are themselves employed might be interested to know what rights they in turn have. Employment law is a huge subject and all that can be done here is to give a very brief outline of the provisions. A comprehensive guide to the subject can be found in Ellis N. *Employing Staff* (4th edition) London: BMJ, 1991.

It is necessary to consider briefly what is meant by employment. The obligations discussed below are only owed by doctor employers to their employees or "servants" and not to "independent contractors", such as a plumber called in to do one job on the partnership premises. In most cases the distinction between the two will be obvious. There is much case law on the more borderline situations but such debates are beyond the scope of this book.

In the following paragraphs the rights available to all employees are dealt with, followed by the special provisions for women and ethnic minorities. The following rights are all contained in the Employment Protection (Consolidation) Act 1978 (not applicable in Northern Ireland).

10.6.1 *Right to have particulars of terms of employment*

Sections 1-6 of the Act deal with this subject. Within 13 weeks of starting their job employees are entitled to receive from their employer a written statement with various details including a recital of who is employing whom and the date the employment began, hours of work, holidays, sick pay, pensions, length of notice either side, job title and, where there are 20 or more employees when the employment began, disciplinary procedures.

10.6.2 *Right to have itemised pay statement*

Section 8 states that this must include gross wage, details of all deductions, and net wage.

10.6.3 *Rights relating to trade union membership*

Section 23 forbids victimisation (as opposed to dismissal: see later) of any employee in relation to his joining or taking a part in trade union activities or in relation to his not joining a trade union.

10.6.4 *Rights to have time off work*

Sections 27 and 28 set out what rights employees have to have time off work in relation to trade union activities. Section 29 states that employees must be given time off (there being no statutory right to be paid while not at work) to perform various public duties. The duties in question are:

- Justice of the Peace (JP)

- member of a local authority

- member of a statutory tribunal

- member of a regional district health authority, family health services authority, health board

- member of governing body of school

The time that must be allowed must be reasonable, consideration being given particularly to certain listed criteria.

If an employee has been given notice by reason of redundancy then he must be given time off to look for work or make arrangements for training (section 31).

10.6.5 *Rights to have minimum periods of notice*

The employer and employee can agree to lengthen the period of notice but the periods below represent the minimum which must be given. If the employee has been employed for a month or more the employee must give at least one week's notice and the employer the following. If the employee has been employed for less than two years: one week. If the employee has been employed for more than two years but less than 12 years: one week per year employed. If the employee has been employed for 12 years or more not less than 12 weeks (section 49).

10.6.6 *Right to have written statement of reasons for dismissal*

If the employee's employment is terminated with or without notice or if a fixed term of employment ends and is not renewed (certain fixed term contracts are not covered at all by the Act if the employee agrees that the Act should not apply) then the employee may demand that the employer give a written statement of the reasons within 14 days. This does not apply, however, if the employment has not lasted for as long as two years at the date the employment terminated (section 53).

10.6.7 *Right not to be unfairly dismissed*

These provisions apply only if the employee has been employed continuously for two years and has not reached retirement age (except when dismissal relates to trade union activities). Dismissal can be deemed to take place not only where the employer ends the employment with or without notice, but also when the employee walks out in circumstances where the employer's behaviour is held to justify his doing so without notice (referred to as "constructive dismissal"). Section 57 attempts to define the meaning of "unfair." It is for the employer to show the reason for the dismissal and that reason either falls within the listed categories below or amounts to some other substantial reason in either case justifying dismissal. The listed reasons are those:

(a)   related to the capability or qualifications of the employee for performing work of the kind which he was employed by the employer to do; or

(b)   related to the conduct of the employee; or

(c)   that the employee was redundant; or

(d)   that the continuation of the employment would be unlawful.

The issue of whether the dismissal was fair or unfair depends on whether the employer acted reasonably or unreasonably in treating the incident as sufficient reason for dismissing the employee, and that question is to be determined in accordance with equity and the substantial merits of the case.

An employee has three months in which to complain to an industrial tribunal about unfair dismissal and the tribunal, if satisfied the dismissal was indeed unfair, may either make an award of damages or order reinstatement.

10.6.8 *Right to redundancy payments*

An employee who has been continuously employed for two years and is dismissed for redundancy is entitled to a redundancy payment (section 81). The Act lays down the criteria for calculating the amount.

10.6.9 *Rights to statutory sick pay*

This is dealt with by the Social Security and Housing Benefits Act 1982 (as amended), which provides that employers must pay sick pay to their employees in certain circumstances (a refund being claimable via national insurance contributions). The employee cannot claim any sick pay for the first three days off sick but thereafter is entitled to claim same at a stated rate up to the equivalent of 28 weeks' pay in any period of up to three years. Thereafter the employee must claim the benefit from the state. The employee need not obtain a medical certificate in the first week but must obtain one thereafter.

10.6.10 *Right to time off for antenatal care*

Section 31A of the Employment Protection (Consolidation) Act 1978 provides that a pregnant woman is entitled to time off work for antenatal care if advised to go for same by a registered medical practitioner, registered health visitor, or midwife. The employer must still pay the woman but can demand a certificate confirming the pregnancy.

10.6.11 *Right to return to work after having a child*

This is set out in section 33 of the Employment Protection (Consolidation) Act 1978. The conditions are as follows. The woman must have been employed before the beginning of the 11th week before the expected week of confinement. The woman must then have been continuously employed for two years by the employer. The woman must give the employer 21 days' written notice of her intention to be absent on grounds of pregnancy (or the notice must be given as soon as is reasonably practicable) and that she intends to return to work for the employer, and the expected week of the confinement.

Forty nine days or more after the expected week of confinement the employer can ask for written confirmation that the woman still wants to

156

return. She must answer within 14 days (or as soon as is reasonably practicable).

The right is to return before the end of the 29th week after the week of confinement to work for the employer (or his successor) on terms and conditions no less favourable, or if this is not practicable the employer may offer suitable alternative employment, and if the woman is redundant he must offer a suitable vacancy if there is one.

If the employer refuses to take the woman back this can be treated as unfair dismissal with the resulting consequences (see above) unless when the woman left the total number of employees did not exceed five and it is not reasonably practicable to permit her to return.

Section 60 also states that in certain circumstances a dismissal on the grounds of pregnancy will be assumed to be unfair.

10.6.12 Right to statutory maternity pay

This right was set out in the Social Security Act 1986 which was superseded by the Social Security Contributions and Benefits Act 1992. As with statutory sick pay the responsibility for paying is imposed on the employer, who can claim reimbursement from the State. The payments must begin not earlier than 11 weeks before the expected week of confinement and be for a maximum of 18 weeks. The woman must have been employed by the employer for at least 26 weeks.

The Still-Birth (Definition) Act 1992 amends the definition of "confinement" in the Social Security Contributions and Benefits Act 1992 by reducing the period of pregnancy after which a labour is treated as "confinement", where a child is born dead, from 28 weeks to 24 weeks. The effect is to make maternity allowance and statutory maternity pay available after a labour which results in the birth of a child born dead and which occurs at this earlier stage of pregnancy.

10.6.13 Right not to be discriminated against

The Equal Pay Act 1970 (not applicable in Northern Ireland) implies an "equality" clause in every woman's contract of employment. This ensures that if a woman is employed on similar work to a man she must not be employed on less favourable terms or be excluded from any benefits.

The Sex Discrimination Act 1975 also makes discrimination in the field of employment unlawful—that is, there must be no discrimination in the arrangements for who should be offered employment or in the terms on which employment is offered. Refusing or deliberately omitting to offer employment on grounds of sex or pregnancy is also unlawful. If a woman is employed it is unlawful to discriminate against her in respect of opportunities for promotion, transfer, or training or any other facility or service.

Partnerships should also note that where there is a partnership of six or more it is unlawful to discriminate against prospective or existing partners.

By virtue of the Race Relations Act 1976 race discrimination, too, is unlawful, the provisions being similar to those for sexual discrimination, including discrimination against prospective and existing partners.

10.7 The GP contract

A new contract for GPs was introduced by the government on 1 April 1990. The contract includes a substantial alteration to the way in which GPs are remunerated. The basis for remuneration is now as follows:

- annual capitation fees for each patient on a doctor's list which vary according to whether the patient is under 65, 65-74 or 75 and over;

- additional fees are payable for patients resident in areas of deprivation;

- payment of a basic practice allowance;

- payment for specific items of service such as maternity services, contraceptive services and home night visits;

- new fees for health promotion clinics, examination of new patients, child health surveillance and minor surgery;

- target payments for cervical cytology and infant immunisation.

In addition to altering the way in which GPs are remunerated, the new contract introduced other factors which were designed to improve services to patients:

- more information about services through the production of a practice leaflet and directories produced by FHSAs;

- annual health checks for all patients over 75, if necessary in the patient's home;

- check-ups for all patients when they first register with the practice. Regular lifestyle check-ups are also offered to all adult patients who have not consulted their GP for three years.

The provision of better information for patients is intended to improve patient choice. A patient is free to choose a doctor from whom he wishes to obtain medical advice and care. Equally, a doctor is free to accept or refuse anyone as a patient, subject to the constraints of his professional and contractual obligations, such as:

- in an emergency, where a doctor is ethically bound to provide any treatment immediately necessary and to ensure that arrangements are made for any further treatment;

- in isolated communities where the doctor is the only source of medical advice.

If a doctor removes a patient from his NHS list he is not obliged to inform the patient of the reason(s) why. Patients are not required to give a reason when changing their doctor. The FHSA has the power to assign a patient to a doctor whether the doctor agrees or not. This mechanism is intended to ensure that patients which doctors might regard as "difficult" have a right to treatment by a GP under the NHS.

10.8 Fund–holding practices

Since April 1991 family doctor practices with 9000 patients or more have been able to apply to become fund holders. They remain in contract with their local FHSA but are allocated a budget to cover the cost of a range of diagnostic tests, inpatient and day case treatment, and outpatient services, their prescribing costs and the costs of their staff and premises. The budget is set by the regional health authority in consultation with the local FHSA. Fund–holding practices are free to negotiate contracts with DHAs and other providers for services to their patients.

10.9 Indicative prescribing budgets

Since April 1991 FHSAs have set individual indicative drug budgets for each practice in their area. Individual practices are expected to keep within the indicative amounts given to them unless there are good reasons for exceeding them.

11 Registered medical practitioners

11.1 Registration of doctors

The statute currently governing the registration of medical practitioners is the Medical Act 1983. Under section 2 of this Act the GMC is obliged to keep two registers of medical practitioners. First, the "register of medical practitioners" which is to contain four lists as follows:

(a) **"The principal list"** This contains the names of all doctors entitled to be fully or provisionally registered (see below) by virtue of United Kingdom or EC qualifications, or who have been directed to be registered by virtue of other foreign qualifications. Not included, though, are those who are entitled to be included in the overseas list.

(b) **"The overseas list"** This contains the names of those qualified as above but who are entitled by reason of residence outside the EC to go on this list instead.

(c) **"The visiting overseas doctors list"** Under section 27 temporary full registration may be granted to visiting overseas specialists if certain criteria apply for a period not exceeding 12 months.

(d) **"The visiting EC practitioners list"** Under section 18 an EC national who is lawfully established in an EC country in medical practice may be permitted to render medical services temporarily in the United Kingdom provided various criteria are met. This temporary registration ends if the doctor becomes established in medical practice in the United Kingdom or if (except in urgent cases) the doctor gives treatment outside the stated criteria.

Secondly, the GMC must keep a register of medical practitioners with "limited registration" (see below).

11.1.1 *Full registration*

United Kingdom doctors

Section 3(a) of the Act provides that the following are entitled to be fully registered. That is a person who:

160

(1) Holds one or more primary United Kingdom qualifications. These are defined in section 4(3) and include:

"(a) the degree of bachelor of medicine or bachelor of surgery granted by any university in the United Kingdom;

(b) licentiate of the Royal College of Physicians of London or the Royal College of Physicians of Edinburgh or the Royal College of Surgeons of Edinburgh or the Royal College (formerly Royal Faculty) of Physicians and Surgeons of Glasgow;

(c) membership of the Royal College of Surgeons of England;

(d) licentiate in medicine and surgery of the Society of Apothecaries of London."

(2) Has passed a qualifying examination. Section 4(2) sets out the bodies who may hold same; and

(3) Has obtained the necessary experience. Under section 10 this involves being employed for the prescribed period in a resident medical capacity in one or more approved hospitals or institutions. A certificate verifying that the necessary experience has been obtained must be applied for and one will not be given unless the doctor has been employed in at least two prescribed branches of medicine for the minimum prescribed period such as to give the doctor the required experience. The doctor's service must additionally have been "satisfactory." (See below for details of provisional registration which enables doctors to obtain the necessary expertise.)

EC doctors

By virtue of section 3(b) doctors who are nationals of EC member states are entitled to be fully registered if they hold one or more recognised primary qualifications obtained in an EC member state (defined in section 17).

Other overseas doctors

If the GMC sees fit so to direct, other overseas doctors may be fully registered if they can satisfy the Registrar of the following:

(a) that they hold one or more "recognised overseas qualifications" (defined in section 19(2)); and

(b) that they have the necessary knowledge of English, and that they are of good character; and

(c) that they have the necessary experience. Under section 20 this means

161

doing the same pre-registration house jobs as United Kingdom doctors or at least the equivalent abroad.

11.1.2 *Provisional registration*
United Kingdom doctors

Section 15 provides for provisional registration so that those wishing to obtain certificates of experience (see above, paragraph 11.1.1) can be employed to that end.

If a doctor would be entitled to full registration under section 3(a) (see above), were it not for the fact that he has not yet obtained the necessary experience, he may be provisionally registered. This operates as full registration "... so far as is necessary to enable him to be engaged in employment in a resident medical capacity" in an approved hospital or institution but not further.

EC doctors

Pre-registration limited registration may be granted to doctors who qualify in EC member states to enable them to undertake pre-registration house officer posts in the United Kingdom. Registration is granted for the period for which an individual post is to be held (usually six months).

Other overseas doctors

Overseas doctors may similarly be provisionally registered if they satisfy all the criteria necessary for full registration under section 19 except the experience requirement. The effect of such registration is as above.

11.1.3 *Limited registration of practitioners with overseas qualifications (excluding EC doctors)*

Under section 22 of the Act the criteria for limited registration are as follows. The person must:

(a) Have "... been selected for employment in the United Kingdom or the Isle of Man as a medical practitioner in one or more hospitals or other institutions approved by the General Medical Council";

(b) Have "... passed the examination necessary for obtaining some acceptable overseas qualification" (defined in Section 22(4));

(c) Have "... the necessary knowledge of English";

(d) Be "... of good character"; and

(e) "... be someone who has the knowledge and skill, and has acquired the experience, which is necessary for practice as a medical practitioner registered under this section and is appropriate in his case."

A person who satisfies the above criteria may be given limited registration if the GMC sees fit. Such registration cannot last longer than the specified period of time (which must not exceed five years in the aggregate), and may be granted either to cover a range of certain types of employment or in respect only of a particular appointment. If registration has been granted only for a particular appointment and the appointment ends earlier than expected then the registration ends also, even if the specified period was for a longer period of time. Limited registration operates as full registration under section 19 in relation to:

"(a) any employment in which he is engaged during the currency of his registration, being the particular employment or employment of a description for the purposes of which he is registered; and

 (b) things done or omitted in the course of that employment; and

 (c) any other thing incidental to his work in that employment which, by virtue of any enactment, may not lawfully or validly be done except by a fully registered medical practitioner, but in relation to other matters he shall be treated as not so registered."

Also note that doctors with limited registration must work under the supervision of a fully registered medical practitioner.

Section 25 of the Medical Act 1983 provides that a doctor who has held limited registration may proceed to full registration if he fulfils the GMC's requirements for so doing.

11.1.4 *Effect of disciplinary proceedings on registration*

Disciplinary proceedings could result in a doctor's name being erased from the register, or in suspension from registration, or in the registration being permitted to continue only on conditions.

Under section 36 of the Act a doctor who is fully or provisionally registered, or who has limited registration and who has been found guilty of a criminal offence, or is judged by the Professional Conduct Committee of the GMC to have been guilty of serious professional misconduct may incur the following penalties.

(1) **Erasure of name from the register** (The doctor can apply for restoration at a later date after at least 10 months.)

(2) **Suspension of registration** The doctor is treated as not being registered

while the suspension operates. The suspension cannot exceed 12 months to start with. The period can be extended by further periods not exceeding 12 months each. Suspension could, alternatively, be followed by erasure or conditional registration as below.

(3) Conditional registration for a period not exceeding three years "... with such requirements so specified as the Committee thinks fit to impose for the protection of members of the public or in his [that is the doctor's] interests." In *Professional Conduct and Discipline: Fitness to Practise* the GMC gives examples of likely conditions that may be imposed, including that he should practise only under supervision or that he should take steps to remedy evident deficiencies in his knowledge, clinical skills, or abilities to manage or communicate. If the doctor fails to keep to the conditions his name can be erased or registration can be suspended (see above). The period of conditional registration can be extended by periods not exceeding 12 months each.

Additionally, under section 37, if the fitness to practise of any doctor, whether fully or provisionally registered or with limited registration, "... is judged by the Health Committee to be seriously impaired by reason of his physical or mental condition" then the Committee may direct suspension of registration or conditional registration as above.

Doctors may appeal against directions for erasure, suspension, or conditional registration, but section 38(1) provides that the Professional Conduct and Health Committees have the power to order immediate suspension pending appeal if the decision was erasure or suspension "... if satisfied that to do so is necessary for the protection of members of the public or would be in the best interests of that person" [that is, the doctor].

11.2 NHS disciplinary mechanisms

Since March 1990 health authorities have implemented revised disciplinary procedures for hospital medical and dental staff, and doctors in public health and community health services. The changes were made under regulation 3 of the National Health Service (Remuneration and Conditions of Service) Regulations 1974 and are described in detail in health circular HC(90)9.

The revised procedures introduce an informal "pre-disciplinary" machinery for reviewing the conduct of consultants who are alleged to have failed repeatedly to honour their contractual commitments. Such allegations are reviewed by a panel consisting of the chairman of the Joint Medical Staff Committee and two other consultants.

There is also a new procedure for dealing with cases of professional misconduct or professional incompetence which merit disciplinary action short of dismissal. This "intermediate procedure" involves the use of independent professional assessors invited by the director of public health to investigate and advise him on matters of professional conduct and competence.

Remedies for breach of contract, maladministration incompetence and professional misconduct are considered in chapter 2.4.

For the criminal offence of pretending to be a registered medical practitioner see 11.3.1 below.

11.3 Privileges and functions reserved to registered medical practitioners

There is no rule of law prohibiting non-registered persons from practising medicine but certain privileges and functions can only be enjoyed or performed by registered medical practitioners.

11.3.1 *Right to use titles*

It is a criminal offence wilfully and falsely to pretend that one is a registered medical practitioner. Section 49 of the Medical Act 1983 states that the offence is committed by a person who "... wilfully and falsely pretends to be or takes or uses the name or title of physician, doctor of medicine, licentiate in medicine and surgery, bachelor of medicine, surgeon, general practitioner or apothecary, or any name, title, addition or description implying that he is registered under any provision of this Act, or that he is recognised by law as a physician or surgeon or licentiate in medicine and surgery or a practitioner in medicine or an apothecary."

11.3.2 *Right to recover fees*

Section 46 of the Medical Act 1983 reserves certain rights to sue for medical fees to fully registered medical practitioners only. The section states: "no person shall be entitled to recover any charge in any court of law for any medical advice or attendance, or for the performance of any operation, or for any medicine which he has both prescribed and supplied unless he proves that he is fully registered." This is subject to an exception for visiting EC practitioners (see chapter 11.1 on registration of doctors, for definition of same).

11.3.3 *Appointments reserved for fully registered medical practitioners*

Section 47 of the Medical Act 1983 provides that only a fully registered medical practitioner may hold an appointment as physician, surgeon, or other medical officer in the following context:

"(a)   in the naval, military or air services;

(b)   in any hospital or other place for the reception of person suffering from mental disorder, or in any other hospital, infirmary or dispensary not supported wholly by voluntary contributions;

(c) in any prison; or

(d) in any other public establishment, body or institution,

or to any friendly or other society for providing mutual relief in sickness, infirmity or old age."

There is an exception to the above whereby a doctor who is not a Commonwealth citizen may act as the resident physician or medical officer of any hospital established exclusively for the relief of foreigners who are ill, if various criteria are met.

Under the terms of the Health and Safety at Work, etc, Act 1974, section 56(2), no person is qualified to be appointed or to be an employment medical adviser unless he is a fully registered medical practitioner.

The National Health Service is also precluded from employing non-registered doctors. See National Health Service Act 1977 and National Health Service (General Medical and Pharmaceutical Services) Regulations (SI 1974 No 160) (as amended) and National Health Service (Scotland) Act 1978.

11.3.4 *Venereal disease*

The Venereal Diseases Act 1917 provides for the prosecution of any unqualified person who treats venereal disease for reward. Section 1 states: "... a person shall not, unless he is a duly qualified medical practitioner, for reward either direct or indirect, treat any person for venereal disease or prescribe any remedy therefor, or give any advice in connection with the treatment thereof, whether the advice is given to the person to be treated or to any other person."

11.3.5 *Attending maternity cases*

Section 17(1) of the Nurses, Midwives and Health Visitors Act 1979 provides: "A person other than a registered midwife or registered medical practitioner shall not attend a woman in childbirth."

11.4 Jury service

The relevant legislation is the Juries Act 1974 (England and Wales only) and the Law Reform (Miscellaneous Provisions) (Scotland) Act 1980. All persons between the ages of 18 and 65 who are registered to vote and who satisfy the necessary residence requirements are qualified and liable to serve on a jury unless they are "ineligible" or "disqualified." Doctors as such are not included in either category, but some doctors are entitled as of right to be excused from jury service if they so wish. Those with this right are doctors who are registered (this included those who are provisionally registered or registered with limited registration) and who are actually practising their profession. Also excused if they fulfil the same criteria are dentists, nurses, midwives, veterinary surgeons, and pharmaceutical chemists. A doctor may also be excused on the same basis if summoned to sit on a coroner's jury (not applicable in Scotland). Persons "ineligible" to serve on a jury are firstly anyone who has ever (during the last 10 years in Scotland) been a member of the judiciary. That category includes JPs, chairmen, vice chairmen, presidents, vice presidents, registrars and assistant registrars of any tribunal. Secondly, "ineligible" persons are those who during the past 10 years (five in Scotland) have been concerned with the adminstration of justice. This category includes medical officers and members of boards of visitors to penal establishments, members of the Parole Board and local review committees, and in England and Wales only deputy, assistant, and actual coroners and persons in charge of or employed in any forensic laboratory. Also ineligible are some categories mentally ill persons. People with serious criminal records are "disqualified" from jury service.

A doctor who decides to do jury service must attend for as many days as he may be directed, and is liable to serve on any jury at the place to which he is summoned. The legislation provides that a juror is entitled to certain allowances for travelling, subsistence, and financial loss which may have occurred through—for example, loss of earnings. The amount allowed is fixed by prescribed rates which change from time to time.

11.5 Medical certificates

The Medical Act 1983 provides that if a medical certificate has to be signed by virtue of any statute that means that it must be signed by a fully registered medical practitioner. Section 48 states: "A certificate required by any enactment, whether passed before or after the commencement of this Act, from any physician, surgeon, licentiate in medicine and surgery or other medical practitioner shall not be valid unless the person signing it is fully registered."

Legislation relating to the National Health Service obliges NHS practitioners to provide certain certificates free of charge.

The National Health Service Act 1977, section 29(2)(d), and the National Health Service (Scotland) Act 1978, section 19(2)(d), state that NHS medical practitioners must issue to patients or their personal representatives such certificates as may be prescribed if such are reasonably required by them under, or for the purposes of, any enactment.

In England and Wales the terms of service for NHS doctors as set out in the National Health Service (General Medical and Pharmaceutical Services) Regulations (SI 1974 No 160), as amended, provide that doctors must issue free of charge to their patients or their personal representatives the certificates listed in schedule 3.

The list is long but includes—for example, certificates supporting claims for payment under the Social Security Act 1975, or for certain disability pensions, certificates to establish pregnancy or other medical grounds to obtain welfare foods, certificates enabling sight to be tested, certificates regarding unfitness for jury service, and certificates enabling a person with a disability to be registered as an absent voter.

The doctor is excused from this obligation "when, for the condition to which the certificate relates, the patient (a) is being attended by another doctor (other than a partner, assistant or other deputy of the first named doctor), or (b) is not being treated by, or under the supervision of, a doctor."

In Scotland similar provisions are made in the National Health Service (General Medical and Pharmaceutical Services) (Scotland) Regulations (SI 1974 No 506) (S41).

11.6 Paramedical professions

The following professions are subject to statutory control by virtue of the Professions Supplementary to Medicine Act 1960: chiropodists, dieticians, medical laboratory scientific officers, occupational therapists, orthoptists, physiotherapists and radiographers. The Act set up the Council for Professions Supplementary to Medicine which coordinates and supervises the work of separate professional boards (also established by the Act, one for each profession).

The Council may recommend to the Privy Council that other professions be brought within the ambit of the Act or that professions currently controlled by the Act be removed from that control. The Privy Council has the power to order accordingly provided both Houses of Parliament agree that such a change should take effect.

The boards are under a duty to promote high standards of professional education and conduct among members of the professions which they regulate. These duties include deciding what qualifications merit registration with the boards, supervising training, registering those who are competent, setting professional standards and removing from the register those whose conduct merits it.

11.6.1 *Education and training*

Under section 4 of the Act the boards have the power to approve courses of training; qualifications granted after taking an examination and attending an approved course of training; and institutions as being suitable to conduct approved training courses. The boards' approval or withdrawal of same must be sanctioned by the Privy Council before it takes effect. Under section 5 the boards also have a duty to supervise approved institutions and examinations for approved qualifications.

11.6.2 *Registration*

It is the duty of the boards to maintain a register of properly qualified persons. Anyone who has attended an approved training course at an approved institution and has obtained an approved qualification is entitled to be registered following application in the prescribed manner.

11.6.3 *Setting professional standards*

As will be seen later, if a registered professional is judged by his disciplinary committee to be "guilty of infamous conduct in any professional respect" that person's name can be erased from the register. The disciplinary committees of each Board are under a statutory duty to prepare and revise from time to time a statement as to the kind of conduct which they consider would amount to infamous conduct. A copy must be posted to each registered member (section 9(6)).

Each board draws up its own rules but some features are common. One clause inserted in all the statements is that no practitioner should by any act or omission do anything or cause anything to be done which he has reasonable grounds for believing is likely either to endanger or to affect adversely in a substantial way the health or safety of a patient.

11.6.4 *Discipline under the Act*

The boards must each establish an investigating committee and a disciplinary committee. The former investigates allegations that a person's name should be removed from the register and decides whether to refer the matter to the latter, which must consider and determine any case referred to it. If a registered professional is convicted of a criminal offence, which a disciplinary committee considers renders him unfit to be "registered" or is "judged to be guilty of infamous conduct in any professional respect," his name can be erased. The fact that the conduct complained of is not specifically listed in the statement mentioned in the above paragraph *does not* preclude the disciplinary committee from directing that his name be erased. The committee can also erase a name if registration was obtained by fraud, and those who make false representations to obtain registration can be prosecuted in the criminal courts.

11.6.5 *Effect of registration*

There is no rule of law which prohibits non-registered persons from practising these professions. However, those who are registered are by virtue of section 6 of the Act permitted to use the title "state registered." Anyone who falsely pretends to be "state registered" when he is not can be prosecuted in the criminal courts.

By virtue of the National Health Service (Professions Supplementary to Medicine) Regulations (SI 1974 No 494) no member of these professions can be employed by the NHS unless he is state registered. There is nothing, however, to prevent non-state registered persons being employed in the private or other sectors outside the NHS. If a licence is required for the operation of private practice premises, local authority bye-laws, for example, may restrict the granting of such licences to state registered personnel.

11.6.6 *Sharing premises*

The sharing of premises between doctors and members of allied professions used to be discouraged, but changes in practice have led to a closer integration of services in the interests of patients. Some GPs employ physiotherapists, chiropodists, etc, and are reimbursed by the district health authority. No charge should be made for services provided to patients of the practice by the associated practitioner if this treatment is provided in conjunction with an NHS GP.

11.6.7 *Complementary therapies*

It is open to any GP to employ a complementary therapist to offer NHS treatment within his practice. The employment of a complementary therapist within general practice is covered by the rules governing the employment of ancillary professional staff in general practice. The parliamentary secretary for health, asked to clarify the position on this, stated, in December 1991:

"GPs may bid for individual posts or sessions to their FHSA, which then allocates its ancillary staff budget to those practices whose bids represent the highest priority in its district. Responsibilities for arguing the individual GP's bid to the FHSA clearly rest with the GP himself, who seeks the proposed additional ancillary staff member in order to develop the medical services available in his own practice.

With regard to fund-holding GPs, the scheme was designed to offer fund-holders more flexibility in the use of NHS resources. It therefore gave them a substantial discretion to decide whether resources should be used in purchasing secondary care from local hospitals, or providing a wider range of services within their own practice.

They can therefore employ a complementary therapist in the same way as a non-fund-holding GP, or can vire additional resources from another part of the fund for this purpose, for which the prior approval of the FHSA is not required.

The critical point in the case of both fund-holding and non-fund-holding GPs, is that the GP remains clinically accountable for the care offered by the complementary therapist.

It is not a "referral" system, whereby one registered practitioner refers a patient for treatment by another. It is a "delegation" system, where the GP asks another professional to provide care for which he remains clinically accountable. It is therefore for the individual GP to decide in the case of each individual patient whether the alternative therapist offers the most appropriate care to treat that patient's condition."

11.7 Indemnity schemes

There is no general requirement that a doctor must be insured against possible negligence or other legal claims. Doctors employed by health authorities are indemnified by the health authority in respect of work undertaken as part of their employment and the authority assumes direct financial responsibility for all claims against them. These arrangements cover all work done as part of the doctor's contract with the authority, for example:

(i)   junior doctor involved in the care of private patients as part of his contract;

(ii) GP providing medical care to patients in hospital under a contractual arrangement;

(iii) university medical staff and research workers in the course of NHS duties;

(iv) doctors in public health medicine carrying out local authority functions under their health authority contract.

Certain activities are not covered by the scheme and it is the doctor's own responsibility to arrange insurance cover—for example:

(i)   a consultant providing medical care for a private patient in an NHS hospital;

(ii) category 2 work;

(iii) GMC disciplinary proceedings;

(iv) a GP providing care for a patient in hospital other than under a contractual arrangement with the authority;

(v)   a GP trainee working in general practice;

(vi)   an NHS doctor working on a contractual basis for another agency (for example, the prison service);

(vii) a doctor attending accident victims ("good samaritan acts").

Doctors who are not obliged to effect insurance or indemnity arrangements—for example, private practitioners and general practitioners—would be foolish not to do so, because apart from being liable for their own negligence, they could also be held legally responsible for any negligent acts perpertrated by their employees. Employers are in law "vicariously" liable for the negligent acts of their employees, regardless of rank or specialty (see chapter 2.2.2).

The three major defence organisations are the Medical Protection Society (MPS), the Medical Defence Union (MDU), and the Medical and Dental Defence Union of Scotland (MDDUS). All three provide essentially similar services. The MDU offers the following:

"The benefits which may be granted to a member include:

(1)   Advice on any matter connected with a member's practice, whether in hospital, in private practice, or while serving in a public or other service;

(2)   Assistance in defending proceedings where a question of professional principle is involved;

(3)   Assistance in vindicating a member's professional interests, honour and character;

(4)   Assistance in proceedings brought by a patient arising from "the act or omission of the member or of ..." various other persons, including partners, assistants, locums, subordinate medical or dental officers, assistants or subordinates who are not registered medical or dental practitioners such as nurses, dispensers etc. However, the MDU will not normally accept responsibility where the member has been engaged in activities outside the normal range of medical or dental practice;

(5)   Assistance when damages and costs are awarded by a court or a settlement is made out of court."

11.7.1 *Medical defence organisations and legal controls*

It can be seen from the above that members of the MDU will not inevitably be guaranteed the assistance they require. If a doctor were to take out insurance with an insurance company there would be a contractual right to insist on any indemnity covered by the policy. Because of the discretionary nature of the cover offered by the MDU and other defence bodies, it was decided in the case of Medical Defence Union *v* Department of Trade [1979] 2 AER 421 that the medical defence organisations are not carrying on the business of insurance and are not therefore subject to the legal controls imposed on insurance companies.

11.8 Fees charged by doctors in NHS hospitals

The BMA guidance note on category 1 and 2 work explains that a doctor employed in NHS hospital work is expected to perform various categories of work in pursuance of that contract. Some examinations and reports that an NHS doctor may be required to do form part of his contractual duties and others do not. The latter, referred to as category 2 work, may be charged for; the former, called category 1 work, may not. The leaflet also explains that where NHS hospital facilities are used for the purposes of category 2 work then one third of the fee payable must go to the hospital as payment for hospital costs.

If a doctor were accused of making a fraudulent claim for payment then criminal prosecution could follow. Section 15 of the Theft Act 1968 (not applicable in Northern Ireland and Scotland) provides that: "A person who by any deception dishonestly obtains property belonging to another, with the intention of permanently depriving the other of it" can be sent to prison for up to 10 years.

"Property" includes money and cheques (section 4(1)). When it comes to the issue of dishonesty the case of R *v* Ghosh [1982] QB 1053 laid down that the court must decide whether according to the ordinary standards of reasonable and honest people what was done was dishonest. If so then the court must decide whether the defendant realised his conduct was dishonest.

Section 17 of the same Act deals with the offence of false accounting defined as follows:

"(1) Where a person dishonestly, with a view to gain for himself or another or with intent to cause loss to another,—

(a) destroys, defaces, conceals or falsifies any account or any record or document made or required for any accounting purpose; or

(b) in furnishing information for any purpose produces or makes us of any account, of any such record or document as aforesaid, which to his knowledge is or may be misleading, false or deceptive in a material particular."

The maximum penalty is seven years in prison.

If a claim was shown to be inaccurate then a successful prosecution could follow if it could be proved beyond reasonable doubt that there was deliberate dishonesty. In other cases the money could be recovered by civil action.

In either event a doctor would risk being disciplined by the GMC. The GMC's guidelines *Professional Conduct and Discipline: Fitness to Practise* detail the categories of improper financial transactions that might lead to disciplinary proceedings. These include a doctor convicted of criminal deception (obtaining money or goods by false pretences), forgery, fraud, theft or any other offence involving dishonesty.

The GMC also takes particularly seriously dishonest acts committed in the course of a doctor's professional practice (whether employed by the NHS or otherwise) or against patients or colleagues. Examples given include the improper demand or acceptance of fees from patients contrary to the statutory provisions which regulate the conduct of the NHS, such as the charging of fees to inpatients or outpatients treated at NHS hospitals, when the proper steps have not been taken to ensure that such patients enjoy the status of resident or non-resident private patients, and improperly seeking to obtain from a health authority any payment to which the doctor is not entitled.

11.9 Relations with the pharmaceutical industry

The GMC, the Association of the British Pharmaceutical Industry (ABPI), and the BMA all take the view that the acceptance of fees by doctors for meeting representatives of pharmaceutical companies is not acceptable.

The Department of Health note HN9(62) 21 covers gifts and hospitality. Independent contractors, such as GPs, are not under any contractual duty to comply with the instructions of this note but they are, like all citizens, subject to the provisions of the Prevention of Corruption Act 1906 and 1916.

The GMC gives further guidance on the relationship between the medical profession and pharmaceutical and allied industries in *Professional Conduct and Discipline: Fitness to Practise*. Its February 1991 edition notes "The seeking or acceptance by doctors of unreasonable sums of money or gifts from commercial firms which manufacture or market drugs or diagnostic or therapeutic agents or appliances may be regarded as improper."

12 Specialised areas of medicine

12.1 Ships' doctors

Legislation provides that certain appointments on board ship are only to be held by registered medical practitioners, and some British registered ships must carry registered medical practitioners on board. There are also provisions for the medical examination of seamen, for the giving of medical treatment in circumstances where no qualified doctor is on board, and for the carrying of medical supplies, etc, in ships. The duty of confidentiality owed by ships' doctors to seamen should also be considered.

Section 47 of the Medical Act 1983 provides that no person who is not a fully registered medical practitioner (see chapter 11.1 for definition) shall hold any appointment as physician, surgeon, or other medical officer in, among other things, the naval, military, or air service. Previous legislation, which has now been repealed, used to extend this provision to appointments in any emigrant or other vessel. However, section 43(1) of the Merchant Shipping Act 1970 gives the Board of Trade power to make regulations requiring certain ships to carry such number of qualified doctors as might be specified. The Merchant Shipping (Ship's Doctors) Regulations (SI 1981 No 1065) made under this section provide the following: every United Kingdom ship which goes to sea with 100 or more persons on board must carry a qualified doctor. Qualified in this context means a fully registered medical practitioner. This provision does not, however, apply to ships going solely between places within the Near Continental Trading area and the Secretary of State does have power to grant specific or general exemptions to this provision.

The Merchant Shipping (Medical Examination) Regulations (SI 1983 No 808) provide that in sea-going ships of 1600 gross register tonnage or over a seafarer must not be employed unless he holds a valid medical fitness certificate. Each applicant must be examined by an approved medical practitioner (approved for the purpose by the Secretary of State). If the practitioner considers that the applicant is fit he must issue him with a medical fitness certificate which may be restricted as to capacity or sea service or geographical areas.

If there is no doctor on board then section 25 of the Merchant Shipping Act 1970 provides that ". . . the master shall make arrangements for securing that any medical attention on board the ship is given either by him or under his supervision by a person appointed by him for the purpose."

Regulations made under Section 22 of the Merchant Shipping Act 1970 may require United Kingdom registered ships to carry specified medicines and other stores, including books containing instructions and advice.

The issue of confidentiality may be important in relation to ships' doctors who have responsibilities to both patients and third parties, in this case, the captain and owners of the vessel. Principles similar to those surrounding the occupational physician apply (see chapter 12.5).

12.2 Prison doctors

The Prison Medical Service predated the National Health Service and its independence was consolidated by the enactment of the Prison Act 1952, section 7 of which provides that each prison must have a medical officer who must be a registered medical practitioner as defined under the Medical Act 1983.

Both in England and Wales, where the prison department is administered by the Home Office, and in Scotland, where it is the responsibility of the Scottish Home and Health Department, there are full time and part time prison medical officers. Full time prison doctors are civil servants on the civil service medical officer grade. In the wake of the Strangeways Prison riot and concern about the extent of HIV infection in prisons there is continuing debate about standards of prison health care. It has been suggested that the Prison Medical Service should be brought under NHS control, and there are calls for the establishment of a Faculty of Prison Medicine to improve training in areas, including mental health, substance misuse, and public health medicine. (At the time of publication of this edition a detailed government review of the function and structure of the Prison Medical Service was underway and may lead to change in its organisation). Part-time prison medical officers are usually GPs in the locality who are contracted for service on the basis of an average hourly commitment per week. Where there is no full-time doctor, the part-time medical officer is "in full medical charge." The Prison Medical Service also engages the services of other GPs and consultants (usually psychiatrists, but also physicians and surgeons) on a casual basis.

A prison does not have to provide the same standard of care as a psychiatric hospital and it is not necessary to provide the same staff to patient ratio. The test for medical negligence is the usual one. In Knight *v* Home Office [1990] 3 AER 237 it was held that neither the prison service nor the medical officer were negligent in failing to keep under continuous observation a mentally ill prisoner known to have suicidal tendencies (he did in fact commit suicide). The decision to observe him at 15 minute intervals was held to be a decision which an ordinary skilled doctor would have made.

12.2.1 *Duties of medical officers*

The Prison Rules (SI 1964 No 388), rule 17(1) states "the medical officer of a prison shall have the care of the health, mental and physical, of the prisoners in that prison." The BMA's longstanding ethical advice is that apart from not being able to choose their own doctor, prisoners have a right to the same medical attention as any other member of society, and a prison medical officer's responsibility to, and professional relationship with, his patients are the same as any doctor working outside prison.

The Prison Rules set out specific duties which the medical officer must perform in the case of any prisoner whose health is likely to be injuriously affected by any condition of imprisonment. The medical officer is required to pay special attention to any prisoner whose mental condition appears to require it, and to make any special arrangements which appear necessary for his supervision or care.

The medical officer must also by virtue of rule 18(3) ". . . inform the governor if he suspects any prisoner of having suicidal intentions." The medical form completed on admission invites the medical officer to comment on possible suicidal intent.

In the case of R *v* Secretary of State for Home Affairs and others ex p Dew ex 16/2/87 (*Law Society Gazette* 1987) a prisoner applied for a judicial review. At the time of his arrest he had sustained a bullet wound and he claimed that he had not received adequate medical care as required by rules 17 and 18. Before the case was heard all the treatment requested had been provided and the case did not continue for procedural reasons.

Rule 21(5) imposes on the medical officer special duties in relation to prisoners' food, and food in this context includes a drink. "The medical officer shall regularly inspect the food both before and after it is cooked, and shall report any deficiency or defect to the governor." Food must be ". . . wholesome, nutritious, well prepared and served, reasonably varied and sufficient in quality."

12.2.2 *Other responsibilities*

Medical officers in prisons also have responsibilities concerning the issue of when prisoners should have to take exercise, work, be shaved or have their hair cut, and be permitted to have alcohol. Special provision is made in relation to prisoners who are pregnant. The provision of needles to known drug addicts is currently under discussion and the medical officer may be called on to exercise clinical judgement.

12.2.3 *Accessibility and choice*

The Prison Rules (SI 1964 No 388), as amended, deal with such issues as accessibility of prisoners to medical treatment, and the duties of prison doctors. The Detention Centre Rules (SI 1983 No 569) and the Youth

Custody Centre Rules (SI 1983 No 570) make similar provision for those institutions.

Prison rule 17(2) provides that "every request by a prisoner to see the medical officer shall be recorded by the officer to whom it is made and promptly passed on to the medical officer."

Rule 17(3) states that "the medical officer may call another medical practitioner into consultation at his discretion, and shall do so if time permits before performing any serious operation."

The prisoner cannot, except to the limited extent set out below, choose to be treated by his own or any outside doctor.

Rule 17(4) provides that if an unconvicted prisoner wants to see an outside doctor or dentist and is prepared to pay any resulting expense the governor may (not must) allow the prisoner to be visited and treated by the outside practitioner in consultation with the medical officer. A prisoner could, of course, write to his doctor under the general provisions regarding prisoners' letters under rule 34. Prison rule 37A also provides that a prisoner who is a party to legal proceedings may see a registered practitioner for the purpose of being examined in connection with those proceedings. Reasonable facilities must be provided for the examination which must take place within the sight but not the hearing of a prison officer.

12.2.4 *Consent to treatment*

There is no rule of law which alters the position of prisoners in this respect. However, because of the situation a prisoner is in it has been alleged that prisoners can be pressurised to agree to treatments or not, and to resist having them for fear of reprisal or hope of advantage in the form of parole, etc. The case of Freeman *v* Home Office [1984] 1 AER 1036 CA arose when a prisoner sued for damages for trespass to the person on the grounds that a medical officer employed by the prison authorities, together with other prison officers, had administered drugs to him by force against his consent. The prisoner argued that the drugs were not for the relief of mental illness but for control and therefore he could not validly consent to taking them as the medical officer was in effect acting not as such but as a disciplinarian. He also argued that consent, to be valid, had to be informed. The appeal court, holding first that the doctrine of informed consent formed no part of English law, then went on to say that the trial judge had been right to find on the facts that the prisoner had consented to the administration of the drugs. The prisoner's claim did not succeed.

In case there is any doubt on the issue there is no legal right to administer drugs to a prisoner without his consent, and for the purposes of sedation as an aid to discipline. The BMA believes that it is unethical for a doctor to administer a drug to a prisoner for any purpose other than for his clinical care and that it is unethical to carry out a research procedure on a prisoner if it is of no direct benefit to the prisoner. This is because the prisoner might expect to derive some benefit from agreeing to participate, thus raising the inference that the consent had been obtained by undue influence.

12.2.5 *Force feeding*

The question of whether prisoners who do not want to eat should be force fed has given rise to difficulties. At one time it was considered that the common law duty of prison doctors to preserve the health and lives of prisoners (Leigh *v* Gladstone [1909] 26 TLR 139) obliged them to force feed. The existence of such a duty or power is now doubted and the Secretary of State has issued guidance to prison doctors on this issue. The guidance is that:

"the common law duty of persons in charge of a prisoner is to take such steps as are reasonable in the circumstances of each case to preserve the life and health of the prisoner. This means that whilst adequate food and drink must be available to a prisoner, there is generally no duty to force him to take it against his will."

The attention of the governor and the medical officer will often be drawn to a prisoner who is refusing food by their examination of the record of returned food (standing order 2B 2). In other cases the staff of the establishment will report to the governor and medical officer their observation that a prisoner appears not to be taking food or fluids or that he has announced an intention not to do so.

The prisoner will normally be admitted to a single room in the prison hospital either:

"(a)   if the prisoner's reported refusal of food continues for more than a few days and

    i   if examination shows that there has been a significant loss in weight; or

    ii   if ketonuria (the presence in the urine of ketones which indicates that the body has begun to metabolise its own tissue) is found; or

    iii   if the prisoner appears mentally disturbed or ill; or

(b)   if it is reported that he is refusing fluids";

and a standard form should be completed and submitted to Headquarters (Medical Directorate).

The guidance also indicates that primary responsibility for the handling of prisoners refusing food and drink rests with the medical officer. There is no rule of practice requiring any medical officer to resort to artificial feeding, but the guidance says that if the prisoner continues to refuse food and his weight falls a worrying amount, or his health appears in danger of being impaired, an outside consultant should be invited to examine the prisoner. If the consultant confirms that the prisoner's capacity for rational judgement is unimpaired by illness, mental or physical, the medical officer should tell the prisoner that he will continue to receive medical supervision and advice; that food and fluids will be made available to him, but that there is no rule of practice which requires any medical officer to resort to artificial feeding; and that the consequent and inevitable deterioration in his health may be allowed to continue without medical intervention unless he specifically requests it.

If the prisoner's capacity for rational judgement is found to be impaired by illness, mental or physical, the medical officer should take such action as he considers necessary.

The Declaration of Tokyo states that where the prisoner's refusal is rational, which should be confirmed by at least one independent doctor, the prisoner should not be force fed, although the consequences of refusal of food should be explained.

Section 28 of the Prison Act 1952 states that the Secretary of State may temporarily discharge a prisoner on account of self-inflicted ill health, but specifically adds that the existence of such power does not detract from the medical officer's duties in respect of any such prisoner whom the Secretary of State decides not to discharge on this ground. Section 22(2)(b) of the Prison Act 1952 (as amended) also provides that the Secretary of State may, if satisfied that a prisoner requires medical investigation, or observation, or medical or surgical treatment, direct the prisoner to be taken to a hospital or other suitable place for the purposes of that treatment. The prisoner is to be kept in custody unless the Secretary of State directs otherwise.

12.2.6 Punishments

The position of prison doctors with regard to prison punishments must be considered. The Prison Rules oblige such doctors to be involved in the processes of removing prisoners from association, placing prisoners under restraint, and cellular confinement. To what extent might such involvement conflict with a doctor's ethical duty?

Rule 43 deals with the right of the governor to remove a particular prisoner from association with the others. This power exists, not as a punishment, but to protect the prisoner being removed or to maintain order. The rule provides, however, that the governor shall arrange for such a prisoner to resume association "if in any case the medical officer so advises on medical grounds."

An award of "cellular confinement", however, is a punishment and under rule 53(2) shall not be made unless the medical officer has certified that the prisoner is in a fit state of health to be so dealt with. Confinement as such is considered acceptable, but the BMA view is that if a doctor is asked to examine a prisoner who is subject to close confinement the doctor must decide if the procedure is excessive and dangerous to the prisoner's health and, if so, make a written report and then refuse to be further associated with the procedure.

Under rule 46 the governor may order a prisoner to be put under restraint "where this is necessary to prevent the prisoner from injuring himself, or others, damaging property or creating a disturbance."

Notice of such order must, however, be given without delay to the medical officer who must inform the governor if he concurs in that order. The governor must comply with any recommendation which the medical officer may make. Prisoners must not otherwise be placed under restraint unless this is done for their safe custody in transit, or on medical grounds, and on the direction of the medical officer. This, too, is not meant to be a punishment. The BMA accepts that individual restraint may be necessary for violent prisoners who are a threat to other prisoners, their guardians, or themselves, and believes that a doctor may give medical advice on individual restraint where the doctor judges that the clinical condition of a prisoner makes restraint necessary. Section 17 of the Prisons Act 1952 states that:

"The medical officer of a prison shall not apply any painful test to a prisoner for the purpose of detecting malingering or for any other purpose except with the permission of the (Secretary of State) or the visiting committee or, as the case may be, the board of visitors."

Even if any of the above did see fit to authorise any such tests any medical officer proposing to carry them out would be well advised to consult his defence organisation first.

12.3 Doctors in the armed forces

In chapter 11.3.3 it is pointed out that only a fully registered medical practitioner may hold an appointment as physician, surgeon, or other medical officer in the naval, military, or air services.

The ethical position of doctors in the armed services is considered in detail in the BMA's ethical advice where the extent to which the general duty of confidentiality may be modified in such circumstances is examined.

In Mason and McCall Smith's *Law and Medical Ethics* (3rd edition) London: Butterworths (1991), page 189 states: "Much loose talk is often voiced as to the status of medical officers in the Armed Forces. In reality, their relationship to individual patients is precisely the same as in civilian practice, with the proviso that the doctor's duty to society is accentuated when this is formulated as a duty to the fighting unit; eventually the lives of many are dependent upon the health of individuals. There is, thus, a wider justification for disclosure than exists in civilian life and the serviceman has tacitly accepted this in enlisting; nevertheless the principle of justification remains valid."

The argument seems to be that by joining the armed forces the patient tacitly agrees that the normal duty of confidentiality which a doctor owes to a patient can, in his case, be modified. However, it is clear that any breach of confidentiality would have to be justifiable.

12.4 Police surgeons

A police surgeon may not only have to examine patients on behalf of the police but also to examine and treat ill patients in custody. The doctor has a clear responsibility to treat the detained person as a patient, and is bound by the ordinary guidelines for confidentiality.

Accused persons are legally innocent and therefore have the same rights as any member of the public. A person in custody is not obliged to submit to medical examination or treatment, or to provide specimens for forensic examination. In the absence of consent any attempt to obtain specimens would constitute a battery. The police surgeon must state that the result of his examination will be reported to third parties and cannot proceed if, as a result, consent to examination is refused. In the interests of justice, however, he may make and transmit the results of observations, which need not be confined to purely visual impressions (Forrester *v* HM Advocate [1952] JC 28). Any examination of a person in custody should, if possible, be witnessed by a third party. In the case of a woman in custody a policewoman or other female should be present. Relatives can be present at the examination of a person under 16 if they request it.

12.5 Occupational health physicians

Doctors employed by companies or other institutions to act as medical advisers on staff health occupy a special position. A doctor must state explicitly before carrying out a medical examination for employment purposes that the results of that examination may be communicated to the employer (or prospective employer), and the consent of the examinee must be obtained in the light of that examination. In the absence of such agreement it is unlikely that the doctor engaged in occupational medicine would be entitled to breach his duty of confidence to a patient on the grounds that the doctor owed a duty as an employee to his employer.

The employee has statutory access to occupational health records maintained on electronic media by virtue of data protection legislation, and since November 1991, to manual records made in connection with the "care" of the individual under the Access to Health Records Act 1990. Medical records held by employers relating to the physical or mental health of their employees may be subject to the Act if made in connection with the care of the employee. Occupational physicians should therefore be aware of its provisions. Illustrative examples include where an occupational physician provides clinical care to employees either directly or through ancillary staff such as nurses or physiotherapists, or where he gives medical advice including counselling on the suitability of an employee's job in relation to his health (see chapter 4.4.3).

In addition, certain reports prepared by occupational physicians may be subject to the Access to Medical Reports Act 1988 which relates to reports prepared by a doctor who has clinical charge of a patient for direct supply to the patient's employer (or prospective employer). Reports by doctors who have had only a casual, non-caring professional association with the patient are excluded. The types of circumstances in which the Act may apply to the reports of an occupational physician, include:

(i) where an occupational physician (whether employed whole time or part time by a public or private undertaking) provides clinical care as defined to the employee of that undertaking being examined;

(ii) where an occupational physician has previously provided medical treatment or advice to any employee in the context of a doctor/patient relationship and thereby holds confidential information which could influence his subsequent report;

(iii) where an occupational physician acts as an employer's agent, seeking clinical information from an individual's GP or consultant. In such a case it is acceptable for the occupational physician, acting for the employer, to notify the employee of his rights under the Act and to obtain his consent to a report being sought on behalf of the employer.

In the case of medical examinations before employment is offered it is unlikely that an occupational physician working full time in the specialty, who is asked to undertake such an examination on a prospective employee, will previously have provided clinical care to that individual. However, many GPs undertake occupational health work on a part-time basis and there could be occasions when they will find themselves undertaking such examinations on patients from their own general practice. The Act will therefore apply to them or to any partners in their practice, who have access to medical records held in the practice.

Many occupational physicians feel that this Act does not apply to internal communications between managers and doctors employed within the same organisation. If clinical care is not provided this interpretation of the Act is correct, but the BMA recommends that frank and open discussion with an employee about whom a report is to be written is the best policy for an occupational physician, regardless of the dictates of the law.

Such reports as are included have always been subject to the patient's consent, but the applicant must now positively seek such consent and must inform him of his rights to access (section 3). The patient can see the report before it is sent, and unless he has done so, issue of the report must be delayed for three weeks (section 4). He has the right to ask the doctor to alter anything that he feels is inaccurate; he may add a dissenting statement should the doctor refuse to do so (section 5). Further details on the provisions of this Act can be found in chapter 4.4.2.

Occupational physicians should only treat patients in cooperation with the patient's GP, except in an emergency. The patient's consent should be secured before telling the GP of any findings or treatment. The BMA advises that if the occupational physician believes that the worker should consult his GP he should urge him to do so.

The Occupational Physician, published by the BMA, gives further detailed advice on this area of medical practice.

12.6 Public health

Public health (formerly called community medicine) is that medical specialty which deals with populations or groups rather than individual patients. In the context of a national system of health care, public health doctors have a particular role in measuring the health needs of the population.

In response to the 1988 Acheson report on public health all health authorities now have a director of public health. He has a responsibility to:

- produce an annual report on the health of the local population;

- develop policies on health promotion and disease prevention;

- provide epidemiological information to enable health authorities to set priorities and purchase services to meet local needs;

- ensure that the health authority has effective policies for the control and reporting of communicable disease, including AIDS.

13 Other activities

13.1 The doctor as company director

13.1.1 *Implications in relation to ethical duties not to advertise*

Until recently the GMC position was that for doctors to indulge in any kind of "self promotion" was unethical. The term proved so difficult to interpret that the February 1991 edition of *Professional Conduct and Discipline: Fitness to Practise* drops references to self promotion.

Indeed, within strict limits, advertising is encouraged. The GMC encourages doctors to provide factual information about their services and professional qualifications. The term "advertising" is used by the Council to mean the provision of information about doctors and their services, in any form, to the public or other members of the profession (see chapter 10.1).

The GMC also provides guidance on the use of the name and qualifications of a doctor in publicity material about companies and other organisations. "The name and qualifications of a doctor who is a director of a company may be shown on the company's notepaper. Doctors should however take steps to avoid the inclusion in material published by any company or organisation with which they are associated, of references which draw attention to their attainments in a way likely to promote their professional advantage, whether or not the business of their company is connected with medical practice."

When is it a statutory requirement to name the directors? The effect of section 305(1) of the Companies Act 1985, as amended, is that a company does not have to name any of its directors on its notepaper. However, if it names one director it must name all the directors and must include in legible characters the Christian name or initials and surname of each individual and the corporate name of every corporate director. If this requirement is violated the company can be fined.

Another mandatory requirement imposed on companies in relation to publicising the identities of directors is that contained in section 288 which obliges companies to keep at their registered office a register of directors and secretaries. The register must contain the following details about each director who is an individual: present name (and any former such name); usual residential address; nationality; business occupation (if any); particulars of other directorships; date of birth.

This register must be open to inspection by members of the public during business hours (for at least two hours a day). Similar details have to be filed with the Registrar of Companies within 15 days of the appointment of directors and be publicly available from Companies House.

13.2 Doctors and patent law

The rationale behind the patents system has been described thus: "It is desirable in the public interest that industrial techniques should be improved. In order to encourage improvement and to encourage the disclosure of improvements in preference to their use in secret, any person devising an improvement in a manufactured article, or in machinery or methods for making it, may upon disclosure of his improvement at the Patent Office demand to be given a monopoly in the use of it for a period of ... years." (See Banks MAL (chairman) *British Patent System; Report of the Committee to Examine the Patent System.* Cmnd 4407, London: HMSO, 1970.)

The Patents Act 1977, as amended, most of which came into force on 1 June 1978, governs applications for patents made after that date and provides that an invention can be patented for 20 years. The Patents Act 1949 governed previous patent applications, and subject to some conditions those known as "old" patents (many of which, of course, still exist) have also had their life extended to 20 years. Even before the Patents Act 1977 methods for the medical treatment of human beings were held not to be patentable as they did not fall within the concept of manufacture. Treatments which were not of a curative nature were sometimes successfully patented—for example, methods of contraception, hair softening, etc. The Patents Act 1977, however, makes the position quite clear. Section 1 of that Act states that an invention can only be patented if, among other things, it is new, it involves an inventive step and it is capable of industrial application. Section 4 then goes on expressly to exclude medical treatment from being interpreted as being capable of industrial application.

Section 4(2) states: "An invention of a method of treatment of the human or animal body by surgery or therapy or of diagnosis practised on the human or animal body shall not be taken to be capable of industrial application."

Drugs and appliances were patentable previously and still are. Section 4(3) of the Patents Act 1977 makes it clear that the exclusion of medical treatment from the patent system does not extend to medicines. Section 4(3) states: "Subsection (2) above shall not prevent a product consisting of a substance or composition being treated as capable of industrial application merely because it is invented for use in any such method" (method of treatment of human or animal body).

There is also an interesting proviso regarding when a substance used for medical treatment can be considered to be "new" for the purposes of satisfying the list of criteria necessary for something to be patentable. Section 2(6) provides: "In the case of an invention consisting of a substance or composition for use in a method of treatment of the human or animal body by surgery or therapy or of diagnosis practised on the human or animal body, the fact that the substance or composition forms part of the state of the art

186

shall not prevent the invention from being taken to be new if the use of the substance or composition in any such method does not form part of the state of the art."

Inventions cannot be patented if they already form part of what is termed the "state of the art". The Patents Act 1977 defines this phrase as being taken to "... comprise all matter (whether a product, a process, information about either, or anything else) which has at any time before the priority date of that invention been made available to the public (whether in the United Kingdom or elsewhere) by written or oral description, by use or in any other way" (section 2(2)).

When something is invented there could be a dispute over to whom the invention belongs, if the inventor was at the time in the employment of somebody else. Section 39 of the Patents Act 1977 sets out the circumstances in which any employee's inventions are to be considered in law as belonging to his employer.

Section 40 provides that if the patent is considered to belong to the employer the employee can in certain circumstances, apply for compensation. The application must be made during the period beginning with the date when the relevant patent is granted and ending one year after it has ceased to have effect.

To register a patent an application should be filed with the Patent Office at State House, 66/71 High Holborn, London WC1, before disclosing any information to other people. The application should include a description of the invention with drawing/s. It can take two to three years from the date of application before the patent is granted. During this period disclosure to others will not damage the prospects of the patent being granted.

Note Bene: See chapter 9.9.5 for future changes to the time limits for patents, under proposed EC legislation.

13.3 Animal experiments

13.3.1 *Animals (Scientific Procedures) Act 1986*

Doctors are not, in the main, placed in any special position so far as the law relating to animal experimentation is concerned. Statute controls the performance of painful experiments on living animals, the administration of beneficial substances to animals in the course of medicinal tests, inhumane operations on animals and the practice of veterinary surgery by unqualified persons.

The Animals (Scientific Procedures) Act 1986, section 3, prohibits the carrying on of "regulated procedures" (see below) in relation to any animal unless certain conditions are fulfilled.

Section 2 defines what is meant by a "regulated procedure" for this purpose as follows:

"... any experimental or other scientific procedure applied to a protected animal which may have the effect of causing that animal pain, suffering, distress or lasting harm" (section 2 (1)). When considering whether any procedure might have the above mentioned effects section 2(4) provides that "... the use of an anaesthetic or analgesic, decerebration and any other procedure for rendering an animal insentient shall be disregarded." The subsection then states that the administration of same to animals for the purposes of experimental or other scientific procedures shall itself be regarded as coming within the category of regulated procedures.

Also regarded as being regulated procedures are scientific or experimental procedures applied to a protected animal, if the procedure is part of a series applied to the same animal and if the series may have any of the above mentioned unpleasant effects (section 2(2)). Also, included is a procedure that might result in the birth or hatching of a protected animal if the procedure may have the above mentioned unpleasant effects (section 2(3)).

Some procedures are excluded from the definition if certain criteria are met. Section 2(5) provides that ringing, tagging, or marking of an animal, or the application of any other humane procedure for the sole purpose of enabling an animal to be identified is not a regulated procedure if it causes only momentary pain or distress and no lasting harm. Section 2(6) excludes from the definition medicinal tests on animals as defined in section 32(6) of the Medicines Act 1968 (see chapter 13.3.2 where the text of this definition is set out) provided the substance or article is administered in accordance with the provisions of that Act as set out in section 32(4) or in accordance with an order under section 35(8)(b).

Killing a protected animal is a regulated procedure only if the animal is killed for experimental or other scientific use, the place where it is killed is a designated establishment (see later), and the method employed is not one sanctioned as appropriate to that particular animal by schedule 1 of the Act, which lists standard methods for humane killing (section 2(7)).

It is obvious from the above that in order to know whether an experiment, etc, comes within the definition of a "regulated procedure" and is thus controlled by the Act it is necessary to know what animals are defined as "protected animals." This point is dealt with in section 1 which states that a protected animal means "... any living vertebrate other than man,"

"... an animal is living until the permanent cessation of circulation or the destruction of its brain" (subsection 4).

A vertebrate means "... any animal of the Sub-phylum Vertebrata of the Phylum Chordata" (subsection 5).

Subsection 2 states that a "... vertebrate in its foetal, larval or embryonic form is a protected animal only from the stage of its development when

(a) in the case of a mammal, bird or reptile, half the gestation or incubation period for the relevant species has elapsed; and

(b) in any other case, it becomes capable of independent feeding."

The Secretary of State may by order extend and alter some of these provisions.

As mentioned above, section 3 of the Act provides that a "regulated procedure" must not be applied to any animal unless certain criteria are fulfilled. Contravention of section 3 is a criminal offence although in England and Wales no prosecution can take place without the consent of the Director of Public Prosecutions, and in Scotland prosecution is at the instance of the Lord Advocate through the Procurator Fiscal. The criteria are as follows:

The person performing the regulated procedure must hold an appropriate personal licence, granted by the Secretary of State (section 4). This qualifies "... the holder to apply specified regulated procedures to animals of specified description at a specified place." The application must (unless the Secretary of State grants exemption from this provision) be endorsed by a person who already holds such a licence or one treated as such by transitional provisions which enable licences granted the Cruelty to Animals Act 1876 to continue until their expiry and who "... has knowledge of the biological or other relevant qualifications and of the training, experience and character of the applicant." The endorser must "... if practicable, be a person occupying a position of authority at a place where the applicant is to be specified by the licence to carry out the procedures authorised in it." A licence cannot be given to someone under the age of 18 and has to be reviewed at least every five years.

Section 10(2) of the Act sets out the required conditions attached to a personal licence.

In relation to the regulated procedure there must be a project licence. Section 5 states that these may be granted by the Secretary of State to specify a programme of work and authorise the application as part of that programme of specified regulated procedures to be applied to animals of a specified description at specified places. A project licence is not to be granted "... except to a person who undertakes overall responsibility for the programme to be specified in the licence." Before granting such a licence the Secretary of State must be satisfied that the programme is being "... undertaken for one or more of the following purposes:

(a) the prevention (whether by the testing of any product or otherwise) or the diagnosis or treatment of disease, ill-health or abnormality, or their effects, in man, animals or plants;

(b) the assessment, detection, regulation or modification of physiological conditions in man, animals or plants;

(c) the protection of the natural environment in the interests of the health or welfare of man or animals;

(d) the advancement of knowledge in biological or behaviourial sciences;

(e) education or training otherwise than in primary or secondary schools;

(f) forensic enquiries;

(g) the breeding of animals for experimental or other scientific use."

Project licences are not to be granted authorising the use of cats, dogs, primates or equidae unless it can be established that other sorts of animals are either not suitable or impracticable to obtain. Additionally (unless the Secretary of State is prepared to make an exception) they must contain a condition to the effect that no cat or dog is to be used unless they have been bred or obtained from a designated breeding establishment. The criteria for these are set out in section 7 (the same condition applies to animals listed in schedule 2—that is, mice, rats, guinea pigs, hamsters, rabbits, dogs, cats, primates).

The regulated procedure must be carried out in the place specified in the personal and project licences. Section 6 provides that no place may be specified in the licence unless it is a designated establishment, and a certificate has been issued to that effect by the Secretary of State. A certificate must not be issued except to a person "... occupying a position of authority at the establishment in question," and must specify:

"(a) a person to be responsible for the day-to-day care of the protected animals kept for experimental or other purposes at the establishment; and

 (b) a veterinary surgeon or other suitably qualified person to provide advice on their health and welfare."

Any certificate issued under the section must contain a condition that the protected animals kept at the establishment for experimental or for other scientific purposes must not be killed except by a method approved under schedule 1 or approved by the Secretary of State even if they are not subjected to regulated procedure or required to be killed by the provisions of section 15.

Section 12 provides that the Secretary of State may revoke or vary any licence granted, but before doing so a notice must be served on the holder who may within the specified period (which must not be less than 28 days) make representations. Section 13 provides for immediate suspension of a licence in cases of urgency, but only for a maximum three month period.

There are other provisions in the Act designed to reduce the suffering in animals used for experiments. Section 14 deals with the issue of the "re-use" of animals; and section 15 with the issue of humane killing at the end of the experiment.

Other provisions in the Act are as follows:

- Section 16 prohibits the showing of regulated procedures to the general public as an exhibition or on the television or advertising any such showings

- Section 17 bans the use of neuromuscular blocking agents in the course of regulated procedures unless their use is expressly authorised by the personal and project licences. The use of any such agent instead of an anaesthetic is banned completely

- Section 18 enables the Secretary of State to appoint inspectors to advise regarding certificates and licences and to visit premises

- Section 19 sets up the Animals Procedures Committee, which advises the Secretary of State regarding the operation of the Act, and "... shall have regard both to the legitimate requirements of science and industry and to the protection of animals against avoidable suffering and unnecessary use in scientific procedures." At least two thirds of the committee's membership must have one of various stipulated qualifications, one of which is full registration as a medical practitioner.

It has already been mentioned that contravention of section 3 is a criminal offence. The same applies to many other provisions. Section 24 also provides for the criminal prosecution of anyone who wrongly discloses information obtained by him in the course of exercising his functions under the Act "and which he knows or has reasonable grounds for believing to have been given in confidence."

13.3.2 Medicinal tests on animals

The legal controls, which exist relating to the import of drugs for use in medicinal tests on animals, were set out in chapter 9.8.4. These are set out in the Medicines Act 1968, and the same Act restricts the circumstances in which substances may be administered to animals in the course of such tests. It should be noted that these provisions are subject to the other laws set out here concerning cruelty.

The phrase "medicinal tests on animals" is defined in section 32(6) of the Act as being "... an investigation or series of investigations consisting of any of the following, that is to say—

(a)   the administration of a medicinal product of a particular description to one or more animals, where there is evidence that medicinal products of that description have effects which may be beneficial to, or otherwise advantageous in relation to, that animal or those animals, and the product is administered for the purpose of ascertaining whether, or to what extent, it has those or any other effects, whether advantageous or otherwise;

(b) the administration of a medicinal product to one or more animals in circumstances where there is no such evidence as is mentioned in the preceding paragraph, and the product is administered for the purpose of ascertaining whether, or to what extent, it has any effects relevant to a medicinal purpose;

(c) the administration of any substance or article, other than a medicinal product, to one or more animals for the purpose of ascertaining whether it has any effects relevant to a medicinal purpose, whether there is evidence that it has effects which may be beneficial to, or otherwise advantageous in relation to, that animal or those animals or not."

Section 132 provides that the term "animal" includes any bird, fish, or reptile.

The terms "medicinal product" and "medicinal purpose" are also defined (these definitions are set out in the glossary).

Section 32(4) of the Act prohibits the administration (or the procuring of the administration) of "any substance or article" to an animal in the course of a medicinal test on animals by any person in the course of a business.

The term "administered" is defined in section 130(9) to include administration: "orally, by injection or by introduction into the body in any other way or by external application, whether by direct contact with the body or not"; and also included are circumstances where the substance has "been dissolved or dispensed in, or diluted or mixed with, some other substance used as a vehicle."

There are some exemptions to this general prohibition, but none of these applies specifically to doctors.

The first of these is set out in section 33(1) and consists of two elements: where,

"the test is, or is to be, carried out in circumstances where there is no evidence that the substance or article has effects which may be beneficial to, or otherwise advantageous in relation to, the animal or animals to which it is, or is to be, administered" and

where there is no prospect of the carcass being eaten by humans.

If the "substance" falls within the definition of "medicinal product" then the test may be carried out if the experimenter holds a "product licence" "which authorises that test and the product is administered in accordance with that licence or in accordance with any instructions required by the licence to be communicated to the person carrying out the test" (section 32(4)(a)).

Section 32(5) defines a product licence for these purposes as "... a licence which authorises a particular medicinal test on animals if—

(a)   the substance or article to be administered in the test is a medicinal product of the description to which the licence relates; and

(b)   the uses of medicinal products of that description which are referred to in the licence are such as to include their use for the purposes of that test."

Whether or not the substance or article used falls within the definition of a medicinal product then the third exception to the prohibition is that where an "animal test certificate" has been issued. Such certificates must certify that subject to the provisions of the certificate, the licensing authority has consented to the test in question" (section 32(2)(b)).

The certificate must also be "for the time being in force and the substance or article is administered in accordance with that certificate" (section 32(4)(b)).

The Act sets out the provisions for obtaining licences and certificates.

The general effect of section 32 can be modified by government order (see section 35(8)(b)). Various orders have been made. (*See* Painter AA, ed. *Butterworths Law of Food and Drugs*. London: Butterworths, 1981: section 170).

13.3.3 *Inhumane operations*

The Protection of Animals Act 1911 (not applicable in Scotland and Northern Ireland) and the Protection of Animals (Scotland) Act 1912 provide that it is a criminal offence to: "... subject, or cause or procure, or being the owner permit, to be subjected, any animal to any operation which is performed without due care or humanity."

The term "animal" in this context is defined to include any domestic or captive animal, and those terms are defined as follows:

"Domestic animal" means "any horse, ass, mule, bull, sheep, pig, goat, dog, cat or fowl, or any other animal of whatsoever kind or species, and whether a quadruped or not which is tame or which has been or is being sufficiently tamed to serve some purpose for the use of man."

The term "captive animal" means any animal "of whatsoever kind or species, and whether a quadruped or not, including any bird, fish, or reptile, which is in captivity, or confinement, or which is maimed, pinioned, or subjected to any appliance or contrivance for the purpose of hindering or preventing its escape from captivity or confinement."

This does not render illegal an operation sanctioned under the Animals (Scientific Procedures) Act 1986 but, as already mentioned, medicinal tests on animals will be illegal if performed contrary to these provisions. Other exceptions relate to killing animals for food, unless unnecessary suffering is thereby caused, and the coursing or hunting of captive animals, unless liberated in an injured, mutilated, or exhausted condition.

It must be noted that the Protection of Animals (Anaesthetics) Act 1954 (not applicable in Northern Ireland) provides that an operation will, for these purposes, be assumed to have been performed without humanity if it is performed on an animal without the use of an anaesthetic to prevent pain during an operation (section 1(1)).

Section 1(2) provides that this proviso applies "... to any operation with or without the use of instruments which involves interference with the sensitive tissue or bone structure of an animal" except for "... the making of injections or extractions by means of a hollow needle." Once again operations sanctioned by the Animals (Scientific Procedures Act) 1986 and certain docking, castration, and other minor operations performed by veterinary surgeons are excepted.

13.3.4 *Veterinary surgery*

The Veterinary Surgeons Act 1966 provides in section 19 that it is a criminal offence for a person who is not a registered veterinary surgeon or practitioner to practise or to hold himself out as practising veterinary surgery. There are some exceptions to this rule, some of which apply to doctors. These are as follows:

(1) An experiment authorised under the Animal (Scientific Procedures) Act 1986;

(2) "The performance by a registered medical practitioner of an operation on an animal for the purpose of removing an organ or tissue for use in the treatment of human beings" (section 19(4)(c));

(3) "The carrying out or performances of any treatment, test or operation by a registered medical practitioner or a registered dentist at the request of a registered veterinary surgeon or practitioner (section 19(4)(d)).

Veterinary surgery is defined to include (section 27):

"(a) the diagnosis of diseases in, and injuries to animals including tests performed on animals for diagnostic purposes;

194

(b) the giving of advice based on such diagnosis;

(c) the medical or surgical treatment of animals; and

(d) the performance of surgical operations on animals."

The term "animal" here includes birds and reptiles.

13.4 Anatomy

13.4.1 *Anatomical examination*

The Anatomy Act 1984 (not applicable in Northern Ireland) (which has replaced the Anatomy Acts of 1832 and 1871, and section 2(1) and section 3 of the Human Tissue Act 1961) regulates the performance of anatomical examinations and the possession of anatomical specimens and the later retention of same.

It should be noted that the Act does not regulate the conduct of post mortem examinations nor the removal of parts of the body when such has been authorised under the provisions of section 1 of the Human Tissue Act 1961 for the purposes of medical education and research, even if the latter involves anatomical examinations. In such a case the Human Tissue Act 1961 regulates the position, although the Anatomy Act 1984 is not thereby prevented from applying after the removal of the tissue has taken place or if there is in the event no removal.

Section 2 of the Anatomy Act 1984 prohibits the performance of anatomical examinations and the possession of anatomical specimens unless certain criteria are met. Before considering the position in relation to anatomical examinations it is necessary to consider what is meant by this expression for the purposes of the Act. Section 1 defines an anatomical examination as follows:

"The examination by dissection of a body for purposes of teaching or studying, or researching into, morphology; and where parts of a body are separated in the course of its anatomical examination, such examination includes the examination by dissection of the parts for those purposes."

Anatomical examinations may be carried out only if four conditions are satisfied, as follows:

(1) Anatomical examinations must only be carried out on premises licensed under section 3(1), which authorises the Secretary of State to issue such licences;

(2) The person who carries out the examination must be authorised to do so under section 3(3). Such authorisation may derive from a licence granted by the Secretary of State to that person or from the fact that the person "... carries out the examination in the course of teaching or

studying, or researching into, morphology and has permission (general or particular) to carry out the examination from a person who is so licensed at the time of the examination;"

(See chapter 13.4.3 for more about licences).

(3) The examination must be lawful according to the provisions of section 4, which deals with the issue of who may authorise the use of the body for the purposes of anatomy. Thus the person who is "lawfully in possession" (see below) may authorise an anatomical examination if the deceased "... either in writing at any time or orally in the presence of two or more witnesses during his last illness, has expressed a request that his body be used after his death for anatomical examination" (provided there is no reason to believe the request was withdrawn before death). Or if having made such reasonable inquiry as may be practicable that person has no reason to believe:

"(a) that the deceased, either in writing or at any time orally in the presence of two or more witnesses during his last illness, had expressed an objection to his body being so used after his death, and had not withdrawn it; or

(b) that the surviving spouse or any surviving relative of the deceased objects to the body being so used."

In those cases where the body is "lying in" a hospital, nursing home, or other institution the Act permits the managers to delegate the right to give authority for anatomical examination to a designated person (section 4(9)).

The subject of who is "lawfully in possession" has already been discussed in chapter 1.4.2. In the footnote to the Anatomy Act 1984 *Halsbury's Statutes of England and Wales* review the English authorities. They point out that in the case of Williams *v* Williams 1882 20 ChD 659 [1881-5] AER rep 840 it was held that the executors have a right to possession of a corpse. The case of R *v* Feist [1858] Dears' B 590; 27 LJMC 164, however, decided that for the purposes of section 7 of the Anatomy Act 1832 (which has been replaced by the Anatomy Act 1984), where a person died in a workhouse, the master of the workhouse was a "party having lawful possession". They also point out that the provision above in subsection 9 implies that in the case of death in a hospital the manager thereof is in lawful possession. They state that the Canadian case Edmonds *v* Armstrong Funeral Home Ltd [1931] 1 DLR 676 decided that there is a general right to possession in the surviving husband, wife, or next of kin. (This case would be of what is termed persuasive authority only in this country, that is, an English court would not have to follow the case but could be persuaded by it). Halsbury's ends by stating that some assistance might be derived from the list of persons responsible for notifying a death under the Births and Deaths Registration Act 1953 (on this, see chapter 5.4). As in the case of donation of tissue, the question of who is "lawfully in possession" could, in theory, be open to debate, but, in practice, this is unlikely to happen in most cases.

There are certain limitations on the right of the person "lawfully in possession" to authorise an anatomical examination:

(a) In England and Wales if a person has reason to believe that an inquest may be required to be held or that a post mortem examination may be required by the coroner then that person must not, without the consent of the coroner, give or act on any authority to perform an anatomical examination.

In Scotland if a person has reason to believe that any inquiry under the Fatal Accidents and Sudden Deaths Inquiry (Scotland) Act 1976 is to be held or that a post mortem examination may be required by the procurator fiscal that person must not without the consent of the procurator fiscal give or act on any authority to perform an anatomical examination;

(b) No authority to perform an anatomical examination may be given by a person entrusted with a body only for the purposes of interment or cremation;

(c) Any authority given expires at the end of the statutory period even if the authority is expressed to be for a longer time. The Act states that the statutory period is three years from the death but power is given to the Secretary of State to vary the length of the period by order;

(4) The last provision which must be complied with in relation to anatomical examinations is that the death must have been registered under section 15 of the Births and Deaths Registration Act 1953, or in Scotland under section 22 of the Births, Deaths and Marriages (Scotland) Act 1965.

A person who carries out an anatomical examination otherwise than as permitted under section 2(1) can be prosecuted in the criminal courts. This is stated in section 11.

Before considering the position in relation to possession of anatomical specimens it is necessary to consider how the Act defines same. The Act states in section 1(2) that an anatomical specimen means for these purposes;

"(a) a body to be used for anatomical examination, or

197

(b) a body in course of being used for anatomical examination (including separated parts of such a body)."

A "body" means a "body of a deceased person."

Section 2 of the Act states that no one may possess an anatomical specimen unless the following criteria are satisfied:

(1) The person in possession must be so authorised under section 3(4). The authority can derive either from a licence granted by the Secretary of State or if the person has "... from a person who is so licensed at that time, permission (general or particular) to have such possession" (see chapter 7.4.2 for more details about licences);

(2) Anatomical examination of a specimen must at the time be properly authorised in accordance with the provisions of section 4 (see above);

(3) A certificate regarding the cause of death must be signed in accordance with Section 22(1) of the Births and Deaths Registration Act 1953 and Section 24 of the Births, Deaths and Marriages (Scotland) Act 1965. (These are the sections requiring a medical certificate to be signed. The provisions are set out in subchapter 6.4).

These restrictions do not apply to a person who comes into lawful possession of a body immediately after death and retains possession prior to the removal of the body to a place where the anatomical examination takes place. Otherwise a person who contravenes these provisions can be prosecuted in the criminal courts.

13.4.2 *Subsequent possession*

Section 5 of the Act regulates the question of possession of a body or parts of a body in circumstances where an authority given under section 4 (see above) has expired or where an anatomical examination has been concluded before such expiry. The general rule is that no one may in such circumstances possess the body or a part of the body unless they do so "for the purpose only of its decent disposal" or if a list of other criteria are satisfied which are as follows:

(1) The person must be in possession of a part of a body concerning which an anatomical examination has been concluded and before the expiry of an authority given as per section 4 (see above);

(2) The part of the body must be such that the person from whose body it came could not be recognised simply be examination of the part;

(3)   The person in possession must have been authorised in accordance with section 5(5). Under this subsection the Secretary of State may license possession "... in the interests of education or research" of parts of bodies or a person may be authorised by permission granted by the person with the licence;

(4)   The possession of the part must be authorised by the person "lawfully in possession" of the body in accordance with the provisions of section 6. These provisions are phrased the same as those under section 4 (above), that is, the person in possession can authorise retention of a part of a body if the deceased has requested this or there is no reason to believe that he would have objected or that his relatives now object.

It is a criminal offence to retain a body or part of one in contravention of these provisions.

13.4.3 *Licences*

Section 13.4 sets out the general provisions about licences under the Anatomy Act 1984. These may be granted to such persons as the Secretary of State considers to be suitable. If a licence is refused the applicant is to be notified in writing of the refusal and the reasons for it. In certain circumstances the Secretary of State can attach conditions to the licence but not in relation to matters covered by regulations laid down under section 8 (see below). The licence can be revoked and ends on the death of the licensee. Any permissions that can be given by the licence holder terminate 21 days after the death of the licence holder (or earlier if so specified).

Under section 8 regulations may be made with a view to securing efficient and orderly examinations and the decent disposal of the bodies (and parts of them) after their examination has been concluded and to ensure that parts of bodies retained are to be decently cared for.

Under section 3 licensed persons must keep such records as may be required by regulations and retain these for such period as is specified.

Lastly, the Act provides in section 9 for the appointment of inspectors of anatomy to, among other things, inspect premises and consider licence applications. Section 10 sets out the rights for such inspectors to inspect records and premises.

13.5 Video recordings

The widespread growth of the video market during the 1980s (and in particular the use of video as a medium for both education and pornography) prompted the Video Recordings Act 1984. The Act makes provision for regulating the distribution of video recordings by sale or hire.

A classification certificate must be issued for each video stating that it is within one of the following categories:

(a) suitable for general viewing;

(b) suitable for viewing only by persons who have attained the age specified in the certificate;

(c) suitable only for supply in a licensed sex shop.

It is an offence to supply or possess for supply an unclassified video or one bearing a false label.

A video which is designed to "inform, educate or instruct" is an "exempted work" and can not be the subject of an offence under the Act. However, this exemption does not apply if the video depicts, to a significant extent, human sexual activity, gross violence towards humans or animals or human urinary or excretory functions or human genital organs (section 2).

Also, the supply of a video is an "exempted supply" in certain circumstances including the supply of a video recording with a view only to its use:

(a) in training or carrying on any medical or related occupation;

(b) for the purposes of services provided in pursuance of the National Health Service Act 1977, the National Health Service (Scotland) Act 1978, or the Health and Personal Services (Northern Ireland) Order 1972;

(c) in training persons employed in the course of services provided under (b) above.

The exempted supply of a video does not constitute an offence under the Act, even if it depicts human sexual activity, etc.

Appendix 1
General Medical Council guidance for doctors on professional confidence (November 1991)

Principles

1 Patients are entitled to expect that the information about themselves or others which a doctor learns during the course of a medical consultation, investigation, or treatment will remain confidential. Doctors, therefore, have a duty not to disclose to any third party information about an individual that they have learned in their professional capacity, directly from a patient or indirectly, except in the cases discussed in paragraphs 6–16 below.

2 Where a patient, or a person properly authorised to act on a patient's behalf, consents to disclosure, information to which the consent refers may be disclosed in accordance with that consent. An explicit request by a patient that information should not be disclosed to particular people, or indeed to any third party, must be respected save in the most exceptional cases—for example, where the health, safety, or welfare of someone other than the patient would otherwise be at serious risk.

3 Doctors carry prime responsibility for the protection of information given to them by patients or obtained in confidence about patients. They must therefore take steps to ensure, as far as lies in their control, that the records, manual or computerised, which, they keep or to which they have access, are protected by effective security systems with adequate procedures to prevent improper disclosure.

4 Most doctors in hospital and general practice are working in health care teams, some of whose members may need access to information, given or obtained in confidence about individuals, in order to perform their duties. It is for doctors who lead such teams to judge when it is appropriate for information to be disclosed for that purpose. They must leave those whom they authorise to receive such information in no doubt that it is given to them in professional confidence. The doctor also has a responsibility to ensure that arrangements exist to inform patients of the circumstances in which information about them is likely to be shared and the opportunity to state any objection to this.

5 A doctor who decides to disclose confidential information about an individual must be prepared to explain and justify that decision, whatever the circumstances of the disclosure.

Disclosures without the consent of the patient

6 Doctors who are faced with the difficult decision whether to disclose information without a patient's consent must weigh carefully the arguments for and against disclosure. If in doubt,

201

they would be wise to discuss the matter with an experienced colleague or to seek advice from a medical defence society or professional association. The following paragraphs discuss circumstances of this kind.

Disclosure in relation to the clinical management of a patient

7 In exceptional circumstances a doctor may consider it undesirable, for medical reasons, to seek a patient's consent to the disclosure of confidential information. In such cases information may be disclosed to a relative or some other person but only when the doctor is satisfied that it is necessary in the patient's best medical interests to do so.

8 Deciding whether or not to disclose information is particularly difficult in cases where a patient cannot be judged capable of giving or withholding consent to disclosure. One such situation may arise where a doctor believes that a patient may be the victim of physical or sexual abuse. In such circumstances the patient's medical interests are paramount and may require the doctor to disclose information to an appropriate person or authority.

9 Difficulties may also arise when a doctor believes that a patient, by reason of immaturity, does not have sufficient understanding to appreciate what the treatment or advice being sought may involve. Similar problems may arise where a patient lacks understanding because of illness or mental incapacity. In all such cases the doctor should attempt to persuade the patient to allow an appropriate person to be involved in the consultation. If the patient cannot understand or be persuaded, but the doctor is convinced that the disclosure of information would be essential to the patient's best medical interests, the doctor may disclose to an appropriate person or authority the fact of the consultation and the information learned in it. A doctor who decides to disclose information must be prepared to justify that decision and must inform the patient before any disclosure is made.

Disclosure required by statute

10 Information may be disclosed in order to satisfy a specific statutory requirement, such as notification of an infectious disease or of attendance on a person known or suspected to be addicted to controlled drugs.

Disclosure in the public interest

11 Rarely, cases may arise in which disclosure in the public interest may be justified—for example, a situation in which the failure to disclose appropriate information would expose the patient, or someone else, to a risk of death or serious harm.

Disclosure in connection with judicial proceedings

12 Where litigation is in prospect, unless the patient has consented to disclosure or a court order has been made, information should not be disclosed by a doctor merely in response to demands from other people, such as a third party's solicitor or an official of the court. A doctor may disclose such information as may be ordered by a judge or presiding officer of the court, as may a doctor summoned to assist a Coroner, Procurator Fiscal, or similar officer either at an inquest or when the need for an inquest is being considered. In such circumstances the doctor should first establish the precise extent of the information which needs to be disclosed, and should not hesitate to make known any objection to the proposed disclosure, particularly when the order would involve the disclosure of confidential information about third parties.

13 Information may also be disclosed at the direction of the chairman of a committee of the

Council which is investigating a doctor's fitness to practise, when the committee has determined that the interests of justice or the public require such disclosure, and provided that every reasonable effort had first been made to seek the consent of the patient or patients concerned.

Disclosure for the purposes of medical teaching, medical research, and medical audit

14 Medical teaching, research and medical audit necessarily involve the disclosure of information about individuals, often in the form of medical records, for purposes other than their own health care. Where such information is used in a form which does not enable individuals to be identified, no question of breach of confidentiality will usually arise. Where the disclosure would enable one or more individuals to be identified, the patients concerned, or those who may properly give permission on their behalf, must wherever possible, be made aware of that possibility and be advised that it is open to them, at any stage, to withhold their consent to disclosure.

Disclosure to employers and insurance companies

15 Special problems relating to confidentiality can arise where doctors have responsibilities not only to patients but also to third parties as, for example, where a doctor assesses a patient for an employer or an insurance company. In such circumstances, the doctor should ensure that at the outset patients understand the purpose of any consultation or examination, are aware of the doctor's obligation to the employer or insurance company, and consent to be seen by the doctor on those terms. Doctors should undertake assessments for insurance, or of an employee's fitness to work, only where the patient has given written consent.

Disclosure after a patient's death

16 The fact of a patient's death does not of itself release a doctor from the obligation to maintain confidentiality. In cases where consent has not previously been given, the extent to which confidential information may properly be disclosed by a doctor after someone's death cannot be specified in absolute terms and will depend on the circumstances. These include the nature of the information disclosed, the extent to which it has already appeared in published material, and the period which has elapsed since the person's death.

Appendix 2
Guidelines to doctors on advertising

Introduction

The General Medical Council, as the statutory body, defines the limitations within which doctors must practise. The GMC issued revised guidance for the medical profession on the subject of advertising in May 1990 outlining professional standards which doctors are obliged to observe. This guidance was further amended in November of that year. The Council's position on various aspects of advertising and the provision of information by doctors had been undergoing review since 1985, but specific pressure for the GMC to examine and modify its guidance stemmed from the Monopolies and Mergers Commission report of 1988.

Similarly, the British Medical Association has looked in detail at its guidance to members on advertising. The Association has produced the revised advice outlined below.

Changes in the way they may distribute information have been perceived by some doctors as undesirable commercialisation of medical practice and many doctors may choose to avoid advertising altogether. Others consider that previous recommendations on advertising were overly restrictive and have cautiously accepted the new freedom. Nevertheless, it is essential that the highest standards are maintained by doctors. Abuse of the freedom to advertise will undermine the traditional doctor–patient relationship and lead to patients losing confidence in the medical profession.

Patients are entitled to be given comprehensive, detailed, and accurate information about medical services available to them. General practitioners need information about specialist services to enable them to advise patients of the need for specialist advice and arrange appropriate referral.

Any information provided by a doctor about his practice must not be false, inaccurate, misleading or reasonably capable of being misinterpreted. It must not compare or contrast the quality of services with those provided by other doctors nor should it imply that the doctor can achieve results from treatment not achievable by other doctors.

The distinction between a GP and a specialist when it comes to advertising is maintained. For the purposes of advertising, ophthalmic medical practitioners are subject to the same rules as GPs.

The GMC draws no distinction between advertising by medical practitioners working within the NHS or in private practice. NHS practitioners, however, have particular obligations imposed on them by their terms of service.

General Practitioners

Practice leaflets

Under the new terms of service NHS GPs must provide members of the public with information about their services in the form of a practice leaflet. There are no specific restrictions as to the size of leaflet, type of paper used in its production, or layout of text. Information provided within the leaflet of NHS practitioners must include the following items. Private practitioners are not obliged to adopt the same content for any leaflet they choose to produce but may find it useful.

Personal and professional details of the doctor

1 Full name
2 Sex
3 Medical qualifications registered by the GMC
4 Date and place of first registration as a medical practitioner

Practice Information

5 The times during which the doctor is available for consultation by patients at the practice premises.

6 Whether an appointment system is operated by the doctor for consultations at the practice premises.

7 If there is an appointment system, the method of obtaining a non-urgent appointment and the method of obtaining an urgent appointment.

8 The method of obtaining a non-urgent domiciliary visit and the method of obtaining an urgent domiciliary visit.

9 The doctor's arrangements for providing personal medical services when he is not personally available.

10 The method by which patients are to obtain repeat prescriptions from the doctor.

11 If the doctor's practice is a dispensing practice, the arrangements for dispensing prescriptions.

12 If the doctor provides clinics for his patients, their frequency, duration and purpose.

13 The number of staff, other than doctors, assisting the doctor in the practice, and a description of their roles.

14 Whether the doctor provides (1) maternity medical services, (2) contraceptive services, (3) child health surveillance services and (4) minor surgery services.

15 Whether the doctor works single-handed, in partnership, part time or on a job share basis, or within a group practice.

16 The nature of any arrangements whereby the doctor or his staff receive patients' comments on the provision of general medical services.

17 The geographical boundary of the practice area by reference to a map.

18 Whether the doctor's practice premises have suitable access for all patients with a disability and, if not, the reasons why they are unsuitable for particular forms of disability.

19 If an assistant is employed, details for him as specified in paragraphs 1-4.

20 If the practice is either a general practitioner training practice for the purpose of the NHS (Vocational Training Regulations 1979) or undertakes the teaching of undergraduate medical students, the nature of arrangements for drawing this to the attention of patients.

Supplementary to the requirements of the NHS terms of service, doctors may also feature:

- Particular interests of the partners such as women's health, or expertise, or qualifications in treatments such as acupuncture or hypnotherapy.

- A general statement about the practice approach to health care.

- Photographs of the premises and doctors.

Advertising and sponsorship

1 A leaflet may include advertising from local businesses, to reduce production costs. Many doctors may wish to avoid carrying advertising altogether.

2 Advertisements should not relate to:

   a   other health care activities, such as pharmacist shops, nursing and residential homes, private hospitals, private clinics.

   b   any business in which a practitioner or a near relative of the practitioner has a pecuniary interest.

   c   the tobacco industry.

3 The inclusion of advertisements should not detract from the purpose of the leaflet which is to provide practice information. Advertisements should therefore normally occupy not more than one third of the leaflet, and doctors must personally ensure that they are "legal, decent, honest and truthful."

4 Sponsorship significantly defrays production costs of a practice leaflet. Advertising in the leaflet by a single sponsoring company should conform to the principles noted above.

5 The leaflet must include a statement displayed prominently that any advertising or sponsorship does not constitute a recommendation by the practice or its doctors.

Distribution of practice leaflets

Leaflets should be freely available within doctors' surgeries and may be placed in local libraries and other locations where patients might seek such information. They may also be distributed to the general public within the area the practice serves provided this does not put the recipients under pressure. As an example, a doctor may distribute a practice leaflet when he establishes a new practice in the area. "Cold calling" in the form of visits to individual homes, or telephone calls is not allowed.

Advertising in other media

General practitioners may publish information about their services in local and national directories, such as *Yellow Pages*. Entries in directories may be in normal or bold typeface and may be "boxed."

Although advertising in newspapers is permissable, GPs are advised to be cautious about "advertising features" in local newspapers in which details of their practice are presented, accompanied by advertisements by local businesses which frequently "offer congratulations" to the practice. This is because the practice information is frequently presented in a promotional and laudatory manner which gives unfair advantage to the practice, compared with others in the area. Doctors usually have no control over the layout of the feature, nor the accompanying advertisements which are a vehicle for increasing advertising revenue by the newspaper. Doctors may be held to account for the overall effect of such features which may imply disparagement of other facilities.

General practitioners also need to think carefully before advertising on local radio and television because of the difficulty of producing advertisements which both comply with the GMC guidelines and are effective in these media.

Specialists

1   Specialists are encouraged to provide information to GP and managerial colleagues, but not directly to the public, except in very limited circumstances (see 4 below). This is to preserve the conventional referral system which operates in this country and which serves in particular to protect patients who are ill enough to merit consultant advice and may therefore be particularly susceptible to external pressures.

2   Specialists may provide information to colleagues on their services and practice arrangements. Material provided should not claim superiority for the specialist's personal qualities, qualifications, experience or skill. These principles apply to specialists working in NHS hospitals, NHS trusts, and in private practice.

3   A specialist's name, qualifications, address and telephone number may be included in local and national directories. Such information should not be distributed directly to the general public.

4   Associations of doctors are now allowed to release lists of their members on request to members of the public. At present the GMC is engaged in discussions with the Royal Colleges and others about the best way of doing this, so as to ensure that such lists are confined to those doctors who are properly qualified to practice the specialty in question. The inclusion in any list of a particular doctor should not imply a recommendation.

Advertising and independent organisations

Some private hospitals, screening centres, private clinics, nursing homes or advisory centres may advertise medical services to the general public. The principles set out concerning the advertising of GP services also apply. Advertisements should not make adverse comparisons with the NHS or other organisations. They should not claim superiority for the professional services offered by doctors within these organisations. It is understood that it is inappropriate for certain services offered by private organisations to be advertised directly to the general public.

A doctor who has a professional or financial relationship with such an organisation or who simply uses its facilities bears some responsibility for its advertising. Ignorance of the content of such advertising is no defence should the advertising fail to conform to the standards set by the GMC. Such doctors are advised to satisfy themselves that any advertising does confirm to these guidelines.

Further Information

The guidance contained within this leaflet is necessarily general in nature. Doctors may obtain advice on specific queries on written application to the Professional Division of the Association. Advice has been produced taking into account the GMC guidelines, which are binding on all registered medical practitioners. Doctors are ultimately accountable to the GMC, as the regulatory body for the profession, but they are unlikely to encounter difficulties if they follow the BMA advice.

General Medical Council. The advertising of doctors' services. In: *Professional Conduct and Discipline: Fitness to Practise.* London: GMC, 1991: paragraphs 59–61 and 90–108.

PSIAD. *Guidelines for Doctors Employed by Private Organisations providing Clinical Diagnostic or Medical Advisory Services*. London: BMA Professional Scientific and International Affairs Division

PSIAD. *Information to Companies, Firms or Associations*. London: BMA Professional Scientific and International Affairs Division

Glossary

A **action** – the formal legal demand of one's rights from another person brought in court; a lawsuit.

ambit – the compass of actions, words, etc.

appeal – the process by which a decision of a lower court is brought for review before a court of higher jurisdiction. The party bringing the appeal is the appellant. The party against which the appeal is taken is the appellee.

assault – both crime and civil wrong. Any examination involving touching the body, investigation, or operation without consent constitutes an assault.

B **bona fide** – in good faith; genuinely.

breach – the breaking of any legal or moral bond or obligation; violation, infraction.

C **cadaver** – a corpse; a lifeless human body used for dissection.

canvassing – soliciting votes, orders, contributions, etc.

civil (courts) – pertaining to the private rights and remedies of a citizen; as distinguished from criminal, political, etc.

claimant – one who makes or enters a claim; one who has a claim on anything.

class A drug – see controlled drugs.

clinical trial – defined in section 31(1) of the Medicines Act 1968 as: "an investigation or series of investigations consisting of the administration of one or more medicinal products of a particular description:

(a) by, or under the direction of, a doctor or dentist to one or more patients of his; or

(b) by, or under the direction of, two or more doctors or dentists, each product being administered by, or under the direction of, one or other of those doctors or dentists to one or more patients of his,

where (in any such case) there is evidence that medicinal products of that description have effects which may be beneficial to the patient or patients in question and the administration of the product or products is for the purpose of ascertaining whether, or to what extent, the product has, or the products have, those or any other effects, whether beneficial or harmful."

common law – the part of Anglo-American law that is derived from

209

court decisions rather than from statutes and regulations. In England the ancient customary law of the land.

confidentiality – the principle of maintaining the security of information elicited from an individual in the privileged circumstances of a professional relationship.

The individual has a fundamental right to privacy; and this is of particular importance in the practice of medicine when the unauthorised disclosure of personal information may have personal, social, or legal repercussions. On the other hand, information about him of a medical nature may have to be released to fulfil a statutory obligation such as the completion of a certificate of the causes of death, a document legally open to inspection by the public. The patient himself may release the doctor from the bond of secrecy by asking him in writing to report on his clinical condition to an employer, insurance company, or solicitor.

congenital disabilities – disabilities existing before birth or at birth; dating from birth.

consent – consent to medical or surgical treatment obtained by implication (implied), word of mouth (verbal) or, on paper, signed (written), necessary to avoid subsequent allegation of operative or other procedure without approval.

contempt (of court) – scorn, disgrace; in law, disregard of the rule, or an offence against the dignity of a court.

contract – a legally enforceable agreement between two parties in which each agrees to do something.

controlled drugs – substances which are controlled drugs are listed in Schedule 2 of the Misuse of Drugs Act 1971 and the degree of legal control depends to some extent on which "class" the substance is in. Drugs considered to be most socially damaging when misused are listed in Part 1, class A drugs. Stringent restrictions are placed on those who may possess, supply, import or export controlled drugs. Section 2(2) of the Act permits amendment of the classes and new additions and removals occur from time to time.

Examples of drugs listed in Schedule 2:

Class A includes: alfentanil, cocaine, dextromoramide, diamorphine (heroin), dipipanone, lysergide (LSD), methadone, morphine, opium, pethidine, phencyclidine, and class B substances when prepared for injection.

Class B includes: oral amphetamines, barbiturates, cannabis resin, codeine, ethylmorphine, glutethimide, pentazocine, phenmetrazine, and pholcodine.

Class C includes: certain drugs related to the amphetamines such as benzphetamine and chlorphentermine, diethylpropion, mazindol, meprobamate, methyprylone, pipadrol, and most benzodiazepines.

coroner – a judicial officer whose duty is to enquire into the manner of death of any person who is suspected of dying an unnatural death, or of one for which the cause is not evident, also of all persons dying in prison, and all deaths among persons certified as having a mental incapacity. Such deaths include those due to violence and industrial disease, and as a result of anaesthetics, and deaths among persons in receipt of disability pensions. He is appointed by the local authority and must possess a legal or medical qualification and have practised for at least five years.

crime – a violation of law, especially if serious: an act punishable by law.

Crown immunity – immunity from prosecution granted by the Crown.

D **damages** – the value estimated in money of something lost or withheld; the sum claimed or awarded in compensation for loss or injury sustained.

decision – form of EC legislation. It is binding in its entirety on those to whom it is addressed which may be member states or groups within them.

defendant – a person sued in a court of law; the party in a suit who defends.

directive – form of EC legislation. It is binding on all member states, but only as to the result to be achieved; it leaves to the national authorities the choice of which form of enactment they will use to achieve that result.

disclaimer – a denial, disavowal, or renunciation.

disparage (ment) – to dishonour by comparison with what is inferior; to match in marriage with an inferior, to lower in rank or estimation; to talk slightingly of, to dishearten.

due care – the legal duty one owes to another according to the circumstances of a particular case. It is that care which an ordinarily prudent person would have exercised in the given situation; the absence of negligence.

E **enact** – to make into an act; hence, to ordain, decree.

enactment – the action of enacting (a law); the state of being enacted.

equitable – 1 Characterised by equity or fairness. 2 Pertaining to the department of jurisprudence called EQUITY; valid in equity as distinct from law.

ethics – the science of moral conduct. Medical ethics: the moral rules and principles which govern a member of the medical profession in the exercise of his profession.

ex parte – on behalf of, on the application of, one party; by or for one party. An ex parte judicial proceeding is one brought for the benefit of one party only without notice to or challenge by an adverse party.

executor – one who executes or carries out; an agent, doer: a person appointed by a testator to execute or give effect to his will after his decease.

exemption – immunity from a liability, obligation, penalty, law or authority; freedom.

exonerate – to free from (a duty, obligation, payment, charge, etc; also, from blame).

F **fraud** – criminal deception; the using of false representations to obtain an unjust advantage or to injure the rights or interests of another.

G **goodwill** – established popularity of a business, treated as a saleable asset.

I **in toto** – entirely.

informed consent – a doctrine that states that before a patient is asked to consent to a risky or invasive diagnostic or treatment procedure he is entitled to receive certain information: (a) a description of the procedure; (b) any alternatives to it and their risks; (c) the risks of death or serious bodily disability from the procedure; (d) the probable results of the procedure, including any problems of recuperation and time of recuperation anticipated; and (e) anything else that is generally disclosed to patients asked to consent to the procedure.

inquest – a legal or judicial enquiry to ascertain or decide a matter of fact, especially one made by a jury in a civil or criminal case. Formerly, a general term for all formal or official inquiries.

inquiry/enquiry – the action of seeking especially (now always) for truth, knowledge, or information concerning something.

inter alia – among other things.

J **Jehovah's Witnesses** – the International Bible Students Association.

K **kin (next of)** – the person (or persons) standing nearest in blood relationship to another, and entitled to share in his personal estate in case of intestacy.

L **legislation** – the action of making or giving laws: the enactment of laws, law giving.

liability – the condition of being liable or answerable by law or equity.

liable – bound or obliged by law or equity; answerable (for, also to); legally subject or amenable to.

licentiate – one who has obtained a licence to exercise some function; for example, one who has received a formal attestation of professional competence or of proficiency in some art from some collegiate or other examining body.

litigation – the action of carrying on a suit in law or equity; legal proceedings.

loco parentis – doctrine which permits a court to appoint a person to stand in the place of parents and assume all of their legal rights, duties, and obligations with respect to a child.

locum tenens – a medical practitioner who acts as deputy for another.

M **maladministration** – inefficient or improper management of affairs especially public affairs.

manslaughter – criminal homicide without malice aforethought.

medical referee – a doctor attached to the Cremation Authority who must have not less than than five years' standing and relevant experience and qualifications.

medicinal – 1 Having curative or healing properties. 2 Belonging to or of the nature of a medicine.

medicinal product – Section 130 of the Medicines Act 1968 defines what is meant by a medicinal product as follows:

The definition includes "any substance or article (not being an instrument, apparatus or appliance) which is manufactured, sold, supplied, imported or exported for use wholly or mainly in either or both of the following ways, that is to say:

(a) use by being administered to one or more human beings or animals for a medicinal purpose;

(b) use, in circumstances to which this paragraph applies, as an ingredient in the preparation of a substance or article which is to be administered to one or more human beings or animals for a medicinal purpose."

Later it is stated that this paragraph applies to "(a) use in a pharmacy or in a hospital; (b) use by a practitioner; (c) use in the course of a business which consists of or includes the retail sale, or the supply in circumstances corresponding to retail sale, of herbal remedies."

Various items are exempt from the definition medicinal product, the most relevant being bandages and other surgical dressings (except medicated dressings where the medication has a curative function which is not limited to sterilising the dressing).

medicinal purpose – is defined as any one or more of the following purposes:

(a) treating or preventing disease;

(b) diagnosing disease or ascertaining the existence, degree of extent of the physiological condition;

(c) contraception;

(d) induction anaesthesia;

(e) otherwise preventing or interfering with the normal operation of a physiological function, whether permanently or temporarily and whether by way of terminating, reducing or postponing, or increasing or accelerating, the operation of that function or in any other way.

minors – under age; below the age of majority (18 years).

misprision – a wrongful action or omission; a misdemeanour or neglect of duty on the part of a public official.

N   **negligent** – inattentive to what ought to be done; neglectful; indifferent of actions or conduct.

notifiable disease – designated infectious disease, the occurrence of which must by law be reported to health authorities.

O   **ombudsman** – (Health Service Commissioner) empowered by Statute to investigate complaints from people who claim that they have sustained injustice or hardship as a result of an alleged failure of a regional or area health authority to provide a service which it was a function of that body to provide, or a result of an alleged failure in a service provided by such a body, or as a result of maladministration in the provision of a service by such a body.

order – the rule of law or proper authority.

P   **patent** – a conditional and limited monopoly granted by the State as a reward for the introduction into the realm of new technology. Inventions in the medical field patentable under British law include new drugs per se, processes for making drugs, synergistic combinations of drugs, and surgical appliances.

plaintiff – the person who brings a lawsuit against another.

post mortem examination – after death examination of a body, including its organs, to establish the cause of death.

precognition – awareness of an event before it has happened, sometimes taking the form of a detailed vision of the event.

Privy Council – a private consultation or assembly for consultation. The private counsellors of the Sovereign.

procurator fiscal – in Scotland the public prosecutor of a shire or other local district.

project licence – granted by the Secretary of State to specify a programme of work and authorise the application as part of that programme of specified places.

product liability – under part 1 of the Consumer Protection Act 1987 producers of defective products are strictly liable.

proviso – 1 A clause inserted into a legal or formal document making some condition, stipulation, exception or limitation. 2 Or on the observance of which the operation or validity of the instrument depends.

pupils – girls under the age of 12 and boys under the age of 14.

Q   **quasi (proprietal)** – as if, as it were. In composition, in a certain manner, sense, or degree: in appearance only.

R **recommendation** – form of EC legislation. It is not mandatory to the member states; it does, however, reflect the views of the EC institutions on a particular question of a particular moment, and is strongly advisory.

regulations – 1 Rules promulgated by an administrative agency, following specified procedures (eg public notice and public hearings), under the authority of a statute. 2 Form of EC legislation. These have general application and are binding in their entirety with immediate effect and without the need to be transposed into national law.

remand – to send back for further proceedings, as when a higher court sends a case back to a lower court.

repealed – 1 To revoke, annul (a resolution, a law, sentence, etc). 2 To recall, withdraw (a privilege, grant, etc). 3 To withdraw or retract a statement.

restrictive covenant – a formal agreement, contract which restricts the setting up of competitive business.

S **standing** (must not have less than five years') – 1 To be or remain valid or of force; to remain good. 2 To be or remain in a specified condition, relation, situation, etc.

statute – 1 A law or decree made by a sovereign or legislative authority. 2 An enactment containing one or more legislative provisions, made by a legislature of a country at one time, and expressed in a formal document; the document in which such an enactment is expressed.

statutory duty – a moral and legal obligation enacted, appointed or created by statute; conformable to the provisions of a statute.

statutory instrument – statutory: enacted by statute; depending on statute for its authority. Instrument: a writing containing a contract; a formal record.

stillbirth – the lifeless state of birth. Failure to breathe or show any other sign of a separate existence upon expulsion from the body of the mother. Term commonly used only for gestations of 24 weeks or more (prior to this, referred to as products of abortion).

subpoena – a court order compelling a witness to appear and testify in a certain proceeding.

sue – 1 To institute a suit for, make a legal claim to; hence to petition or appeal for; to seek to obtain. 2 To institute legal proceedings against (a person): to prosecute in a court of law; to bring a civil action against.

summons – 1 An authoritative call to attend at a specified place for a specified purpose. 2 A call or citation by authority to appear before a court or judicial officer.

T **third party** – other person/s; not self.

tort – 1 Injury, wrong. 2 The breach of a duty imposed by law, whereby some person acquires a right of action for damages.

215

treason – 1 The action of betraying. 2 Violation by a subject of his allegiance to his Sovereign or his State.

tribunal – a court of justice; a judicial assembly; place of judgement or decision.

U **ultimus haeres** – in law, the Crown or the State, which succeeds to the property of those who die intestate, or without next of kin.

V **vested** – not contingent or suspended, hence (law) already acquired.

vicarious liability – filling the place of another: exercised, performed or suffered by one person or thing instead of another.

W **ward of court** – someone (usually a child) under the protection of a court.

warrant – a writ for arresting a person or for carrying a judgement into execution.

witness – one who sees or has personal knowledge of a thing: one who gives evidence.

Index